CONTEMPLATION & COUNSELING

| *An Integrative Model for Practitioners* | P. GREGG BLANTON |

IVP Academic

An imprint of InterVarsity Press
Downers Grove, Illinois

InterVarsity Press
P.O. Box 1400, Downers Grove, IL 60515-1426
ivpress.com
email@ivpress.com

InterVarsity Press® is the book-publishing division of InterVarsity Christian Fellowship/USA®, a movement of students and faculty active on campus at hundreds of universities, colleges, and schools of nursing in the United States of America, and a member movement of the International Fellowship of Evangelical Students. For information about local and regional activities, visit intervarsity.org.

All Scripture quotations, unless otherwise indicated, are taken from The Holy Bible, New International Version®, NIV®. Copyright © 1973, 1978, 1984, 2011 by Biblica, Inc.™ Used by permission of Zondervan. All rights reserved worldwide. www.zondervan.com. The "NIV" and "New International Version" are trademarks registered in the United States Patent and Trademark Office by Biblica, Inc.™

While any stories in this book are true, some names and identifying information may have been changed to protect the privacy of individuals.

Cover design and image composite: Autumn Short
Interior design: Jeanna Wiggins
Image: floral shapes: © Softulka / iStock / Getty Images Plus

ISBN 978-0-8308-2865-4 (print)
ISBN 978-0-8308-6519-2 (digital)

Printed in the United States of America ∞

InterVarsity Press is committed to ecological stewardship and to the conservation of natural resources in all our operations. This book was printed using sustainably sourced paper.

Library of Congress Cataloging-in-Publication Data
A catalog record for this book is available from the Library of Congress.

P	25	24	23	22	21	20	19	18	17	16	15	14	13	12	11	10	9	8	7	6	5	4	3	2	1
Y	38	37	36	35	34	33	32	31	30	29	28	27	26	25	24	23	22	21	20	19					

"This book lays out the fascinating links between the tradition of Christian contemplation, mindfulness, and the process of change in psychotherapy. It puts all of these in the context of the vibrant literature that makes up these three fields. Christians everywhere will find it enthralling and practical."

Sue Johnson, author of *Created for Connection*, developer of the emotionally focused model of couple and family therapy

"Brilliantly written, *Contemplation and Counseling* provides a practical guide to integrating contemplative practices into contemporary counseling drawing upon scientific research, clinician theory, and spiritual understanding."

Diane R. Gehart, professor and author, *Mindfulness and Acceptance in Couple and Family Therapy*

"It is easy to be confused by the extravagant claims made for mindfulness in the media today. Here is a wise and measured guide to understanding the connections between the Christian-contemplative tradition and clinical-mindfulness practices. The book provides a rich survey of a wide range of helpful contemplative sources. It is more than a mere survey of practices and perspectives, it contains a clear invitation for readers to draw close to God through contemplative prayer."

James C. Wilhoit, professor of core studies and Scripture Press Professor of Christian education, Wheaton College

"Gregg Blanton immerses us in a rich integration of the pattern of contemplative prayer, the discoveries of relational neuroscience, and the practice of psychotherapy. In lovely detail, he traces how the attributes of the relationship with God that emerge in centering prayer are identical to the attributes that help us be a healing presence for our clients. While this is stated in Christian terms, the process is applicable to anyone—both client and therapist—who senses that spirituality and psychotherapy are intertwined processes. In many ways, it is an invitation to clients as well as therapists to open to the inherent healing wisdom within and become mystics at the same time. This book is beautiful, inspiring, thorough, wise, and filled with heart."

Bonnie Badenoch, author of *The Heart of Trauma: Healing the Embodied Brain in the Context of Relationships*

"Gregg Blanton has provided a needed service to the integration world. *Contemplation and Counseling* sheds light on how a contemplative view of psychology and theology can enhance the therapeutic process. His approach is practical and intervention focused in nature and wisely underscores that contemplative prayer has the potential of leading to deeper awareness of the power of love through real relational connection with a present and communicating God."

Gary W. Moon, founding executive director of Martin Institute for Christianity and Culture and Dallas Willard Center, Westmont College, author of *Becoming Dallas Willard*

"This is a must-read book for any Christian mental health professional wanting to cultivate the practice of contemplative prayer and to cultivate an experience of love in counseling. Blanton courageously illustrates how love is at the center of the contemplative counseling model that he is proposing, both as the goal and as the means to achieve that aim. He creatively blends findings from neuroscience and attachment science with a Christian theology of love as an antidote to human stress and fear. His contemplative-oriented style of counseling creatively weaves interventions influenced by Carl Rogers, Sue Johnson, Dan Siegel, and others together with interventions grounded in openness to receive God's love. In this inspiring and motivating book, Blanton presents a simple and accessible guide to centering prayer as a practice that can be taught to clients but only after the professional develops their own contemplative practice."

Lorrie Brubacher, author of *Stepping into Emotionally Focused Couple Therapy*, ICEEFT certified trainer in emotionally focused therapy

To Ana

CONTENTS

ACKNOWLEDGMENTS

EVEN THOUGH MY NAME is on this book, there is no way I could have written it by myself. There are so many people who have knowingly and unknowingly contributed to this project. Thinking back many years ago, I am thankful to Greg Robinson, who introduced me to the tradition of Christian contemplative thought. His suggestions of books to read set me on this path. I am grateful to my pastor, John Rice, for introducing me to a personal practice of contemplative prayer. My thanks go to my colleague Marlene Van Brocklin for sharing her love of lectio divina with me. The practice of lectio divina ushered me into the wonderful world of centering prayer.

Speaking of centering prayer, I cannot express enough my gratitude to Thomas Keating. His many books on centering prayer have guided my thinking and practice of contemplative prayer. It was because of his influence that I was able to get my first book published, so I am indebted to him for getting me started as an author. Everyone needs that first break. I feel so blessed to have been part of a centering prayer group led by Judy Harris.

I am grateful for the teachers in mindfulness and psychology who have helped shape my concepts about the integration of contemplation and counseling. I am especially thankful for the work of Daniel Siegel and his colleagues in the discipline of interpersonal neurobiology. The ideas of Sue Johnson have also made a deep impression on my way of doing counseling and being a counselor. I am grateful for the trail that Jon Kabat-Zinn blazed in mindfulness. My own training in MBSR motivated me to seek my own path within the Christian tradition.

I am indebted to the clients who have encouraged me in my attempts to integrate contemplative prayer into our work. I have learned so much from them as we have explored the ramifications of contemplative prayer for their lives. I appreciate the times when we have sat together in silent prayer during our sessions. Those have been precious moments.

Other folks have knowingly contributed to this project, and I am deeply grateful to them. First, I could not have done this without the masterful guidance of my editor, Jon Boyd. Thanks to Jon for believing in this project and for thoughtfully and skillfully leading me through the process. Next, the sabbatical offered to me by my institution, Montreat College, provided me with the opportunity to complete much of this project. Many thanks to Greg Kerr, academic dean, for standing behind this endeavor.

I am especially thankful to my daughter, Juliana Blanton, for her investment in this project. As I was in the process of writing this book, Juliana was completing a graduate program in clinical mental health counseling. I am indebted to her (she probably won't let me forget it) for carefully reading each chapter and for offering her constructive suggestions. It was truly a gift from her to me for which I am grateful.

And finally, my biggest thanks go to my lovely wife and companion, Ana. There is no way that I could have reached this point in my journey without her. Her support, encouragement, and belief in me have been constant and abiding. She has patiently spent countless hours talking with me about this book, reading early renditions of it, and offering her keen insights. I am grateful for the times we have spent together with God in contemplative prayer. Those moments capture the way in which she has been a solid, sustaining, and loving presence in my life. Ana, it is to you that I dedicate this book. I love you.

INTRODUCTION

AS INTEREST IN CONTEMPLATIVE thought is growing among Christians, it is time to consider the place of contemplative prayer within the field of counseling. Can contemplative prayer be integrated into therapeutic work? If so, how? How can this spiritual practice be used as a counseling intervention? Is the counselor's own practice of contemplative prayer important? If so, why? What exactly is contemplative prayer?

As we entertain these questions, an even larger issue inspires us. Can contemplative prayer actually serve as a foundation upon which to build a new approach to counseling? Does it provide clear insight into the client's situation? Might it offer us sound guidance for establishing a therapeutic relationship? Can contemplative prayer illuminate the purposes of counseling and suggest interventions for accomplishing these goals?

A robust model requires the use of many parts, and the integration of these various elements is essential. Because of their differences, these diverse components may not fall easily into place. The very essence of these divergent features can create tension, but my goal in this project is to achieve some degree of equilibrium and complementarity between these different pieces. And, as a result, I hope that we will create a sound and effective way of working with clients.

This new paradigm brings together many disparate components. It works to build an alliance among science, theology, and Christian contemplative thought in an effort to create a dynamic approach to counseling. It balances various dimensions of the human person: emotion, cognition, and action. It highlights and honors both the conscious and unconscious functions of the mind. And, by understanding the power of both words and silence, it equalizes and harmonizes their functions.

Ultimately, contemplative prayer leads us to the power of love. At each step along the way, as we construct a contemplative way of counseling, we are confronted with the healing capacity of love. How we view our clients, the ways we relate with them, and the strategies we use to help them change are all informed by our loving search for God in contemplative prayer.

In chapters one and two, I introduce the three voices that you will hear throughout this book. They are science, theology, and Christian contemplative thought. As we listen to the dialogue between these three disciplines, we discover complementary ideas that form the structures for this novel approach to counseling.

Chapters three and four offer an integrative understanding of the client's situation. The human person is multidimensional: physical, mental, spiritual, soulful, and relational. How does this viewpoint help us assess the client's relationships with God, others, and self? And, what mechanisms of change are revealed by our balanced perspective?

In the fifth chapter, we arrive at seven qualities needed of counselors. We discover that these traits are the product of a regular and consistent practice of contemplative prayer. So this raises the following questions: Do counselors who employ this new contemplative model need to engage in contemplative prayer themselves? If so, how do they go about establishing their own practice?

Based upon a multidimensional and integrative understanding of counseling, chapters six and seven reveal the core skills of this innovative paradigm. We see how a contemplative view of the human experience sheds light on the therapeutic process. Eleven fundamental interventions are examined in detail, one of them being the hallmark of this original approach: teaching contemplative prayer.

Bringing together the principles, practices, and basic tenets of the contemplative-oriented method of counseling, chapter eight sets forth a four-stage process for helping clients change. At each step along the way, we consider basic questions: (1) What is the client's process? (2) What are the counselor's objectives? (3) What is the nature of the counselor-client relationship? (4) What interventions are employed?

Chapter nine examines the element that pervades every aspect of this new method of counseling: love. This is a model by and for love. Once again, we approach our discussion from three angles: scientific, theological, and contemplative. We discover how love informs our view of human beings, the therapeutic relationship, counseling strategies, and the goal of counseling.

Speaking in unison, theology and science are calling counselors to a deeper engagement—on both personal and professional levels—with Christian contemplative prayer. This is my invitation to you as well. I have two wishes for you. First, I hope you will experience contemplative prayer for yourself. Second, I trust that the ideas of this book will support you as you venture into a contemplative-oriented approach to counseling.

ABBREVIATIONS

ACC	anterior cingulate cortex
ACT	acceptance and commitment therapy
COAL	curiosity, openness, acceptance, love
DBT	dialectical behavior therapy
EFT	emotionally focused therapy
EPE	elicit-provide-elicit
fMRI	functional magnetic resonance imaging
GABA	gamma-aminobutyric acid
IPNB	interpersonal neurobiology
MBCT	mindfulness-based cognitive therapy
MBSR	mindfulness-based stress reduction
MI	motivational interviewing
PACE	playfulness, acceptance, curiosity, empathy
PART	presence, attunement, resonance, trust
REBT	rational emotive behavior therapy

TWO VOICES

OUR JOURNEY INTO a Christian contemplative-oriented approach to counseling begins. We are building an integrated, holistic model for understanding Christian contemplative prayer in psychotherapy. Our goal is to comprehend what happens in counseling from the perspective of Christian contemplative prayer.

The design that guides our treatment rests on three pillars: Christian contemplative prayer, theology, and science. This approach is similar to that of Mark McMinn (2012), who argues for a model that integrates psychology, theology, and spirituality. However, the plan we are devising is different in that it includes other disciplines of science—such as neuroscience—alongside psychology. In addition, instead of addressing the broad topic of spirituality, this approach focuses on one particular area of spirituality: Christian contemplative prayer.

Where do we begin? In this chapter, we will examine two underpinnings of our model: science and theology. In the process of listening to these two voices, we will uncover several principles that will become central to our model for integrating Christian contemplation and counseling.

THE SCIENCE OF CONTEMPLATION

In our study of the science of contemplation, we must seriously consider the extraordinary interest that clinicians and researchers have shown in mindfulness over the past forty years. The *New York Times* recently described mindfulness as "perhaps the most popular new psychotherapy technique in the past decade" (Carey, 2008). A recent survey of over two thousand practicing social workers, counselors, and psychologists found that 41% of the sample utilized mindfulness as part of their counseling practice (Stratton, 2015). However, mindfulness has not always been so well embraced by the counseling community. What happened in order for the field of mental health to alter its original skeptical view of mindfulness? How did mindfulness move into mainstream psychotherapy? To answer these question, we must become acquainted with the premier pioneer of mindfulness work: Jon Kabat-Zinn.

Origins of mindfulness work. Jon Kabat-Zinn, professor of medicine at the University of Massachusetts, began his work in the late 1970s. His goal was to apply mindfulness in a modern medical setting. With the support of the medical faculty at the university, Kabat-Zinn developed a clinic that brought mindfulness to individuals with a wide range of medical conditions.

As his work progressed, Kabat-Zinn made the following contributions to the integration of mindfulness and psychotherapy: (1) an operational definition of mindfulness, (2) a treatment model, (3) a bridge to the mindulness-based treatment of psychological disorders, and (4) an emphasis upon scientific research.

Most of the literature and practice around mindfulness focuses on its Buddhist roots, and this was indeed Kabat-Zinn's original source of inspiration. However, Kabat-Zinn was searching for a way to make mindfulness available and accessible to a Western audience. His goal was to develop a secular definition of mindfulness that was also true to the essence of Buddhist teaching.

Kabat-Zinn (2003) settled on the following definition: "An operational working definition of mindfulness is: the awareness that emerges through paying attention on purpose, in the present moment, and nonjudgmentally to the unfolding experience moment by moment" (pp. 145-46). The key elements of Kabat-Zinn's definition are (1) paying attention, (2) the present moment, and (3) without judgment. Mindfulness is about focusing the mind in a very specific way. "On purpose" includes the intention of focusing on the present moment (D. Siegel, 2007). Being nonjudgmental means letting go of judgments of how the present moment should be and simply accepting what is.

With this secular-sounding definition of mindfulness, Kabat-Zinn went on to develop a treatment procedure to serve patients with difficult-to-treat medical issues. Kabat-Zinn introduced his program at the mindfulness-based stress reduction (MBSR) clinic at the University of Massachusetts in 1979. By 2012, there were over seven hundred MBSR programs being offered worldwide.

MBSR is an intensive eight-week program with a well-defined curriculum. The core program of MBSR consists of two- to three-hour weekly classes and one daylong class. The curriculum includes mindfulness breath meditation, mindfulness-based body scans, yoga with mindfulness, and loving-kindness meditation. Group members are expected to engage in a daily practice of twenty to forty-five minutes during the eight-week period. In the first phase of the program, participants are encouraged to pay attention to sensations within the body. After gaining this skill, group members then learn how to expand this awareness to their thoughts and feelings. Although MBSR is a demanding program, follow-up studies indicate that 80-95% of participants continue to practice mindfulness (Gehart, 2012).

From the outset, Kabat-Zinn and his colleagues wanted to demonstrate scientifically that MBSR training could improve physical health and accelerate rates of healing. A range of studies now demonstrates that mindfulness can help improve the medical conditions of people with psoriasis, fibromyalgia, multiple sclerosis, and hypertension. Mindfulness has been shown to enhance immune function and even raise the level of the enzyme telomerase, which is instrumental in maintaining and repairing the ends of chromosomes (D. Siegel, 2017).

MBSR, which originally proved effective in bringing about physiological improvements, has since produced remarkable results in the treatment of psychological concerns. The first counseling model to apply Kabat-Zinn's program to the treatment of psychological problems was mindfulness-based cognitive therapy (MBCT). In consultation with Kabat-Zinn, the originators of MBCT included many of the same mindfulness practices used in MBSR. Even though MBCT was designed to prevent relapse in participants with a history of depressive episodes, recent research indicates that it is effective for people with ongoing depression (Baer, 2010).

Within a few short decades, the mental health community has moved from a skeptical view of Kabat-Zinn's MBSR program to an enthusiastic embrace of his mindfulness-based approach. His remarkable success can be attributed to the careful, systematic research of his program. New research continues to provide growing evidence of the efficacy of mindfulness-based approaches in the treatment of both physical and psychological concerns.

Mindfulness-oriented therapies. Based on the success of MBSR, other mindfulness therapies emerged in the application of mindfulness to other symptoms and concerns. The three most widely known mindfulness therapies used in the treatment of psychological disorders are MBCT, acceptance and commitment therapy (ACT), and dialectical behavior therapy (DBT). All these approaches, which have received increasing empirical support for their efficacy, are rooted in the cognitive-behavioral tradition.

Described as the third wave of behavioral therapy, mindfulness therapies add a twist to traditional cognitive-behavioral therapies (Gehart, 2016). Mindfulness models are designed to help clients relate to their thoughts and internal dialogue with acceptance. Rather than approaching cognitions and feelings with the intention of changing them, clients are encouraged to deal with disturbing thoughts and emotions with inquisitiveness and compassion. The goal is to teach clients to approach their problems with curiosity and acceptance rather than with avoidance.

Mindfulness approaches are typically classified as either mindfulness based or mindfulness informed. MBCT, patterned after MBSR, is an example of a mindfulness-based model. MBCT is designed for small groups with up to twelve participants. In contrast to MBSR, which focuses on stress and the stress response, the teaching material of MBCT applies to depression. However, like MBSR, MBCT emphasizes formal guided meditations and requires therapists to have their own practice of mindfulness.

Even though MBCT is rooted in the tradition of cognitive therapy, it emphasizes the acceptance of thoughts rather than trying to get clients to change the content of their thinking. Instead of trying to replace negative thoughts with positive ones, as traditional cognitive therapy might do, MBCT focuses on noticing the effects of negative thoughts on the body in terms of body sensations.

The other two dominant mindfulness approaches—ACT and DBT—fit within the mindfulness-informed category. DBT was developed at the University of Washington in the late 1970s by Marsha Linehan. To learn more about acceptance, her area of interest, Linehan studied Zen Buddhism. With the concepts she acquired, Linehan began to integrate acceptance and mindfulness with traditional cognitive-behavioral strategies.

DBT is characterized by the tension between acceptance and change (Gehart, 2016). On the one hand, the counselor accepts the client just as he or she is at the present moment. DBT acceptance involves embracing the good and bad without judgment or the need to change anything. On the other hand, the counselor recognizes that change is continuous and necessary. The counselor embodies this synthesis by balancing acceptance of the client with recognizing that change is needed.

DBT is a well-regarded, widely used evidence-based treatment for borderline personality disorder (Gehart, 2016). Over time, it has been used increasingly to treat eating disorders, depressive disorders, bipolar disorders, substance-abuse disorders, and self-harming disorders in adolescents. Treatment of clients generally involves attendance at weekly individual sessions and weekly group sessions. In their group meetings, clients are taught four basic sets of skills. One of these core components is mindfulness. (Linehan, along with Kabat-Zinn, was one of the first to include mindfulness as part of her therapeutic model.) The six mindfulness skills taught in DBT are divided into three "what" skills—observing, describing, and participating—and three "how" skills—nonjudgmentally, mindfully, and effectively.

The second major mindfulness-informed therapy is ACT. ACT, like the other third-wave behavioral approaches, asserts that any attempt to control thoughts is the problem, not the solution. Instead, ACT incorporates mindfulness exercises that facilitate awareness and acceptance of thoughts and feelings. The acronym, ACT, outlines the basic process of this model: (1) *A* refers to the acceptance of difficult thoughts and feelings, (2) *C* refers to the client's choices and commitment to a life direction that reflects who the client truly is, and (3) *T* refers to the action steps that the client is willing to take toward her or his life direction.

ACT has been used to treat a variety of client problems. The current literature describes the use of ACT with depression, anxiety, anger, substance abuse, chronic pain, and work stress (Baer, 2010). The empirical evidence supporting the effectiveness of ACT, which has grown significantly over the past decade, is both noteworthy and promising.

The mindfulness approaches discussed in this section share some similarities, yet they also differ. They all encourage clients to mindfully experience thoughts and feelings that they typically avoid. Using these mindfulness approaches, clients learn to accept cognitions and emotions; then they commit to choosing more effective behaviors. MBCT, the mindfulness-based approach, teaches formal mindfulness to clients as a primary intervention. In contrast, clients who participate in the mindfulness-informed approaches—DBT and ACT—are not expected to engage in formal mindfulness practices. Instead, these clients are introduced to mindfulness principles and informal mindfulness skills within the context of broader therapeutic models.

The neurobiology of mindfulness. In 2003, the path of Jon Kabat-Zinn intersected with that of Daniel Siegel, professor of psychiatry at the UCLA School of Medicine and co-director of UCLA's Mindful Research Center. Since the early 1990s, Siegel had been working on an interdisciplinary view of the mind and mental health. Soon after meeting Kabat-Zinn, Siegel attended a series of trainings in mindfulness being led by Kabat-Zinn. Siegel began to practice mindfulness in his personal life and included mindfulness as an important element of his model, called interpersonal neurobiology (IPNB).

Siegel and his IPNB model are now at the forefront of research in the interconnections of mindfulness, mental health, psychotherapy, and the brain. Siegel's work has been important in (1) explaining mindfulness, (2) exploring the effects of mindfulness, (3) researching how mindfulness affects the brain, and (4) enlarging mindfulness research to include other forms of religious contemplation.

Siegel's perspective of mindfulness. Daniel Siegel (2017) builds his work upon a simple assertion: "What we do with our mind matters" (p. 308). What are we supposed to do with our minds? According to Siegel, we have the wonderful opportunity of using our minds to focus our attention. This is what mindfulness is about, focusing the mind in specific ways (D. Siegel, 2007).

Focusing is about paying attention in the present moment. This creates a special form of awareness called mindfulness. Daniel Siegel (2007) divides attention into three dimensions: orienting, alerting, and executive. We are orienting when we select an object upon which to focus. Orienting is the "aiming" part of attention. Alerting is when we maintain our focus on the selected object. Alerting is the "sustaining" part of attention. When we notice that our focus has drifted away from our selected target and then return our focus to that object, we are using the executive function.

Aiming and sustaining our attention are central to the practice of mindfulness. To practice mindfulness, we must have the intention of aiming and sustaining our focus on a selected object. We must also have the capacity to realize that our attention has wandered and then be able to refocus our attention. Orienting, alerting, and executing are the essential elements of mindfulness.

For example, a common first step in mindfulness is for practitioners to focus their attention on their breath. When they notice that their attention has drifted off to something else, as it invariably does, they return their attention to their breathing. Over and over again, by returning their focus to their breath, they develop the aim and sustain dimensions of the mind's attention.

Drawing a direct line between mindfulness and attention, Siegel (2007) observes, "Mindfulness involves attuning our attention to our own intention" (p. 164). This description highlights two vital concepts that are related to attention: intention and attuning. What is intention? Siegel (2017) explains that intention is about "developing a state of mind with purpose and direction" (p. 284). Practitioners must be aiming their attention at a selected object (e.g., breath, a candle, the sound of a bell, etc.). And they must have the purpose of sustaining their attention on that object. For example, practitioners of breath awareness must first have the intention of aiming and sustaining their attention on their breathing.

Focusing is about paying attention to one's intention in the present moment. Can I be aware this moment of what I am doing (e.g., typing, reading, drinking a cup of tea, etc.)? Or is my mind on something else, such as the meeting I had yesterday or my plans for tomorrow? Often our minds are preoccupied with the past and worried about the future, but mindfulness brings us into the present. What am I doing, thinking, feeling, and sensing at this precise point in time? Can I be aware that I am typing as I am typing? That is the nature of mindfulness—paying attention in a specific way to the experience of this moment.

In addition to intention, mindfulness and attention are also about attuning. What is attuning? Attunement is about attending to one's own intentions. For example, when I sit down to contemplate, do I bring my intention into focus?

From a Christian perspective, am I paying attention to my intention of focusing on God? Do I get distracted from my intention by memories of the past or plans for the future? It doesn't matter. I simply return my attention to my intention, to be with God. That is attunement.

Another example of attunement, from a mindfulness perspective, would be the practice of breath awareness. You select your breath as your object of attention. You are aware that your intention is to focus upon your breathing for a period of time. When your mind shifts its focus to some other object—such as an event that is coming up later in the day—you notice that your mind has wandered from its intention. Then you bring your attention back to your intention. That is attunement.

Siegel (2007) explicitly describes mindfulness as a "form of internal attunement" (p. 132). Just as focusing on the inner world of another person—paying attention to their thoughts and feelings—creates interpersonal attunement or intimacy with that person, concentrating on your own cognitions and emotions fosters an attunement or companionship with yourself. By paying attention to your own intentions, you create an internal closeness that allows you to become your "own best friend" (D. Siegel, 2007, p. 172). Siegel (2007) argues that this "form of self-relationship" (p. 17), this "form of attention and care focused on oneself" (p. 215), fosters a "secure relationship with the self" (p. 191).

The effects of mindfulness. Siegel's research into mindfulness led him to three core concepts: (1) presence, (2) integration, and (3) love. Siegel (2017) writes, "Presence is the portal for integration to arise" (p. 283). Finally, he concludes that integration is made visible through love. It goes like this: presence → integration → love.

First, Siegel observed that mindfulness—paying attention in the present moment—fosters a state of mind or trait called *presence.* Siegel (2010a) observes, "Presence means being open, now, to whatever is" (p. 13). Presence is about (1) being open, (2) being in the now, and (3) being accepting. The first quality of presence is openness, which can be described as receptivity. Instead of being closed, we are in a stance of receiving. Rather than reacting and turning away, we turn toward and accept the experience (e.g., thought, feeling, sensation) that is happening right now.

The next element of presence is being in the now. *Now* can be defined as this present moment. Our minds seem to be so easily drawn to the past and the future, but they avoid the present. However, mindfulness is about paying attention to the present moment. What is happening now?

The final component of presence is acceptance. Acceptance is about receiving things as they are at this moment. When we exercise acceptance, we are being nonjudgmental. Instead of judging the activities of our mind, acceptance says, "You don't have to change or remove any thought, feeling, or sensation that you are experiencing at this moment." If we want, we can observe these inner workings with curiosity or we can gently turn our awareness to something else that is happening at this present moment.

Siegel (2017) argues that the concept of presence is captured by the three O's of mindfulness: observation, objectivity, and openness. First, there is the choosing of an object to observe. For example, we choose our breath as the target of our attention. During the observation, we are aware that we are observing the object of our attention. Objectivity is the ability to have a thought or feeling and not get caught up in it. With objectivity, we realize that the thought is just a thought instead of perceiving it as reality. And finally, openness means that we can be receptive to what arises as it arises.

Presence is the opposite of unfocused attention. Often we have a blurry notion of what is happening. In a cloudy way we know that something is happening in and around us. However, with mindfulness, we develop a sharp focus. With observation, objectivity, and openness, our minds begin to see things with greater depth and clarity. This sharp awareness is called presence.

For Daniel Siegel (2017), presence is the doorway that leads to integration. And integration is the basis of health and well-being. But what is integration? Integration is about making connections. It is the process by which separate elements are linked together into a working whole (D. Siegel, 2010b). Siegel identifies nine domains of integration. As one moves toward integration, one is also being transformed. For Siegel (2010a), "Transformation is how we move from nonintegrated ways of being to integration" (p. 235). Integration, for Siegel (2010a), is at the heart of psychotherapy. The changes that occur through psychotherapy and mindfulness are brought about by "releasing the transformative power of integration" (p. 248).

Finally, Siegel concludes that integration is the route to love. Love is Siegel's ultimate destination as a researcher, educator, and counselor. Siegel (2007) observes that mindfulness and attunement activate a system that is similar to "love without fear" (p. 130). (Without realizing it, Siegel is quoting from 1 Jn 4:18.) Love is about approaching the moment with curiosity, openness, and acceptance.

Mindfulness and the brain. Daniel Siegel is recognized as the premier researcher into the interconnections between mindfulness and the brain (Gehart, 2012). His studies examine the neural mechanisms associated with contemplative practices. Siegel argues that the way we focus our minds can actually change our brains. Even though our understanding of how contemplative practices affect the brain is still in its infancy stage, Siegel offers three observations about how these ancient practices can alter the structure and function of the brain.

First, Siegel (2007) asserts that a contemplative practice alters the connections between the prefrontal cortex and limbic zones of the brain. (It is important to know that there are neural connections that descend directly from the middle prefrontal cortex to the amygdala.) As contemplative practitioners focus their attention, the inhibitory neurotransmitter gamma-aminobutyric acid (GABA) is released from the middle prefrontal cortex to the amygdala, thus soothing painful emotions. Bonnie Badenoch (2008) says that, because of mindfulness, our fears are calmed as axonal fibers connecting the middle prefrontal region and the amygdala carry GABA to the fear-encoding neurons of the amygdala. The influence of GABA then modulates the excited amygdala.

Second, Siegel (2007) associates mindfulness with nine functions of the prefrontal cortex. For example, as practitioners engage in mindfulness—thus enhancing these brain functions—their body regulation systems improve, they become more attuned to and empathic with others, they achieve greater emotional stability, their ability to pause before responding increases, they get better at calming their fears, and they engage in more behaviors that contribute to the welfare of others. To summarize, the practice of mindfulness is associated with and improves these important functions of the brain.

Finally, Siegel (2007) observes that mindfulness produces a left shift in frontal activation. What does this mean? It indicates that mindfulness shifts brain activity from the right hemisphere to the left prefrontal regions of the brain. The amazing discovery is that this shift to the left is associated with an approach state. In other words, you are now willing to turn toward or face the mental activities that you previously avoided—fear-producing thoughts, old memories, painful emotions.

Neuroscience is telling us that contemplative practices literally modify the structures and functions of the brain. But what are practitioners actually doing during their practice that invites these changes? Researchers agree that the refocusing of attention produces these amazing alterations (Gehart, 2012). Over and over again, as practitioners engage in a twenty-minute period of formal contemplation, they focus their attention, lose focus, and then refocus. Refocusing is the simple mechanism that rewires the brain and develops new neural pathways.

Enlarging the tent. As he continued to study the nature of mindfulness, an important truth dawned on Siegel. That is, he realized that this special way of focusing the mind was not only practiced in Buddhism but also in Christianity. He discovered that this way of paying attention was a fundamental part of Christian contemplative prayer (D. Siegel, 2007). Realizing that a contemplative tradition existed within Christianity, Siegel began to enlarge the tent of his discussion. Instead of referring to only one form of contemplation—mindfulness—Siegel (2007) began using a broader term, "contemplative mindful practice" (p. 9). This was the beginning of a scientific curiosity in contemplative practices outside of Buddhism, an interest that included Christian contemplative prayer.

An evangelical response to the science of mindfulness. *A response to Siegel's IPNB model.* The emerging field of interpersonal neurobiology (IPNB) has recently caught the attention of the evangelical mental health community. Leaders within this group view Daniel Siegel's model as a useful fulcrum for integrating contemporary neuroscience with Christian counseling (Clinton & Sibcy, 2012; Jennings, 2013; Thompson, 2010). IPNB is also seen as a useful bridge between neurobiology and Christian formation practices, such as contemplative prayer (Edwards, 2015).

Two of these authors, Thompson (2010) and Jennings (2013)—both psychiatrists—share an appreciation for Siegel's emphasis on the nine functions of the prefrontal cortex. Along with Siegel, they stress the importance of strengthening and healing the prefrontal regions of the brain. As Christians, both Thompson and Jennings turn to biblical methods for accomplishing this end.

Evangelical authors share a propensity to accept certain elements of Siegel's model—neuroscience, behavioral development, and attachment theory—while sidestepping an essential component of interpersonal neurobiology: mindfulness. In Thompson's case, he downplays Siegel's emphasis on mindfulness, simply saying that Siegel integrates "spirituality" (rather than "mindfulness") into IPNB. Jennings makes a similar mistake. He replaces the term *mindfulness* with the word *meditation*.

Using the term *meditation* instead of *mindfulness* (or *contemplation*) is troubling because it misleads the reader. (We will explore the difference between contemplation and meditation in chapter two.) Jennings suggests that practitioners are meditating when they are intently focusing their mind on a spiritual idea, such as a passage from the Bible or an attribute of God. However, this is not what Siegel means by the terms *mindfulness meditation* and *contemplative mindful practices*—such as Christian contemplative prayer. Instead, both mindfulness meditation and Christian contemplative prayer are practices that teach practitioners how to let go of thoughts—versus ongoing rumination or concentration on an idea—so that they can rest in silence.

If we are to embrace Siegel's model, we must come to terms with an essential element of IPNB—mindfulness (or contemplative practices). This brings us to the next section, in which we explore how evangelicals are responding to the integration of mindfulness and counseling.

A response to mindfulness and counseling. To date, evangelical counselors have offered us three responses to mindfulness-oriented therapies. The first option is to embrace mindful-based interventions. The second possibility is to treat clients with a Christianized version of mindfulness. The third recourse is to use Christian contemplation as an intervention within a mindfulness-informed model of counseling. My goal in this book is to offer a fourth approach, a Christian contemplative-oriented approach to counseling.

Siang-Yang Tan (2011) and David Wang and Tan (2016) represent the first camp. Their approach to mindfulness-oriented models is first to offer empirical evidence that supports the efficacy of MBCT, ACT, and DBT. Based upon this scientific support, they encourage Christian counselors to employ mindfulness-based interventions with their clients. Wang and Tan (2016) then proceed to add a couple of ideas from the Christian contemplative tradition: "learning to be mindful of the sacrament or sacredness of the present moment, and surrendering to God and his will" (p. 73).

Tan and Wang offer us a mix of useful and inadequate guidance. We can applaud their efforts to educate counselors about the scientific support for and effectiveness of mindfulness-oriented models of counseling. We need to be informed about these interventions. We can also appreciate Tan and Wang's attempt to bridge the divide between Buddhist mindfulness and Christian contemplative prayer. However, the fact that they offer us only two principles that are grounded within the Christian contemplative tradition leaves us wanting more.

The second possibility, recommended by Scott Symington and Melissa Symington (2012), is to offer clients a Christianized model of mindfulness. Their goal is to create a brand-new design, one that utilizes both Buddhist and Christian thinking. In the end, they offer counselors a model that rests upon three basic concepts: presence of mind, acceptance, and internal observation. Using an eight-week program (modeled after Kabat-Zinn's MBSR), they employ mindfulness skills that fall into three categories: breath meditation, informal mindfulness throughout the day, and watching internal sensations. Symington and Symington (2012) supplement their model with only two ideas from the Christian contemplative tradition: "attuning to God's presence and appreciating the sacredness of the present moment" (p. 76).

The third choice is to offer Christian contemplative practices within the context of mindfulness-informed theoretical orientations. The contribution of Joshua Knabb and Thomas Frederick (2017) represents this approach. Employing ACT, they utilize contemplative strategies as interventions for their clients.

Even though we can commend the efforts of these researchers at interdisciplinary integration, something important is missing from these three options. We need a theoretical frame of reference that contains insights from the Christian contemplative tradition in general and contemplative prayer in particular. Teaching clients how to practice contemplative prayer is a good first step. However, we must go further, offering clients goals, techniques, and principles that are thoroughly rooted in a Christian contemplative worldview.

Why is this fourth option important and necessary? I hope to address these questions in the next section.

An argument for a Christian contemplative-oriented approach. I believe that a dialogue between mindfulness and Christian contemplation is important. They both have important contributions to make to clinical practice and research. There are similarities, but they are also different. It is their differences that motivate me to offer a fourth option for counselors.

What are the commonalities shared by mindfulness and Christian contemplative prayer? According to Stephen Stratton (2015), they possess similar concepts and constructs. Both contemplative prayer and mindfulness place an emphasis upon our embodied natures, breathing, present-moment awareness, and nonsuppressive strategies for managing distracting thoughts. Both of these contemplative practices overlap in their use of two processes, that is, concentration and insight (or open awareness). Concentration refers to a laserlike focus on a specific sound, object, or bodily sensation. When practitioners concentrate, they are intent on not letting their attention wander from the selected target. Insight, on the other hand, allows for broader awareness. In other words, insight promotes nonspecific attention or wider awareness. Practicing awareness, when distracting thoughts appear practitioners watch them appear and then let them pass. Aware that their focus has wandered, they stay with their thoughts briefly, observing their rise and fall.

Christian contemplative prayer overlaps with mindfulness and shares an emphasis on attentional regulation (Stratton, 2015). Contemplative prayer blends elements of both concentration and insight, situating itself somewhere in the middle. When a person practices contemplative prayer, his or her attention is shifting back and forth between a laserlike focus and broader awareness. This means that people who practice Christian contemplation first pick a target of attention—God. When their minds wander, they may observe the distracting thought briefly before returning their focus to God.

Theologian Martin Laird's view of Christian contemplative prayer dovetails with Stratton's scientific understanding. Laird (2011) writes, "The practice of contemplation is as much concerned with the expansion of awareness as it is with the concentration of our attention" (p. 5). Both processes—awareness and concentration—are two components of Christian contemplative prayer. The practice of contemplative prayer is not one or the other. It is both.

Even though there are clear similarities between mindfulness and Christian contemplative prayer, I do not suggest that they are identical processes.

Because they are distinguishable, a model informed by Christian contemplation is remarkably distinct from one that is oriented toward mindfulness. What are the major differences between these two contemplative practices, and where do these dissimilarities lead us in terms of counseling practice? In other words, what are their implications for therapeutic strategies?

The first distinction is that contemplative prayer integrates the client's faith into counseling, whereas this is not the case with mindfulness (Stratton, 2015). Mindfulness has intentionally separated itself from its historical roots in Buddhism and presents itself as a secular contemplative practice. The term *secular* is used to indicate that a religious or spiritual worldview is absent. When a technique or counseling model is secular, it purposefully eliminates concepts and practices that are religious or spiritual.

By teaching a Christian client contemplative prayer, the counselor is intentionally integrating the client's faith into the counseling experience. The counselor is embedding a technique, contemplative prayer, within a specific religious framework, that is, Christian. By using contemplative prayer, the counselor is sending the message, "I value your Christian experience." Emphasizing a religious/spiritual experience—contemplative prayer—allows the counselor to then incorporate ways of relating, thinking, and behaving that are situated in the Christian faith.

The main difference between Christian contemplative prayer and mindful contemplative practice is one of purpose. The principal contrast is that contemplative prayer is built around a relationship with God, whereas mindfulness is not (Ferguson, Willemsen, & Castañeto, 2010). When clients engage in contemplative prayer, they are aiming at greater communion with God. The clear message to our clients is, "When you become present and open to God, God's power will change you."

The purpose of mindfulness-informed models is different. The objective is for clients to grow by means of their own efforts, through the practice of mindfulness (Madagáin, 2007). For this reason, mindfulness-informed therapies place an emphasis upon "skills." In DBT the core skills are interpersonal effectiveness, emotion regulation, and distress regulation, while in ACT the main skills are creative helplessness, cognitive diffusion, acceptance, self as context, and valuing (Germer, 2005). Through their own abilities, clients are taught that they can overcome problems and give meaning to their lives.

Even Buddhist authors recognize this main distinction between mindfulness and contemplative prayer. Gehart (2012) points out the primary difference: "Christians use contemplative prayer as a means of having direct contact with God. . . . Buddhism does not use mindfulness to directly connect with God" (p. 9). At the heart of Christianity is the belief in our need for a relationship or friendship with God through the Son. Jesus said, "I have called you friends" (Jn 15:15). Christianity is about turning to or depending upon God because we cannot solve our problems. Only God can save us from our condition and give our lives purpose.

In contrast, Buddhist mindfulness is a turning to self for a solution. For Daniel Siegel (2007), mindfulness is about creating—on your own—an internal closeness that allows you to become your "own best friend" (p. 172). Siegel teaches us that mindfulness is about focusing on yourself and establishing a relationship with yourself. On this point, the purpose of the contemplative practice, Christian contemplative thought and mindfulness clearly disagree.

Are the two distinctions that we have identified between mindfulness and a Christian contemplative-oriented approach significant? This question is only beginning to receive attention in the literature. Wachholtz and Pargament (2005, 2008) conducted two relevant studies that compared secular and religious contemplation—a form of contemplation that admittedly emphasized the concentration side of contemplation. The participants in the religious meditation group focused on phrases such as "God is peace," "God is joy," "God is love," and "God is good," whereas subjects in the secular group concentrated on the following language: "I am content," "I am joyful," "I am good," and "I am happy."

Wachholtz and Pargament wanted to determine if spirituality—one that attends to the subject's relationship with God—is a critical component of contemplation. They found that participants benefitted significantly more from the religious than from the secular form of contemplation. The subjects in the spiritual group reported a greater increase in their closeness to God over the course of research. The study also revealed improvement in mood and decrease in anxiety among the people who were assigned to the spiritual group. Wachholtz and Pargament (2005) concluded, "Spiritual techniques may be more effective than secular techniques" (p. 383).

What are the implications of these scientific studies? The results indicate that Christian clients respond well to a counseling approach that integrates contemplative prayer with treatment strategies that are embedded in Christian contemplative thought. The practice of contemplative prayer is important because it is built upon a relationship with God and emerges from within the client's own faith. As the counselor uses principles—God's love, the counselor's presence, and therapeutic techniques—that arise from contemplative prayer, clients benefit and change. As Fox, Gutierrez, Haas, Braganza, and Berger (2015) contend in their review of the scientific literature on contemplative prayer, "There is evidence accumulating that contemplative practices produce the largest psychological and spiritual gains when they are practiced within a spiritual context. It is therefore becoming increasingly important to understand contemplative practices as they exist within their faith origins" (pp. 804-5).

The Christian tradition of contemplative prayer is rich with ideas that inform our approach to counseling. My contention is that the Christian contemplative heritage provides counselors with a clear perspective on the three components of counseling: (1) a useful understanding of the client's situation, (2) guidance for establishing a helping relationship, and (3) effective interventions for resolving the client's presenting problem (Gehart, 2016).

Mindfulness has produced numerous effective models of counseling, but it is time for an integrated Christian contemplative-oriented approach to counseling. A host of mindfulness authors have invited advocates of Christian contemplative prayer to engage in the scientific discussion about the integration of contemplative practices and psychotherapy (Gehart, 2012; Kristeller, 2010; D. Siegel, 2007; R. Siegel, 2010). But so far the call to introduce a truly Christian contemplative-informed model of counseling has gone unanswered.

Why has the evangelical mental health community failed to introduce a Christian contemplative-oriented model of counseling? First, until recently, the evangelical Christian community has largely overlooked the Christian contemplative tradition and the practice of contemplative prayer (Stratton, 2015). The second impediment has been the lack of an evangelical theological framework for understanding contemplative prayer. What is the broader theological perspective from which we are to view contemplative prayer? What is the biblical nature of contemplation? For too long, the evangelical community has not had answers to these essential questions. However, within the past few years, evangelical authors have offered us reasonable theological responses to our questions about contemplative prayer. It is to these theological underpinnings of a Christian contemplative-based model of counseling that we now turn.

A THEOLOGY OF CONTEMPLATIVE PRAYER

We need an inherently Christian description of contemplation. A truly Christian approach to contemplative prayer must be consistent with historical theology and the Scriptures. Contemplative prayer must be grounded in a theological understanding of fundamental biblical themes such as sin, the revelation of God, God's grace, the Word, the Holy Spirit, and the saving work of our Lord Jesus Christ. This theological approach to contemplative prayer must answer these basic questions: (1) What makes contemplation possible? (2) What is our role in contemplation? (3) What is contemplative prayer?

An examination of faulty views of contemplative prayer provides a useful backdrop for our study of the theological underpinnings of Christian contemplation (Coe, 2014). Contemplative prayer is considered by some as a technique for reaching and knowing God. Others think of it as an attempt through human effort to bridge the gap between God and humanity. Sometimes contemplative prayer is viewed as a method for meeting our deep hunger for God.

Theologian John Coe (2014), building upon Nicene theology of the fourth century, offers theological corrections to these faulty views. The orthodox Christian position is that there is a giant chasm between God and humanity. This gap cannot be bridged by human effort. Instead, knowledge of God is grounded solely in God's sovereign choice to reveal himself. For God to be known by humanity, God must take the initiative to reveal himself, which is what he did in the incarnation and in sending the indwelling of the Holy Spirit. Personal knowledge of God is made possible in the work of Christ on the cross, which makes a relationship with or knowledge of God possible.

As we begin to slowly examine the themes offered by Coe, we see the application of important theological themes to the subject of contemplative prayer. First, there is the truth about the human condition. Humanity is lost in sin. That is, we are separated from God, and there is nothing we can do on our own to reconcile ourselves with God. Contemplative prayer is not an attempt on our part to reach or know God.

Then what makes contemplative prayer possible? It is only achievable by God's initiative to reveal himself to us. This is exactly what God did by sending his Son and the Holy Spirit. It is not our effort but God's initiative that provides us with access to the Father through the Son by the Spirit. In the words of theologian Kyle Strobel (2014), "God creates the possibility for contemplation" (p. 90).

God makes contemplation possible through the work of his Son (Strobel, 2014). First, Jesus acts as a high priest who leads us before the Father (Heb 6:20). By sacrificing himself, Jesus became a mediator between God and humanity. Second, Jesus invites us to participate in his Sonship. By receiving Christ, we become children of the Father. Due to our adoption into his Sonship, we come to God within the very person of Christ. We become "hidden with Christ in God" (Col 3:3). Because of his Sonship, we are able to proclaim with Christ, "*Abba*, Father" (Mk 14:36). Contemplation is possible because we are united to the Son and because the Son leads us before the Father.

The movement of God toward us is also evident in the indwelling of the Holy Spirit. What is the work of God's Spirit? By receiving the Spirit, we become children of God, thus allowing us to address God as "*Abba*, Father" (Rom 8:15). The third person of the Trinity assures us that we are God's children (Rom 8:16). God himself, through the Holy Spirit, communicates with us (Rom 8:16). In a wonderful way, the third person of the Trinity assures us of God's love for us (Rom 5:5). And finally, God's Spirit prays for us at a level that is too deep for words (Rom 8:26). Contemplation is possible because of the indwelling of the Holy Spirit.

Our discussion so far makes it clear that contemplation is possible only because of God's initiative. Contemplative prayer is not our effort to get to God. Instead, God comes to us through the work of the Son and the Holy Spirit. So what is our role in contemplative prayer?

The question of our role in contemplation is an important one. In contemplative prayer, we do not exert effort but we are active. We are performing an important work when we are receptive of God. Receptivity, an attitude of waiting on God, is a difficult kind of activity. Even though we are alert and animated in contemplative prayer, we are not putting forth effort. The term *effort* connotes that we are trying to make something happen, such as ushering in God's presence. But God's presence is a gift, one that we cannot control. We can only be open to and receive this gift. As Christian contemplative teacher Thomas Keating (1999) writes, "The chief act of the will is not effort but consent" (p. 71). He adds that the activity of the will is to "consent to God's coming, to the inflow of grace" (p. 71). Keating concludes, "To receive God is the chief work of contemplative prayer" (p. 71).

The last important question that calls for a theological answer is, What is contemplative prayer? First, theologian, Evan Howard (2014) tells us that contemplative prayer is about communicating with God.

As we know, communication between two parties involves both speech and listening, with rich gaps in between. Contemplative prayer, as communication with God, exhibits these important dimensions. Contemplative prayer is not wordless, as some would suppose. As we begin to pray, we may be bombarded with a multitude of thoughts and words, but then we may slowly transition into a period of silence. During this time of quietness, being in God's presence is sufficient. There is no need for talking or even thinking. Howard (2014) writes, "It seems good and natural that we would—and even should—permit a communicative presence with God that takes place without particular words or even thoughts" (p. 135). After a brief period of silence, we may find ourselves entertaining other distracting thoughts and words. Contemplative prayer is not a static state. Instead, in this type of prayer, we are in a continuous state of flux between words and silence.

Some may question whether this description of contemplative prayer fits with the prayer life of Jesus. How much of Jesus' prayers involved words, and how much of the time was he sitting in silence with his Father? We cannot be sure because we know little about Jesus' prayer practices (Howard, 2014). How much of the time was he talking when he spent the whole night praying (Lk 6:12)? We know that he prayed for one hour in Gethsemane, but only three sentences are recorded (Mk 14:35-37). We can only deduce that Jesus' prayer fluctuated between words and silence, and that is the nature of contemplative prayer.

In response to our third question—What is contemplative prayer?—contemplative prayer is essentially about knowing God and being known by God (Strobel, 2014). Strobel (2014) asserts, "The ultimate grounding of contemplation is being contemplated as one who is known; caught up in the contemplation of God as one who is in Christ" (p. 96). God gazes at us as *in Christ*. The only thing that we can do in response is to look back at God. In contemplative prayer, we experience a type of face-to-face knowing. The Father gazes upon our face, and we respond by seeking his face (Ps 27:8). That is the nature of contemplation.

By now, you will have noticed that I have not actually defined contemplative prayer. My intention was to first establish a sound theological foundation for our definition. Now that we have established a broad theological perspective, it is time to take on a distinctively Christian definition of contemplation. That is the subject of chapter two.

CONCLUSION

Before moving on to the next chapter, I want to revisit the scientific and theological foundation of contemplative prayer. How do these underpinnings inform the Christian contemplative-oriented approach that I am presenting? I wish to suggest that we as counselors recognize the following principles and concepts as essential for integrating contemplative prayer and counseling:

1. *An operational definition of contemplative prayer.* We will work on establishing an operational definition of contemplative prayer.

2. *Scientific grounding.* We will promote a dialogue between science and faith. I agree with Christian psychiatrist Timothy Jennings (2013), who writes, "To maintain a healthy balance, we must use the Bible and harmonize it with science" (p. 12).

3. *Contemplative prayer as an intervention.* We will teach clients how to practice contemplative prayer as a way to address their presenting problems.

4. *Practice by the counselor.* Counselors need their own personal contemplative prayer practice. (You can't teach what you haven't experienced.) I will offer ideas to support counselors as they establish their own practice.

5. *Conversant with current models of counseling.* We will create a model that integrates ideas from contemplative prayer with complementary features from present-day psychotherapy models.

6. *Integration.* We will concentrate on the following types of integration: (1) left and right brain functions; (2) words and silence; (3) past, present, and future; (4) body, mind, and heart; (5) acceptance and change; (6) sitting and action; (7) body, mind, emotions, and behavior; and (8) conscious and unconscious mind.

7. *Prefrontal functions.* We will emphasize the following prefrontal functions in our model: (1) attunement with God, others, and self; (2) emotional balance; (3) fear modulation; (4) self-awareness; (5) attention to the body; and (6) loving behavior.

8. *Love.* We will establish love as the means and end of our contemplative-oriented approach to counseling.

9. *Presence.* We will promote an approach that begins with the presence of God and includes the quality of presence in the counselor.

10. *Historical theology.* We will attempt to support every therapeutic strategy with Scripture, historical theology, and Christian contemplative thought.

CONTEMPLATIVE PRAYER

IN THE LAST CHAPTER, I pointed out that the scientific and mental health communities lean toward one form of contemplative practice—mindfulness—which has a more secular orientation. But scientific evidence is mounting to support the need for counselors to use Christian contemplative practices with certain clients because it may fit more appropriately with the clients' faith origins. As we proceed to establish a Christian contemplative-oriented approach to counseling, an inherently Christian account of contemplation is called for. We began to develop this understanding in chapter one by erecting a theological foundation for contemplative prayer. In this chapter, we will continue to build upon this underpinning by exploring three questions: (1) What is contemplative prayer? (2) What is a useful context for engaging in this practice? (3) Is there a good method for practicing contemplative prayer?

WHAT CONTEMPLATIVE PRAYER IS NOT

There are many misconceptions and much misinformation about the properties of contemplation. Therefore, before saying anything about what contemplative prayer is, it may be helpful to clarify what it isn't. Let's examine four common myths about contemplative prayer in order to better understand the true nature and dynamics of contemplative prayer:

- Myth 1: Contemplative prayer is a relaxation technique.
- Myth 2: The goal of contemplative prayer is to free our minds of thoughts.
- Myth 3: Contemplative prayer is employed in an effort to reach and know God.
- Myth 4: Meditation and contemplative prayer are synonyms.

Many people think that contemplative prayer is a relaxation strategy (Keating, 1999), but contemplative prayer is not a technique. It is prayer. In prayer, we are entering into a relationship with God. Yes, a relaxation response often results from contemplative prayer, but it is strictly a side effect. Relaxation is a byproduct rather than the goal of contemplative prayer.

Another misconception about contemplative prayer is that it involves clearing the mind of thoughts. Contemplative prayer is often considered a way to stop the activities of the mind. But contemplative prayer is not opposed to thoughts. Thomas Keating (1999) advises us to simply accept the fact that thinking is going to happen when we practice contemplative prayer. When we recognize this reality, we are less likely to be upset when thoughts arise. The goal of contemplative prayer is not to be free of all thinking. Instead, as Keating (1999) reminds us, the aim "is to deepen our relationship with Jesus Christ" (p. 50).

A third myth is that contemplative prayer is a human method for bridging the chasm between ourselves and God (Coe, 2014). As I argued in chapter one, this gap cannot be crossed by human effort. Therefore, contemplative prayer is not a technique that we can use to reach or know God. Instead, contemplative prayer is made possible only because God has taken the initiative to reveal himself to us. Our role is simply to respond and accept the gift that God makes of himself (Wilhoit, 2014).

Finally, the terms *contemplation* and *meditation* are not interchangeable. It is understandable that these terms can be confusing. In the Eastern religious traditions, the words *meditation* and *contemplation* have the opposite meanings from their use in the West (Madagáin, 2007). In the East, the definition for *meditation* is identical to the West's understanding of *contemplation*: becoming silent, going beyond thoughts and words. On the other hand, the East's view of *contemplation* is the same as the West's idea of *meditation*: reflecting on an idea or devotional passage. The bottom line is that *meditation* and *contemplation* refer to two completely different processes.

WHAT IS CONTEMPLATIVE PRAYER?

Historical background. At the core of Christianity is the question, How can human beings come to know God? Throughout the history of the church, theologians have developed a twofold schema for answering this query (Howard, 2008). One approach has been referred to as the affirmative or *kataphatic* way, while the other response has been termed the negative or *apophatic* way.

The kataphatic way of doing theology affirms that God is knowable. The focus is on things that can be stated firmly about God: God is love, God is light, God is the Lord of Hosts, God is Father, and so on. This type of spirituality utilizes words and images that represent the things that we have come to know about God.

On the other hand, the apophatic type of spirituality asserts that God is ultimately unknowable. Howard (2008) quotes the theologian Maximos the Confessor (580–662): "If you come to theologize in a negative or apophatic manner . . . you come in an admirable way to know Him who transcends knowing" (p. 136). Citing another influential theologian of this camp who went by the pseudonym Dionysius (fifth or sixth century), Howard (2008) writes, "Now as we plunge into the darkness which is beyond intellect, we shall find ourselves not simply running short of words but actually speechless and unknowing" (p. 139). In the negative way, we arrive at a point where we run out of words to speak of God. We find ourselves in silence.

The two ways arrive at different conclusions. Affirmative theology finds that we can comprehend God by statements, names, and images, whereas the negative way prefers a silent recognition that God is beyond knowing and words. The kataphatic approach claims that God can be known, while the apophatic method asserts that God is unknowable. The first proclaims that God has revealed himself, but the second claims that God is hidden. The kataphatic way says that God is present, while, in contrast, the apophatic way observes that God can be absent.

It stands to reason that these two types of spirituality—affirmative and negative—which promote two contrasting ways of knowing God, would spawn two different devotional practices. The kataphatic way places emphasis on meditation while the apophatic way applies a different practice—contemplation.

Meditation and contemplation are different. Meditation emphasizes words, statements, and images that capture what we know about God. Good examples of meditation can be found in the use of icons in the Eastern church, the meditations of Ignatius of Loyola's *Spiritual Exercises*, and the exercises used in Puritan devotional life. On the other hand, contemplation removes images and words from the mind. It finds the worshiper in silence before God. Examples of contemplation are found in the fourteenth-century English classic *The Cloud of Unknowing*, the work of Spanish mystic John of the Cross (1542–1591), and the more recent works of Thomas Merton (1915–1968).

From a distance, we see that contemplative prayer reflects a negative or apophatic way of knowing God. But in order to draw closer to a definition of contemplative prayer, we will explore several different descriptions of this devotional practice.

Defining contemplative prayer. Just as mindfulness researchers have carefully defined the term *mindfulness*, we want to establish an operational definition of contemplative prayer. Before doing so, it may be helpful to review a few different descriptions of contemplative prayer. I will set forth the views of Richard Foster, John Coe, Thomas Merton, and Saint John of the Cross to help us see the various ways in which Christians view this form of prayer.

Richard Foster's view of contemplative prayer. For our purposes, I will highlight three key elements that Foster (1992) identifies within contemplative prayer: (1) attentiveness, (2) presence, and (3) silence.

Contemplative prayer rests on a basic truth about the mind: it needs something upon which to concentrate. An attentive person is focused on something. In contemplation, the mind's attention is centered upon God. As Paul instructed us, "Set your minds on things above, not on earthly things" (Col 3:2).

In contemplative prayer, we follow the example set by Mary (Lk 10:38-42). Unlike Martha, who was "distracted" (Lk 10:40), Mary was focused on Jesus. She was tuned in to one thing. Mary's attention allowed her to filter out unimportant data in order to narrow her focus onto the one thing that mattered the most at that moment: Jesus.

Recognizing the relationship between attention and prayer, Simone Weil (2009) writes, "Prayer consists of attention. It is the orientation of all the attention of which the soul is capable toward God. The quality of the attention counts for much in the quality of the prayer" (p. 57). Weil's use of the phrase "orientation of all the attention" highlights the fact that our attention is often directed away from God. We are occupied with thoughts about one thing or another. So what do we do when we notice that our attention has wandered? We return our attention away from the thought and back to God.

Presence is the next key ingredient in contemplative prayer. In the story of Mary and Martha, we observed that Mary "sat at the Lord's feet" (Lk 10:39). Contemplative prayer is about sitting. Wilhoit and Howard (2012) write, "In contemplation, we just sit. God's Spirit is present. We are present" (p. 124). God makes his presence known to us, and we respond by making ourselves present to him.

During the conversation, beneath the level of words—and this is where contemplative prayer occurs—there is the fundamental presence of the other party. You can actually feel the other person's presence. What does it feel like to be with the other person? Does the other person give you a good or not-so-good feeling? That is his presence.

Contemplative prayer is about dwelling with God. But when we take a seat, are we really there? Are we present? As Foster (2008) points out, "There is a big difference between simply being in the same room with others versus truly being present to them" (p. 22).

Too frequently we are in another location. Yes, our bodies are seated, but we are someplace else. When we sit down, we must begin the process of re-collecting ourselves. That is, we must join our minds, hearts, and souls with our bodies. We must come fully into the room with Jesus. Once we are completely present, we can turn to God and say, "I am here. Here I am." Foster (1992) encourages us to "let go of all competing distractions until we are truly present where we are" (p. 161).

Being present means more than being *here*. It also means being here *now*. Even though our bodies are here, our minds become distracted and wander off. And where do they go? Our minds are prone to forget about the Lord and to focus on memories of the past or worries about the future. Our minds find it difficult to stay in the present moment. However, in contemplative prayer, we learn how to bring our attention back to our divine guest, who is with us now. As Paul wrote, "Now is the day of salvation" (2 Cor 6:2).

Finally, for Foster (1992), contemplative prayer is "progress toward silence" (p. 155). Theologian Martin Laird observes the theme of silence among great contemplatives in Christian history. Laird (2011) quotes Augustine, "God speaks in the great silence of the heart" (p. 92). Citing John of the Cross, Laird (2006) says, "Our greatest need is to be silent before this great God, . . . for the only language he hears is the silent language of love" (p. 2).

But what is silence? There are two kinds of silence: outer and inner (Hempton, 2009). We know the difference between a noisy environment and a quiet one. But what of interior silence? Inner silence is what we encounter when we find an interior place that is free from words. Dallas Willard (1988) writes, "In silence we close off our souls from sounds, whether those sounds be noise, music, or words" (p. 163). Christian philosopher Peter Kreeft (2000) reminds us that contemplative prayer is the "practice of God's presence without words" (p. 28).

Silence is not only the absence of external noise but the scarcity of words. When speech is missing, two things are happening. First, we are not speaking. Second, we are not thinking. Therefore, when we are silent, we are free from speech—both talking and thinking.

The idea of interior silence beckons us, but when we seek it, we notice an amazing phenomenon. The attempt to be silent immediately involves us in a struggle with our thoughts. There is so much noise in our heads. There are so many distractions. We want to be silent, but there is anything but silence.

How do we arrive at interior silence? We must first make peace with the fact that thoughts are part of contemplative prayer. There is nothing wrong with the chatter in our heads. In contemplative prayer, we are not batting away any idea or feeling that appears. We are not resisting thoughts or trying to have blank minds. That involves too much effort.

So what are we to do? In order to arrive at the land of silence, we must follow two steps. First, we must simply acknowledge and observe the thought. We must listen to the advice of Evagrius, the desert father: "Let him keep careful watch over his thoughts. Let him observe their intensity, their periods of decline and follow them as they rise and fall" (as cited in Laird, 2006, p. 82). But we often do the opposite in contemplative prayer. A thought arises and we chase after it.

This brings us to the second step: as soon as we notice the thought, we must release it. Contemplative prayer is about letting go of thoughts. Thomas Keating (1999) provides a metaphor to illustrate this step. He uses boats drifting down the river as an analogy for thoughts. We can either watch the boats (thoughts) appear and pass by, or we can climb on board. Once we climb on board, it may be a period of time before we even realize that we have attached ourselves to a thought. Instead of chasing after thoughts, in contemplative prayer we cultivate the skill of letting go. These steps prepare us for silence.

John Coe's view of contemplative prayer. John Coe offers us an evocative image of contemplative prayer. His image is relational, interactive, and emotional. Coe (2014) writes, "Christian contemplative prayer is attending to the presence of the Spirit of Christ" (p. 151). From this brief definition, we can ascertain that contemplative prayer is about (1) love and (2) openness.

In contemplation, we are attending to the presence of the Spirit of Christ. The first important question is, What is the primary quality of the Spirit of Christ? It is one of love. Paul makes this point in his letter to the Christians in Rome: "God's love has been poured out into our hearts through the Holy Spirit" (Rom 5:5). When we are in the presence of the Spirit of Christ, we are in the presence of love. In contemplative prayer, we recognize that we are located in the love of God (see 1 Jn 4:16).

Contemplative prayer originates in love and culminates in love. During this time of prayer, God invites us into his loving presence, we respond in love, and then God answers with love. With loving attention, we put ourselves in God's loving hands. We surrender ourselves to his care. With love, we sit at Jesus' feet. Foster (1992) quotes Augustine as saying, "True, whole prayer is nothing but love" (p. 255).

Bruce Demarest (1999) agrees that in contemplative prayer we are practicing—or entering into—God's presence. But what is the manner in which we come into his presence? The foremost attitude we need for joining God's company is openness. According to psychologist David Benner (2010), openness is a main component of communications. Even when there are no words, a person can still be open.

The concept of openness is captured by the following verse: "Here I am! I stand at the door and knock. If anyone hears my voice and opens the door, I will come in and eat with that person, and they with me" (Rev 3:20). Notice that the idea of openness—that is, opening a door—is situated in the middle of this verse.

What do we observe about openness in this passage? First, we notice that it involves consent. In contemplative prayer, we say yes to God's Spirit: "Yes, I am giving you permission to come in." Second, openness connotes receptivity. We no longer resist his request to come in. Instead, we welcome him with enthusiasm. Rather than being guarded, we make ourselves vulnerable. Instead of holding back, we now entrust ourselves into his care.

Thomas Merton's view of contemplative prayer. Some would argue that it was the writings of Trappist monk Thomas Merton in the 1950s and 1960s that reawakened Western Christianity to its contemplative heritage. For Merton (1962), contemplative prayer occurs when "the will rests in a deep, luminous and absorbing experience of love" (p. 276). Here we see the qualities of (1) love and (2) rest.

In contemplative prayer, we sense the love of the Spirit, and this love changes us. Merton describes this experience as deep, luminous, and absorbing. When one senses the love of the Spirit, a "beautiful, deep, meaningful tranquility floods your whole being" (Merton, 1962, p. 276). The love of the Spirit is personal. You know that this presence is God. Even though God is hidden, he is also somehow obvious.

What do we do in the presence of God? The picture that Merton uses for contemplative prayer is one of rest. Picking up on this idea, Thomas Keating (1999) says of contemplative prayer, "It is a resting in God" (p. 20). It behooves us to understand this image. First, what are we resting? Our minds. We rest or still our minds of thinking. As we let go of thoughts, we find ourselves in a state of tranquility and interior peace.

Does rest mean that we suspend all action? No, there are a few simple acts that we participate in during contemplative prayer. We turn ourselves toward God, we open ourselves to God, and we receive his love. As Madagáin (2007) says, "The Lord wants to do more of the work in us and only asks us to be quiet and to rest in this silence" (p. 5). The concept of rest does not exclude action. Our small part is to consent to the love of the Spirit. We cannot initiate the love of God or sustain the love of God, but we can dispose ourselves to it. Rest allows us to remain in the presence of God.

For Kreeft (2000), resting in the presence of God is like bringing ourselves into the sunlight. We're not trying to produce anything by our own efforts. We are just standing in the light. In contemplative prayer, we are not exerting effort to produce any specific outcome. Instead, we are merely basking in God's love for us. We are not employing some type of technique. We are simply receiving and returning God's love.

John of the Cross's view of contemplative prayer. For John of the Cross (1991), contemplative prayer happens when we "preserve a loving attentiveness to God with no desire to feel or understand any particular thing concerning him" (p. 92). Since we have already discussed the importance of attention, we will concentrate on another concept that illuminates our understanding of contemplative prayer, that is, gazing.

Augustine, using language similar to that of John of the Cross, described prayer as a "loving gaze of the human spirit toward God" (Demarest, 1999, p. 164). The notion of *gazing* or *seeing* offers us a useful way of thinking about contemplative prayer. What are we looking for in contemplative prayer? Theologian Kyle Strobel (2014) responds that we are "seeking God's face in Christ by the Spirit" (p. 103). We know that we are looking for God's face, but why? And why is it so difficult to see his face? The answers to these questions are crucial to our understanding of contemplative prayer.

We are wired to search for faces. In the first hours of life, babies begin to scout out the faces and eyes of those around them. And what are they looking for? Each one is searching for his or her mother's face. *Out of all the female faces peering at me, which one belongs to my mother?* The mother's face is the one that says, "You are my beloved. You are my special child. You are mine. You have infinite value." These are the eyes that the baby recognizes.

Observing an infant's early instinct to search for his or her mother's face gives us insight into why we have a natural drive to seek God's face. Neuroscience has taught us that facial expressions tell us everything we need to know about the nature of our important relationships. Of course we are driven, like our heroes in the Bible, to seek God's face. We are informed in Scripture that Moses wanted to see God's face (Ex 33:18-23). David proclaimed, "Your face, LORD, I will seek" (Ps 27:8). In another passage, David pleaded, "Do not hide your face from me" (Psalm 102:2). This drive seen in Moses and David seems to be supported by God's message for his people to "pray and seek my face" (2 Chron 7:14).

In terms of our relationship with God, it makes sense that we are looking for a heavenly face. We are searching for that face that is looking at us with love. In contemplative prayer, we experience God gazing at us with that same look of love that he had for his Son when he said, "This is my Son, whom I love; with him I am well pleased" (Mt 3:17).

Why does God gaze at us with that special look that says, "You are my child. I love you. I am pleased with you. You have immense worth in my eyes"? Because he sees us as *in Christ*. Nearly 250 times phrases like "in Christ" or "in him" are used in the New Testament to remind us of our relationship with God through Jesus Christ (Wilhoit & Howard, 2012). We begin contemplative prayer by knowing that we are "in Christ" and that God looks upon us with love.

The kind of seeing that we do in contemplative prayer assures us that we are loved, secure, and safe. When we see his face, we know that we don't need to hide or be afraid. Instead, we know that we are invited into his presence, assured of his love for us. When we see the gleam in his eye, we know that we are special and that, to him, we are of great worth.

The process of mutual gazing begins with God. As Strobel (2014) has said, "The ultimate ground of contemplation is being contemplated as one who is known; caught up in the contemplation of God as one who is in Christ" (p. 96). Before we even began seeking his face, he was looking upon us in love. And, when we see that keen look of love, we gaze back in love.

Although we are instructed to seek God's face and even though we have an intense drive to watch his face, the type of seeing we do in contemplative prayer comes with certain inherent difficulties. Our ability to see God's face is limited and unclear. When we look at his face, it is not face-to-face. Instead, we see his face as a reflection in a mirror (1 Cor 13:12). It is important to remember that, unlike the mirrors of today, mirrors in Bible times were generally made of metal, not clear glass. Even though they were highly polished, their reflecting abilities were limited.

Even though we have an intense drive to see God's face, we actually are unable to behold it fully. John asserts, "No one has ever seen God" (1 Jn 4:12). The truth is that we need special eyes for observing God's face during contemplation. The eyes for catching sight of God are "eyes of your heart" (Eph 1:18). During our prayer we must rely upon faith because we do not see and may not feel God (Heb 11:1). By faith, we know that God is present with us. He told us that he is always with us (Mt 28:20), so we have faith that this is true when we pray.

It seems that the gazing we do during contemplative prayer is in anticipation of the time when we will behold God in heaven (Strobel, 2014). Only then will we see him face-to-face (1 Cor 13:12). John reminds us of this: "See what great love the Father has lavished on us, that we should be called children of God! . . . When Christ appears, we shall be like him, for we shall see him as he is" (1 Jn 3:1-2). In contemplative prayer, we look—in faith—at the face of our loving Father, knowing that we will not see him clearly until we behold him face-to-face in heaven.

Operational definition of contemplative prayer. I have tried to illustrate that there are numerous ways to understand and think about contemplative prayer. However, several qualities do appear again and again in these descriptions of contemplative prayer. We will use these properties in our definition:

1. *Love.* Contemplation is an experience of love. The entire encounter can be understood as God gazing at us, and us looking back at God, with love. Contemplative prayer is simply our loving response to the love that God initiates toward us.

2. *Attention.* Contemplative prayer is a prayer of attention. We are focusing our minds on God in Christ. Yes, our minds will naturally wander away from God, but we want to return our focus to him. Over and over again, we return our attention to the indwelling Spirit of Christ.

3. *Openness.* Contemplative prayer is about opening ourselves to the Spirit of Jesus. We offer him consent to act as he pleases during our time of prayer. We receive him with enthusiasm. We entrust ourselves into his care. We rest from our efforts, knowing that the work is his.

4. *Silence.* Contemplative prayer is letting go of words and thoughts. This letting go of words is called silence. In silence, we sink beneath the dimension of words. We communicate with God at a different level, the level of spirit. Our spirits commune with the Spirit of God in silence.

5. *Rest.* What do we do in contemplative prayer? We are taking a break from words and thoughts. We are resting in God's presence. God is doing most of the work, but we also have a job to do. We must continue to turn toward God, to be open to his presence, and to receive his love.

6. *Presence.* Contemplative prayer is about presence, God's presence and our presence. By faith, we know that God is with us as we pray. We come into his presence, which is characterized by love. Then we make ourselves present in love to him.

In conclusion, our operational definition is as follows: Contemplative prayer is loving attentiveness—characterized by openness, silence, and rest—to the presence of God. This definition contains the six key elements of contemplative prayer: (1) love, (2) attention, (3) openness, (4) silence, (5) rest, and (6) presence.

CONTEXT FOR CONTEMPLATIVE PRAYER

So far, our description of contemplative prayer reveals a type of prayer that makes space for silence. In contemplative prayer, we are communicating with God without words or even thoughts. However, as we venture into contemplative prayer, we find that silence and words are intermingled. Our time of prayer may begin by soaking in the Scriptures. This may be followed by a verbal conversation with God. Then we may find ourselves moving silently—with a loving gaze—into God's presence. After a time of silence, we may transition back into a verbal prayer such as the Lord's Prayer. Silence and words go together. Silence is simply the space between words.

From the earliest days of the church, Christians have sought a way to navigate between words and silence. How does one listen to God's Word, respond with words to what we hear, and then move into God's presence beneath the words? As early as the third century, the Christian theologian Origen used the Greek phrase *thea anagnosis* (divine reading) as a way to describe this transition between Scripture and silence. The practice described by Origen became widespread among the desert fathers and mothers as they established the Word of God as the basis for their prayer lives (Benner, 2010).

By the fourth century, much of the Christian church had accepted this practice, the devotional reading of Scripture (Wilhoit & Howard, 2012). Lectio divina—as the practice was then called—was a way to immerse people in Scripture, eventually leading them into God's loving presence. Benedict (480– 547) was one of the earliest church leaders to use the phrase *lectio divina*, which literally means "divine reading." Due to the influence of Benedict, lectio divina became central to Western monasticism. With the recent rise of interest in classical Christian spiritual practices, lectio divina has been rediscovered and is being practiced by Christians.

Over time, lectio divina has come to be understood to have four components, which were first outlined by Guigo II in the twelfth century. He labeled the four stages of prayer *lectio, meditatio, oratio*, and *contemplatio*. Benner (2010) suggests that these four Latin terms describe four dimensions of prayer—prayer as attending, prayer as pondering, prayer as responding, and prayer as being.

Lectio: prayer as attending. *Lectio* means "reading." Wilhoit and Howard (2012) describe it as the kind of reading done by a lover. To the lover, the letter—or text—is important, but so too is the relationship. In the stage of lectio, a small portion of Scripture is selected, and this portion is read in a relational way—looking to our relationship with God and how he is revealing himself through the text.

In lectio, we turn to a passage of Scripture and read it slowly, phrase by phrase. We are listening for the still, small voice of God. Is there some word or phrase that God's Word has for us today? We are never reading the Scriptures alone. The Spirit is always nearby. We pray for the Spirit to be active as we read the Bible, revealing God to and within us. Jesus reminds us of our need of the Spirit: "The Holy Spirit, whom the Father will send in my name, will teach you all things" (Jn 14:26).

Meditatio: prayer as pondering. *Meditatio*, from which we get the word *meditation*, is a prayer of pondering or ruminating. The concept of ruminating can be captured in the image of cows, sheep, or goats chewing their cud (Wilhoit & Howard, 2012). They first chew their food until it is partially digested, then they regurgitate it as cud, and then they gnaw on it once again. When we ponder God's Word, we bite off a small portion. We chew on it and then bring it back up to munch on it again and again. With this kind of ruminating, we savor and leisurely dwell on the Scripture passage.

As we meditate on Scripture, we allow it to soak into us. As it sinks in, we engage our minds and think about the passage. As we mull over the text, we look for connections to our lives. Where does it meet us in our lives? Is God's Word speaking to an issue or concern that we are dealing with? Is God calling us to address some area of our lives? Is God giving us an example to follow? As you can see, meditatio often engages our minds through the use of questions.

Oratio: prayer as responding. *Oratio* literally means "speaking." This is what we most often think of as prayer: worded prayer. This third element of lectio divina flows naturally out of the first two components: reading and meditating on Scripture. At this stage of prayer, we are responding. In this stage of lectio divina, we are talking to God about what happened in us as we were listening to his Word.

What stirred in your spirit as you listened to the voice of God's Spirit? Did you feel led to some type of action? Did some longing arise in your heart? Was some emotion touched? Did you experience a sense of God's presence with you? Was some seed planted in your heart?

At this point in prayer—oratio—we notice and water this seed (Wilhoit & Howard, 2012). This component of prayer speaks to the response that happened in our spirits as we listened to the voice of God's Spirit. In oratio, we give voice, or words, to what we heard in the text. We speak to God about the seed that was planted. With words, we address our relationship with God. It may sound like this: "I sense you calling me to take some action in my life. I feel a desire to be part of some pursuit." "I am feeling so sorry about this thing I have done." "I am so happy to be aware of your presence."

It is important to realize that the elements of prayer do not necessarily follow in some linear fashion. Oratio, which sometimes follows reading and meditating, can also precede each of them. For example, we may engage in worded prayer before we read a passage of Scripture. It only makes sense to ask the Spirit for assistance prior to opening the text. Worded prayer can also emerge in the middle of reading or meditating upon Scripture.

Contemplatio: prayer as being. So far, in lectio divina, we have been talking about things we do. But *contemplatio* is a prayer of being (Benner, 2010). At this stage of prayer, the Word has led us into the quiet rest of God's presence. In contemplatio—from which we get the English word *contemplation*—we are simply being with God in Jesus. We are resting in his presence.

We are opening ourselves so that we might be acted upon by the indwelling Spirit of Christ.

Until this point in our prayer, we have been depending upon words—God's Word to us and our words to God. But there is another level of conversation that is beneath words. On this plane—in contemplatio—we are simply present to God and God is present to us. After engaging in worded conversation for a while, we slow down enough to simply pay attention to this mutual presence. In contemplation, "we rest, present with the God of the text" (Wilhoit & Howard, 2012, p. 111).

Benner (2010) writes, "Contemplative prayer is wordless, trusting openness to the God who dwells at the center of our being" (p. 133). At the contemplatio stage of prayer, we open all that we are to God—mind, body, soul, and spirit. We open to God in whom we dwell (Acts 17:28). We no longer rely upon words or thoughts because, at this level of prayer, being with God does not require words. Our spirit is simply communing with the Spirit of God. We are not trying to eliminate words or thoughts. They just seem unnecessary. Instead, we are turning toward God with openness. The rest is up to God.

After a time of quiet repose, after a period of simply gazing into his face, we may return to a worded prayer. We may express our thanks for this time of receiving his Word. We may once again chew upon the Word or talk to God about the seed that he has planted in our hearts. Words flow into silence; then silence returns to words. As Kreeft (2000) puts it, "The road to wordless prayer is paved with words. . . . The wordless sense of God's presence is a flower that grows from the plant of prayer in words" (p. 28).

CENTERING PRAYER

Up to this point, we have been answering the question, *What* is contemplative prayer? However, this leaves us with another query: *How* does one practice contemplative prayer within the context of counseling? Is there a method for engaging the client in contemplative prayer? Actually, many approaches to contemplative prayer have been practiced over the history of Christian spirituality. However, the procedure that has gained the greatest recognition in recent history is called centering prayer. This is the method we are adopting for our Christian contemplative-oriented approach to counseling.

As we move into our discussion of centering prayer, we are faced with several important questions: What is the history of centering prayer? What are the guidelines for practicing centering prayer? What is the relationship between contemplative prayer and centering prayer? How are centering prayer and lectio divina connected? Is there scientific support for the use of centering prayer?

Introduction to centering prayer. Centering prayer is a simple form of contemplative prayer that was developed by three Cistercian monks—William Meninger, Basil Pennington, and Thomas Keating—during the 1970s. It is important to note the timeframe in which centering prayer was developed—the 1970s. During this decade, there was a movement among spiritual teachers of major Eastern religions to come to the United States and present their respective methods of meditation. (Note: In 1977, the American Psychological Association sounded the call for research into the clinical effectiveness of meditation.) Numerous young people who learned these other traditions came to Saint Joseph's Abbey in Spencer, Massachusetts, where Keating was abbot, asking for a Christian method of contemplation. Since there was not a contemporary method of Christian contemplation, Meninger, Pennington, and Keating were prompted to create one. The result was centering prayer, a new name and a new package for the ancient Christian tradition of contemplation.

The unique intent of the originators of centering prayer was to provide a simple method for practicing Christian contemplation. Before I introduce this method, it is important that I issue a warning. The word *method* can be misleading because it implies that we now have some special technique for making something happen. For example, by pushing a button, we can make a light go on (Kreeft, 2000). We want to avoid the belief that we can use some technique to kindle God's loving presence or to initiate some special experience. No, we are simply spending time with God and responding to his initiative. We are not trying to achieve some end. Instead, we are simply opening ourselves to God.

God's presence is not something that we can control or make happen. Centering prayer is not a technique that enables us to achieve some predetermined experience. No, we simply turn to God. We spend time with him, believing by faith that he is there with us. In this way, turning toward God in faith and openness can be called a method. However, whatever happens during this time of centering prayer is up to God. We don't control the outcome or expect a particular result.

The four guidelines of centering prayer. Having acknowledged this warning, we can now examine the four guidelines for centering prayer proposed by Keating (1999, p. 139):

1. Choose a sacred word as the symbol of your intention to consent to God's presence and action within.

2. Sit comfortably and with your eyes closed, settle briefly, and silently introduce the sacred word as the symbol of your consent to God's presence and action within.

3. When you become aware of thoughts, return ever so gently to the sacred word.

4. At the end of the prayer period, remain in silence with eyes closed for a couple of minutes.

Guideline 1. When we begin our time of centering prayer, we are aware that we have a special purpose, an intention. What is that intention? It is to "consent to God's presence and action within" (Keating, 1999, p. 139). Our aim is simply to be open to God in Jesus and to the work that he wants to do inside us.

We select a short word—such as *love, peace, Jesus*—to remind us of our intention. Keating says that this word is a symbol of our intention. A symbol is a mark, sign, or word that represents an idea, object, or relationship. For example, one of the most recognizable symbols in the world is the *M* for McDonald's. As soon as we see the golden arches, we begin to think about McDonald's. In centering prayer, the word one selects reminds one to focus the mind on the indwelling Spirit of Christ.

What is the difference between a sacred word and a mantra? In some contemplative practices, such as Transcendental Meditation, a word is used to focus attention. When the word is repeated over and over, we call this a mantra. The idea is to use the mantra to block out thoughts.

In centering prayer, the sacred word is used differently. We only use the word when it is necessary. It becomes essential when we become aware that we are distracted with some thought. The intention of the sacred word is not to block out thoughts. Instead, its purpose is to remind us of our intention to be in God's presence, to be open, and to consent to his presence. We are not using the sacred word as a bat to knock away thoughts. Instead, we are using it as a gentle reminder of our purpose, that is, to be present to God (Madagáin, 2007).

Guideline 2. The second guideline highlights two central components of centering prayer. First, we are reminded that contemplative prayer is an embodied experience. We bring our bodies before God. We are reminded to sit in a comfortable posture. That way we can calm and relax our bodies. Then we are instructed to close our eyes. This allows us to shut out the visual distractions around us.

In addition, the second guideline causes us to remember that centering prayer is a prayer of silence. And we recall that the road to silence is paved with words. So in centering prayer we begin with a word, the special word that we have selected as a symbol of our intention. Then we settle into silence and let go of thoughts that might distract us from our focus: God.

Guideline 3. Within a brief period of time, you may notice that your mind has wandered away from its intention—to focus on God in Jesus. This, the presence of distracting thoughts, is a normal part of contemplative prayer. There is no need to fret or get upset about the fact that your mind has drifted away from God. Instead, silently use your word to call to mind your intention.

Keating reminds us how to handle distracting thoughts. First, he tells us to be gentle with ourselves. Being gentle is the opposite of being harsh with or judgmental of yourself. You have not been bad, inadequate, or incompetent in some way. No, it is expected that your mind will wander. But when you become aware of the distraction, use your word as a way to return your wandering mind to the indwelling Spirit.

Guideline 4. In this last step of centering prayer, Keating reminds us again that silence is a space between words. Our time of silence is coming to an end, and we will soon be returning to words. Perhaps these last few minutes will serve as a transition into the world of verbal expressions. Maybe these last moments will give us time to build a foundation for the words that we will use after our time of contemplation. When centering prayer is done in a group, it often ends with recitation of the Lord's Prayer.

History of centering prayer. Centering prayer is not something new. Rather, it draws upon a long history of Christian contemplative prayer. The roots of centering prayer can be traced back to the desert fathers of the fourth and fifth centuries, to the anonymous fourteenth-century spiritual classic *The Cloud of Unknowing*, to Teresa of Ávila of the sixteenth century, and to Thomas Merton in the twentieth century.

The origins of the Christian contemplative tradition are located in the writings of the desert fathers. Here we will mention three of these writers because of their clear influence upon centering prayer: Evagrius Ponticus, John Cassian, and John Climacus. Evagrius Ponticus was the first important writer among the desert fathers. He succeeded in compiling what these early monks taught about prayer. Evagrius captures one of the early principles of contemplative prayer: "When your spirit . . . turns away from every thought, . . . then you can be sure that you are drawing near that country whose name is prayer" (as cited in Madagáin, 2007, p. 89).

Madagáin (2007) shows how centering prayer draws upon the contemplative practices of the early desert fathers. He quotes John Cassian as saying, "The soul must be restrained from meandering, from all slippery wanderings, so that it may rise bit by bit to the contemplation of God into the gazing upon the realms of the spirit" (p. 95). Here we see the instruction to let go of thoughts during prayer. John Climacus is also cited: "If it happens that, as you pray, some word evokes the delight or remorse within you, linger over it" (p. 99). The use of a sacred word was practiced even by the early Christian contemplatives.

Moving on to the influence of *The Cloud of Unknowing*, Madagáin (2007) quotes the author: "A naked intent toward God, the desire for him alone, is enough" (p. 107). Likewise, in centering prayer one's intention is key. Every time practitioners notice that their minds have wandered and use their sacred word, they are repeating their intention of being present to the presence of God.

How do the originators of centering prayer draw upon the teachings of Teresa of Ávila (Madagáin, 2007)? In her book called *Life*, Teresa uses an analogy of how a garden can be watered in four ways: drawing water from a well, getting water by means of a water wheel, using irrigation to allow the water to flow directly from a stream into the garden, and letting rain fall on the garden. The four methods of watering a garden represent four stages of prayer. Clearly, the techniques range from those that require much effort to those that are less difficult. The idea of using less effort is captured by Keating (1999) when he writes, "The more God does and the less you do, the better the prayer" (p. 71).

Finally, the word *centering* was inspired by the writings of Thomas Merton (1966): "At the center of our being is . . . a point or spark which belongs entirely to God which . . . is like a pure diamond, blazing with the invisible light of heaven" (p. 142). Centering prayer, which follows in the tradition of Christian contemplative prayer, is simply about opening up and receiving God at that point inside.

Contemplative prayer and centering prayer. In the previous section, we identified several key principles of contemplative prayer—letting go of thoughts, using a sacred word, the emphasis on intention, action but not effort—that are employed in the practice of centering prayer. Centering prayer undoubtedly draws upon the tradition of contemplative prayer. The founders of centering prayer were simply attempting to renew the teaching of the Christian tradition of contemplative prayer. Before these writers began their work in the 1970s, all too many Christians had a relatively negative view of contemplative prayer. So it was their desire to present contemplative prayer in an up-to-date form. Their goal was to develop some method by which people could practice contemplative prayer.

Madagáin (2007) refers to centering prayer as a "stepping-stone to contemplation" (p. xviii). What does this mean? It indicates that centering prayer is a method that leads the practitioner into a deeper relationship with God. Sharing the custom of all Christian contemplatives throughout history, the person who practices centering prayer is learning to set aside thoughts so that he or she can rest in the presence of God. The goal of centering prayer is identical to the objective that contemplatives have had since early times, that is, to accept the love of God and to look back at God in love.

Centering prayer and lectio divina. Another aim of centering prayer was to build upon the tradition of lectio divina. You will recall from an earlier section that much of the Christian church had accepted the practice of lectio divina by the fourth century. The four components of lectio divina—lectio, meditatio, oratio, and contemplatio—were all practiced during a person's time of prayer. The four phases were interwoven and not treated as clear-cut or discrete categories. (These distinctions did not exist prior to the sixteenth century.) Prayer was naturally assumed to progress from thinking—the first three elements—to the letting go of thoughts, or contemplation.

Over time, the fourth component of lectio divina, contemplatio, was lost by the Christian church. As the sixteenth century progressed, the idea that prayer could open up into contemplation was regarded as highly unlikely. The belief that prayer could progress from thinking to silence was discarded. The creators of centering prayer wanted to restore this forgotten fourth element of lectio divina. Keating (1999) writes, "The method of centering prayer empha-sizes the final stage of *lectio* because it is the phase that has been most ne-glected in recent times" (p. 29).

In my contemplative-oriented way of counseling, following Keating's example, I emphasize the final stage of lectio divina, contemplatio. However, if a client is familiar with and wants to practice all four stages of lectio divina, I accept and work with this client's decision.

Scientific support for centering prayer. Research into centering prayer is in its early stages. This fact becomes apparent when we compare the research done on other contemplative practices with that which has been conducted on centering prayer. Fox, Gutierrez, Haas, Braganza, and Berger (2015) report that most of the research—over eight hundred studies—providing evidence for the efficacy of contemplative practices have focused on Transcendental Meditation and mindfulness. In contrast, only four important studies have been conducted to examine centering prayer.

A significant amount of work is yet to be done in order to answer questions about centering prayer from a social science and data-driven perspective. For instance, do practitioners of centering prayer experience physical and mental health benefits? Do people experience noticeable changes in their lives after practicing centering prayer? How do we compare centering prayer and mindfulness?

When we examine the four qualitative and quantitative studies of centering prayer (Ferguson, Willemsen, & Castañeto, 2010; Fox et al., 2015; Johnson et al., 2009; Newberg, Pourdehnad, Alavi, & d'Aquili, 2003), what do they reveal? According to Gutierrez, Fox, and Wood (2015), the collective evidence that we have thus far suggests that centering prayer can yield worthwhile psychological, spiritual, and physiological effects.

Counselors need to be aware of these four studies conducted on centering prayer. First, centering prayer appears to produce neurological responses similar to those of mindfulness. Newberg et al. (2003), measuring the brain activity and cerebral blood flow of Franciscan nuns practicing centering prayer and of Tibetan Buddhists, discovered similar findings. Subjects in both groups experienced increased activity in the prefrontal cortex and altered blood flow to the parietal areas of the brain when they engaged in their respective contemplative exercises.

The second study advances the idea that centering prayer can serve as an effective means of coping with cancer treatment. Johnson et al. (2009) found clinically significant improvements in the psychological and spiritual dimensions of the lives of the participants. Despite progressive cancer symptoms, subjects in the research showed gains in their mood, anxiety levels, and faith.

The final two studies offer evidence that centering prayer impacts the relational dimension of people's lives. The research by Ferguson et al. (2010) revealed that participants experienced improvements in their relationships with God and others. In addition, they met with an overall reduction in stress. Subjects in the study indicated that centering prayer led to a sense that they were loved by God. In addition, they reported less conflict and greater intimacy in their interactions with others (e.g., children, coworkers, spouse). Ferguson et al. (2010) explained the participants' reduction in stress this way: improvements in interactions with others led to a decline in stress, since relationships are the primary source of stress.

The final study by Fox et al. (2015) suggested that the pathways of change in centering prayer may be different from those in mindfulness. The participants in their research described their experience in interpersonal terms—their relationship with God, self, and others—reminiscent of the study by Ferguson et al. (2010). This emphasis on relational terms sheds more light on a major difference between contemplative prayer and mindfulness.

In summary, the scientific studies of centering prayer yield some important data for counselors. First, there seems to be mounting evidence to support the claim that centering prayer is similar, yet different, from mindfulness. Newberg and Waldman (2009) emphasize how they are alike when they write of the practitioners of centering prayer that "the neurological changes were nearly the same as those we recorded from a group of Buddhist practitioners" (p. 48). However, centering prayer is distinguishable from mindfulness in that it integrates the client's faith into the process, featuring the subject's relationship with God.

Second, data are accumulating that centering prayer can foster psychological and spiritual benefits when it is practiced in a spiritual context. Third, support is growing regarding the efficacy of centering prayer as a therapeutic intervention. Finally, the findings of scientific studies suggest that centering prayer can yield significant psychological, spiritual, and physiological benefits for practitioners.

APPLICATION TO AN INTEGRATED APPROACH

How does our discussion of contemplative prayer inform the Christian contemplative-oriented approach to counseling that we are developing in this book? I find the following principles and concepts useful as we move toward an effective integration of contemplative prayer and counseling:

1. *Love.* A contemplative approach to counseling is grounded in the concept of love. Everything we do is focused on the goal of building the client's love for God, others, and self.

2. *Presence.* This paradigm of counseling emphasizes the concept of presence. Can clients be fully present in the counseling room? How can we help them learn to be present to themselves, God, and others? Can we, as counselors, learn to be fully present with our clients?

3. *Body.* Contemplative prayer is an embodied experience. In the counseling process, we help our clients become more aware of physiological processes. We assist them in becoming more sensitive to their posture, movement, responses to facial expressions, and breathing.

4. *Attention.* Contemplative prayer is a prayer of attention. We are learning to focus our minds. Likewise, in counseling, we assist clients in becoming more aware of their mental activities. The counseling process is one of helping clients notice and then let go of negative thinking.

5. *Gentleness.* This model of counseling, just like contemplative prayer, engages in a gentle process. The counselor consistently demonstrates acceptance and validation. The foremost goal of the counselor is to offer a safe environment. This objective requires the counselor to be sometimes firm but always gentle.

6. *A circular and integrative process.* In this paradigm, just as in contemplative prayer, we experience a natural flow between words and silence. Active conversation between client and counselor may be followed by a statement such as, "What you said was really important. Let's pause and think about that." The counselor may be able to prompt a lively exploration of the client's behavior or thought processes by asking, "Can you notice your body right now. What is it saying?"

ON BEING HUMAN

AT THIS POINT, you have developed a deeper understanding of Christian contemplation and have learned a method for practicing contemplative prayer. The question you may be asking is, What do I do now? One option is to tell your clients that you have learned about contemplative prayer and that they might want to try it. After sharing this information, you continue with psychotherapy as usual using your preferred model of counseling.

However, we are seeking another option, one that may radically alter the way we do counseling. We are striving to create a new paradigm of counseling, a Christian contemplative-oriented approach to counseling. In determining what you should do now, you may decide to embark upon a way of doing therapy that is informed at every dimension by insights that are gained from contemplative prayer.

Theory building requires three building blocks: (1) a useful understanding of the client's situation, (2) guidance for establishing a helping relationship, and (3) effective interventions for resolving the client's presenting problem (Gehart, 2016). In this volume, my goal is to allow reasonable responses to each of these elements to arise from our study of Christian contemplative thought. The objective is to propose therapeutic strategies that are shaped by insights and principles from the practice of contemplative prayer. In this chapter, we examine the first building block.

Theory provides us with a powerful lens through which we can assess or view the client's condition. How we understand the client's situation is typically referred to as case conceptualization. Assessing the client's predicament, or case conceptualization, has two components: (1) understanding human nature and (2) comprehending the client's presenting problem. In this chapter we will build a model of the human person, while chapter four will address how to develop an understanding of the presenting problem.

Beneath every theory of counseling we find a narrative about the human condition (Simon, 2003). This deeper story may not be told explicitly, but it is still there between the lines. This account is answering the question, What is the fundamental nature of human beings? This deeper narrative is the underpinning of every therapeutic model. This foundation gives us direction for what to do and say in counseling.

PRINCIPLES FROM CONTEMPLATIVE PRAYER

The Christian contemplative tradition offers us a distinctively Christian view of human nature. Contemplative prayer provides us with propositions that serve as a base for our understanding of human nature. Resting upon this foundation, Christian theology then helps us build a more complete model of the person. The principles that have emerged from our study of contemplative prayer can be captured by three themes:

- love

- transformation

- integration

The principle of love. The meaning of contemplative prayer is captured in one word: *love.* Following a theologically informed perspective of this word *love* leads us to a deep understanding of our essential nature. The path of love reveals a human person who is a complex unity of body, mind, heart, and soul. We discover a human being with several key abilities—physical, mental, spiritual, and relational—that assist a person in loving and being loved.

The principle of transformation. Richard Foster (1992) observes, "The primary purpose of prayer is to bring us into such a life of communion with the Father that, by the power of the Spirit, we are increasingly conformed to the image of the Son. The process is transformation" (p. 57). The end goal of contemplative prayer is to become like Jesus. Through contemplative prayer, we are being shaped more and more into the image of God. We are being transformed.

The principle of integration. The great Puritan theologian Richard Baxter (1615–1691) is quoted as saying that contemplation "opens the door between the head and the heart" (Beck & Demarest, 2005, p. 250). This image of an open door speaks to the opportunity for a connection between the mental and spiritual abilities of the human person. The different dimensions of the person—head, heart, body, and social—are intertwined. One part does not act separately from the others. Beck and Demarest (2005) write, "God designed us to be integrated whole beings, with emotion, mind, imagination, will, and body working together in complete harmony. Inner unity, not fragmentation, is our heritage. Wholeness is our birthright" (pp. 229-30). Contemplative prayer unites the different dimensions of the human person.

DIMENSIONS OF HUMAN NATURE

Building upon these foundational themes from contemplative prayer, we begin to establish a distinctively Christian and biblical view of human nature. Jesus captured the essence of human nature when he said, "Love the Lord your God with all your heart and with all your soul and with all your mind and with all your strength." He continued, "Love your neighbor as yourself" (Mk 12:30-31). These words by Jesus reveal that the human person is

- body
- mind
- heart
- soul
- relational

In the next sections, we will carefully examine each of these dimensions of the human person. In the process, we will see how each ability manifests itself within the context of contemplative prayer.

Human nature as physical. Contemplative prayer is clearly an embodied experience, a physical act. Moving to a place of prayer, sitting down, and taking a particular posture are all activities of the body. Our contemplative practice raises and addresses numerous questions concerning the body: What's an appropriate sitting posture? What do I do with my hands? Do I close my eyes? What if my body becomes uncomfortable? Am I supposed to sit still?

During our time of sitting with God, we learn a great deal about the body. We learn to be at home in it, listen to it, and work with it. We discover the value of the bodies that we are. For twenty minutes we sit with and notice a variety of physical sensations: an itchy nose, a pain in the back, tension in the neck. We become better connected to our bodies. We learn to listen to the messages that our bodies are sending to God. Contemplative prayer clearly teaches us to be at home in our bodies.

Christian theology teaches us the immense importance of the body. It is the instrument by which we encounter and respond to life experiences. By means of our bodies, we interact with our physical, social, and spiritual worlds. Dallas Willard (2012b) reminds us that the body is an essential—but often misunderstood—part of the human person. We must learn to embrace it without making it the central part of human life.

Human nature as mental. We experience contemplative prayer as an embodied mind. The activities of the mind, both cognitive and emotional, are key elements of our contemplative practice. The functions of the mind are on full display as we sit in silence with God. Contemplative prayer addresses various questions about the mind: What do I do with thoughts and emotions that arise while I am engaged in centering prayer? How should I respond to them? Should I fight them? Do I give in to them?

Contemplative prayer leads us to deeper understanding of the mind. Our practice of turning to the presence of the indwelling Spirit of Christ can be instrumental in training our minds. Jonathan Edwards (1703–1758) is quoted as saying, "The business of the Christian ought to be very much [in] contemplation and the improvement of the faculties of the mind in divine things" (Strobel, 2013, p. 129). Through contemplative prayer, we learn to observe and direct the activities of the mind.

Scripture teaches us that what we do with our minds matters. What will we allow our minds to dwell upon? Which ideas and emotions will we entertain with our minds? Will we be mastered by our thoughts and feelings? Learning to focus our minds on the right things is of paramount importance (see Col 3:2). We must ascertain how to be good thinkers and feelers.

Human nature as spiritual. In addition to physical and mental abilities, we are equipped with spiritual capabilities. Our spiritual dimension allows us to relate to God (Willard, 2012b). We can refer to this human dimension as *spirit*, but I will use the term *heart*. (Just remember that these terms are interchangeable in the current discussion.)

Just as the human heart is at the center of the physical body, the spiritual heart is at the core of the human being. Here at the midpoint, working with our bodies and minds, our intention is to meet with God. At the heart, at the core of our being, our spirit (or heart) rests in God's Spirit.

The human heart is a physical organ that pumps blood—the source of life—throughout the body. Likewise, the spiritual heart, once it receives life from God, transmits life throughout the human person. Recognizing the importance of the heart, Scripture admonishes us, "Keep your heart with all vigilance, / for from it flow the springs of life" (Prov 4:23 NRSV). Interacting with the indwelling Spirit of Jesus evokes a powerful internal response, one that can be likened to a wellspring of fresh water. This heart-based reaction is on full display in the story of two men who spent the day with Jesus, walking, talking, and eating together (see Lk 24:13-32). Reflecting on their encounter with Jesus, they observed, "Were not our hearts burning within us?" (Lk 24:32). Being in God's presence stimulates the spiritual heart, bringing life to the human person.

The heart is at the center of contemplative prayer. As we turn our loving attention to God, we sink to the center of our being, where the spirit (or heart) communicates with the Holy Spirit. Paul writes, "The Spirit himself testifies with our spirit that we are God's children" (Rom 8:16). At this level, our hearts are organizing our bodies and minds around the goal of relating to God.

The spiritual heart has a wonderful ability, that is, to see. Did you know that the heart has eyes (see Eph 1:18)? The eyes of the heart are so different from the eyes of the body or the eyes of reason. This kind of seeing sees things that are invisible. This kind of seeing is called faith, and faith sees things that are unseen. The author of Hebrews wrote, "Now faith is confidence in what we hope for and assurance about what we do not see" (Heb 11:1).

Contemplative prayer utilizes the eyes of the heart. Gazing in silence, we are looking for the invisible face of God. We are casting about for a face that cannot be seen—at least for now. Jesus said, "Blessed are the pure in heart, for they will see God" (Mt 5:8). Jesus understood the heart to be an organ of spiritual perception. In contemplative prayer, we are using the ability of our hearts to "see God."

Human nature as soulful. So far, we have explored three main systems of the human experience: physical, mental, and spiritual. These operations allow us to interact with God, our physical environment, and the inner workings of our mind. Any one of these dimensions of the person cannot be understood without the other. Christian thinking leads us to think of these different features as being intertwined with one another.

The process of interrelating these three systems is called integration, and integration is the task of the soul (Willard, 2012b). The function of the soul is to intermingle the body with the mind, the mind with the heart, and the heart with the body. One part cannot operate alone without the other dimensions. The intellect depends upon the body and heart. Our spiritual capacity, that is, our ability to relate to God, depends upon the activities of the body and mind. Ultimately, we are an integrated whole being—body, mind, and heart—that works together in harmony. *Soul* is a term that refers to the whole person.

Contemplative prayer brings all the dimensions of the human person together in harmony. As we seek God's face in Christ by the Spirit, all the human systems are undivided in their purpose. We come into the presence of the indwelling Spirit of Jesus as a body, well aware of cognitive and emotional processes. In contemplative prayer, discovering stillness in our bodies and minds, we turn the eyes of our hearts toward God. During this time of silent prayer, we discover that our bodies have the capacity to be spiritual, that focusing our minds can assist our spiritual abilities, and that our spiritual hearts can be embodied. In contemplative prayer, we find true integration of body, mind, and heart. We find out what it is to experience wholeness.

Human nature as relational. So far, contemplative prayer, along with Christian theology, has helped us develop a model of the human person. We are a complex unity of body, mind, and heart, which work together as a whole person—which we call soul. However, we are still missing a fundamental tenet of human nature, that is, that we are created in the image of God. This view of humans as *imago Dei*—"image of God" (see Gen 1:26)—informs us that human nature is like God's nature. In order to understand our own lives, we must look at divine life.

The most obvious thing we see about God in Scripture is that God is not individual but relational (Grenz, 2006). The Christian doctrine of the Trinity reveals the nature of God. The God we know is the triune one. There are three trinitarian persons united in love as one. Because God is community, humans—who are created in God's image—must be relational as well.

The image of God can be understood as our capacity for various relationships. Utilizing the entire person—body, mind, and heart—we have been created to relate to self, others, and God. In the next section, we will examine each of these vital relationships from a Christian contemplative perspective.

Relationship with self. As we enter God's presence in contemplative prayer, there is little that we need to do other than be ourselves. However, this can be a complicated task because it confronts us with this tiny word *self.* What is the self? How does the self show up in the context of contemplative prayer? How do we relate to it? We will address these questions in this section.

Psychologist David Benner (2011) explains why the experience of self is so difficult. He suggests that we actually have two selves. The first one he refers to as the Self. He capitalizes the word in order to highlight the fact that there is something immensely bigger than what we experience as *me.* This Self is the *imago Dei,* the imprint of the divine that we are. We began life with this Self. This Self is the true self or our self-in-God. From this place, we are one with the Spirit of Christ.

Within months of being born, we begin to develop a sense of being a separate identity—having an *I* or being a *me.* Within a short period of time, we move from the Self we had at birth to a sense of *me* that is connected to my thoughts, my emotions, and my body. We actually become disconnected from our true self. This small self is the one that we have constructed. Having concluded that I am these thoughts and feelings, this self defines *me* in a narrow and meager way. According to Daniel Siegel (2010a), the findings of neuroscience support this idea of a small self: "My own reading of the neuroscience of self is that the cortex is naturally inclined to create a smaller and limited sense of self" (p. 257).

In the context of contemplative prayer, we find ourselves repeatedly in a state of self-reflection, thinking about the small self. Our minds get attracted to and focused on what we think, feel, and desire. The challenge of contemplative prayer is to withdraw our attention from this self in order to focus on

God. When, for a fleeting moment, we experience this state of being empty of our small self, we momentarily return to our true self. As we return to the Father's love, we may experience brief reminders of the Self, the self-in-God.

Situated within contemplative prayer, we gain awareness of the self that we have created. This self-made image is the one we want others—and even God— to see. But these people we have created are simply the masks that we wear. We come to believe that these masks are our true faces.

But we do have a true face or Self. We find it when we turn our faces to our heavenly Father. We discover our real Self in the context of God's love for us. We move from the false self that we have constructed to the true self that we are in Christ. As Paul writes, "You have taken off your old self with its practices and have put on the new self, which is being renewed in knowledge in the image of its Creator" (Col 3:9-10).

Within the context of contemplative prayer, we leave behind our self-made identities and assent to who we truly are. As Basil Pennington (2001), co-creator of centering prayer writes, "When we leave off all our superficial activity, when we leave behind our thoughts, feelings, our flow of images, and simply settle down to assent wholly to being who we are, we are essentially prayer—response to God" (p. 89). With one simple word, *prayer*, Pennington answers the question, Who am I?

Relationship with others. Human beings are social beings, and as such we are created to form relationships with others. It is clear that we are not designed to live alone. Speaking of Adam, God said, "It is not good for the man to be alone" (Gen 2:18). So God created a wife for Adam. Marriage is the first social relationship that is described in Scripture. With time, humans entered into other relationships with children, extended family, friends, and neighbors. Humans are part of a large web of relationships. The life of humans is one of relating to others.

At first glance, it appears as if contemplative prayer is devoid of social relationships. Aren't I sitting alone with God as I engage in silent prayer? On a physical level, the answer is obviously yes. However, on a psychological level, my practice has taught me a very different lesson. As I sit with God, a multitude of social interactions enters my mind. I find myself replaying (or conjuring up) the interchanges that I have had—or will have—with my wife, family members, coworkers, and neighbors. In contemplative prayer, far from being alone, I often find myself engaged in vibrant conversations with past, present, and future members of my social community.

Clearly, a contemplative perspective of persons embraces the truth that we are part of a web of relationships. Further, a contemplative-informed view of relationships highlights certain relational questions: (1) Am I accepting responsibility? (2) Am I being present and attentive? (3) Am I remembering my intentions? (4) Am I demonstrating acceptance?

Responsibility. Modern systems theory informs us that our interchanges with others can be thought of in terms of interactional cycles. This means that our interactions with others repeat a predictable set of behaviors. I will do one thing, which is then followed by a response by the other person, which is then followed by a response by me, and so on. This pattern gets repeated again and again. We tend to concentrate on the other person's part in the cycle. We think, *Things would go so much better between us if you would change.* We find ourselves focusing on the other person's flaws and shortcomings. Even during contemplative prayer, I have observed my mind fabricating criticisms, complaints, and accusations of the people in my social web.

The antidote to this blaming mentality is an attitude of responsibility, a posture that is generated within contemplative prayer. Just as I take responsibility for the direction of my attention in contemplative prayer, I must assume accountability for my part in the interactional cycle. I must accept liability for my half of the interaction. Perhaps my wife has contributed to the problem by being late, but I show self-responsibility by saying, "I'm sorry for reacting so quickly in anger." Notice that my statement does not address my wife's behavior. That is her responsibility. Contemplative prayer leads me to focus on my part in the problem. Richard Foster (2008) reminds us that spiritual disciplines, such as contemplative prayer, can teach us to be "response-able—able to respond appropriately" (p. 18).

Presence. In contemplative prayer, we learn about sitting and being present. Being present is a basic component of good relationships. Presence is the ability to be here, but we have a tendency to be there. Being there typically refers to where our minds are. Instead of being with the other person, we are often preoccupied with other thoughts. We may be sitting right beside the other person, but are we really there?

The problem so often is that we are having trouble paying attention. The essence of being with another person is the ability to pay attention. What is it that people want most from us? Our attention. They want us to turn toward them. Turning toward them means that we are actually present, instead of distracted and preoccupied. We are focused on them and making the other the center of our attention.

Contemplative prayer teaches us to notice all the thoughts that carry our attention away from God. We are learning to withdraw our attention from these distractions and turn our focus back to God. We are learning to sit in the same room with God, to be present. This quality of presence is essential to good relationships.

Intentions. In contemplative prayer, we learn three important lessons: (1) we get easily lost; (2) by establishing our intention, we get oriented to our desires; and (3) we must persevere in returning again and again to our intention. During our time of silent prayer, we often lose sight of what we really want. In other words, we get lost. Our aim is to focus our minds on God, but we quickly find ourselves chasing after a host of different thoughts. However, by reminding ourselves of our intention—to be open to the presence of God—we can get ourselves back on track. For a short amount of time, we may be empty of thoughts that distract us from the indwelling Spirit of Jesus, but inevitably we get sidetracked once again. We learn to return over and over again to our intention. First and foremost, contemplative prayer is a prayer of intention.

These contemplative-informed principles can be directly applied to relationships. Relationships always start out with some sort of direction. We set out to be a loving parent, faithful spouse, dependable coworker, good friend, and helpful neighbor. Originally, we wanted to have a certain type of relationship. But we can lose our way.

Intention aims us in the right direction. Intention lets us know where we are pointing. We must remember our intention. We must stop and ask ourselves, What were my intentions for this relationship? Did I want love, enjoyable times together, good communications, teamwork, something else? When we remind ourselves of our intentions, we get headed in the right direction. Our relationships—as well as contemplative prayer—require clear intentions.

Acceptance. From our practice of contemplative prayer, we are learning to be gentle with ourselves. In our times alone with God, we confront the weaknesses of the mind. It is unruly, distracted, and easily wanders away from God. We could blame, criticize, and berate our minds. Instead, we learn to respond with gentleness. When we observe that our attention has drifted away from God, we gently return our focus to the face of God.

The gentleness that we practice toward ourselves in contemplative prayer alerts us to the judgmental tendency of the mind. Instead of blaming and finding fault with the mind when it finds something new upon which to focus, there is only acceptance. The weighty question we face in contemplative prayer is, Will I respond to a wandering mind with judgment or gentle acceptance?

Contemplative prayer teaches us important lessons that we can apply to our relationships. Will we be quick to criticize and look for flaws in others? Will we set up predetermined expectations for how others "should" act and believe? Will we lash out in anger and judgment at the people in our lives? Or will we engage in acceptance? Acceptance is the antidote to judgmentalism. Rather than expecting others to think or behave in a certain way, we can receive them as they are. Of course, we cannot condone certain behaviors—for example, cases of abuse, such as physical, substance, and verbal. But we can withhold condemnation and let go of judgment in order to support the worth of the other person.

Relationship with God. Persons are created to be in relationships with others, and the primary other for human beings is God. Humans are designed to be in kinship with God through the saving work of Jesus. This connection is what spirituality is all about (Howard, 2008). In this regard, a Christian contemplative-oriented approach to counseling diverges from most traditional models of counseling because the traditional models seldom assess a client's relationship with God. Our model is different.

Assessing a client's relationship with God is central to a contemplative-informed model of counseling. The view of human nature that I am espousing in this chapter looks at all the elements of the human person with a particular question in mind: How does this ability—physical, mental, social—support or undermine this client's connection with God? For example, how is my client's use of his body affecting his relationship with God? In what ways are my client's mental capacities, both cognitive and emotional, shaping her affiliation with God? Questions about spirituality are a key part of the assessment process.

TRANSFORMATION

Ultimately, the goal of this contemplative-informed approach to counseling is the transformation of each element of human nature: physical, mental, spiritual, and relational. Our desire is for each of these dimensions of the person to be transformed into Christlikeness. According to C. S. Lewis in *Mere Christianity* (1956a), as transformation occurs Jesus "is beginning to turn you into the same thing as Himself. He is beginning, so to speak, to inject His kind of life and thought into you" (p. 28).

The paradigm that we are constructing has an endpoint in mind: love. Our objective is for clients to emerge from counseling with more ability to love and be loved. As we noted before, Jesus said, "Love the Lord your God with all your heart and with all your soul and with all your mind and with all your strength." He continued, "Love your neighbor as yourself" (Mk 12:30-31). These words by Jesus capture his primary goal for humans—to be lovers. And he instructs us in terms of how to love. We are to love with all our hearts, souls, minds, and bodies.

The radical changes that we are aiming at through this counseling model require the transformation of each component of human nature. First, this model welcomes the body and employs interventions for utilizing the physical dimension of humans. Second, our paradigm places an emphasis on the mind—both cognitive and emotional abilities. Transformation comes about as we assess and intervene at the levels of body and mind. As Paul observed, "Offer your bodies as a living sacrifice, holy and pleasing to God. . . . Be transformed by the renewing of your mind" (Rom 12:1-2).

A contemplative-informed model of counseling cannot downplay the capabilities of the heart. Our objective is to enhance our clients' abilities to see with the eyes of their hearts. We want to improve their spiritual eyesight. Their relationship with God will be examined and a healthy connection with God encouraged. We hope that the process of counseling will change their hearts. This transformation of heart is captured by Ezekiel: "I will give you a new heart and put a new spirit in you; I will remove from you your heart of stone and give you a heart of flesh" (Ezek 36:26). This approach to counseling is not for the weak-kneed; we are working on a total heart transplant.

Finally, this paradigm for counseling aims at integrating the various dimensions of the human person. We are focused on the whole person. The task of bringing all the parts together in unity is the role of the soul. Our goal is to help each dimension work to support the other parts of the person.

Our model of persons is a complex unity: body, mind, heart, soul, and social. We want to carefully assess each dimension, observing how each feature is intermingled with the other parts. Ultimately, we will use this assessment to understand the client's presenting problem, establish appropriate goals and interventions for counseling, and build a supportive relationship with the client.

GUIDELINES FOR ASSESSMENT

In this section, we return to the first building block for theory building—an assessment or view of the client's situation. We call this "case conceptualization." My aim in this chapter has been to approach this component of theory building from a Christian contemplative perspective. My objective has been to offer a view of human nature that is grounded in contemplative prayer. Wanting to flesh out a contemplative-informed assessment, I offer an outline and specific questions that a counselor, using contemplative thought, might employ during an assessment. Adopting a structure suggested by Gehart (2012), this assessment examines three key areas: (1) relationship with self, (2) relationship with others, and (3) relationship with God.

Relationship with self. When conceptualizing in this area using contemplative prayer, the counselor can consider focusing on four areas:

- experience of body

- encounter with mind

- acceptance of self

- construction of self

Experience of body. The contemplative-oriented counselor is curious about how clients experience their bodies. Approaching clients from a contemplative perspective, the counselor wants to know if clients are able to attend to their internal physiological experiences. If they are aware of their physical sensations, the counselor wonders about the clients' abilities to reflect upon their experiences. Once this area is assessed, the counselor will want to focus on developing clients' abilities to tune in to, experience, and express their internal physiological sensations.

These are some of the questions that the contemplative-informed counselor may want to explore in terms of clients' experience of their bodies:

1. Are you able to identify what you are experiencing in your body?

2. Can you tune in to and stay with your physical sensations without reacting to them?

3. To what extent can you reflect upon and describe your internal physiological experiences?

Encounter with mind. How clients experience their minds is of utmost importance when a counselor is conducting an assessment based upon this new contemplative paradigm. Once again, the counselor is interested in clients' abilities to monitor their emotions and thoughts. The contemplative counselor wants to know if clients can observe and express these inner experiences without reacting to them. After the assessment, the counselor may want to help clients tune in to, experience, and express their emotions and thoughts.

When exploring clients' experience of mind, the contemplative-oriented counselor will be curious about the following areas of inquiry:

1. Are you able to identify your emotions and thoughts?

2. Can you tune in to and stay with these mental experiences without reacting to them?

3. To what extent can you reflect upon and describe your feelings and thoughts?

Acceptance of self. Most clients do not stop to assess their level of self-acceptance. Perhaps, unbeknownst to them, feelings of shame are buried under surface emotions of anger and a sense that something is missing. These clients may not notice how often they engage in self-attacking or self-blaming behavior. These clients may not be aware of the voice of self-criticism that drones in the background. Operating from a contemplative perspective, the counselor will want to lead the client to a place of greater self-acceptance and less self-judgment.

Some of the questions that contemplative counselors may want to pose as they assess clients in this area are as follows:

1. Are you aware of self-criticism, self-blame, and self-judgment?

2. Do you have a knee-jerk reaction of trying to ignore, fix, or defend these areas where you feel defective?

3. Are you willing to simply engage with and examine these areas in a spirit of kindness?

Construction of self. Contemplative-oriented counselors are interested in the client's definition of self. Most clients come to counseling with a limited sense of self. They are often attached to the selves that they have (or someone else has) created. In contrast, the contemplative counselor wants to help clients enlarge their sense of self. After the assessment, this counselor will want to help clients open up to other ways of defining who they are.

The following questions may help the contemplative counselor assess construction of self:

1. How did you learn to define yourself in this way?

2. Are you committed to this view of self?

3. Are there times when you have another view of yourself?

Relationship with others. In addition to assessing clients' relationship with self, we want to examine their relationships with others. When conceptualizing in this area using this contemplative-oriented approach, the counselor may want to focus on four areas:

- taking responsibility

- practicing presence

- remembering intentions

- demonstrating acceptance

Taking responsibility. When working with individuals and couples, it is vital to consider how they relate to others. Using a contemplative-informed model, the counselor will want to first identify the interactional cycles in which clients find themselves. Then the contemplative counselor will explore the client's level of responsibility. After assessing this feature, the counselor will want to help the client grow in this area.

These are some of the questions that contemplative counselors will want to employ as they assess this element:

1. Can you describe the interactional cycle that you and the other get into?

2. Do you have a tendency to blame the other person, or can you take responsibility for your part in the cycle?

3. Can you reflect on your behavior in a kind way?

4. Can you engage with the physical sensations, emotions, and thoughts that accompany the behavior?

Practicing presence. As we evaluate how clients relate to others, we want to assess their level of presence. Their ability to move the attention from themselves to others is very telling. As contemplative-oriented counselors, we want to explore our clients' capacities to be in the here and now. Knowing more about this area will help us assess how effective our clients will be in their interpersonal relationships. As we move on in treatment after the assessment, we will want to help our clients practice presence.

These are some of the questions that the contemplative-informed counselor may want to explore in terms of the client's presence:

1. How well do you pay attention to others' thoughts, desires, and emotions?

2. What internal sensations, emotions, or thoughts interfere with your ability to pay attention to others?

3. What's going on when you aren't present with me during our session?

4. Can you catch yourself not paying attention and then rein in your attention?

Remembering intentions. Intentions are vital to our clients' relationships with others. Many times, our clients do not have clear intentions, they have forgotten their intentions, or they don't know how to reorient themselves to their intentions. The contemplative-informed counselor emphasizes this area of assessment. And after the assessment the counselor helps clients work on this area of their lives.

When exploring clients' intentions, the contemplative-oriented counselor will be curious about the following areas of inquiry:

1. Did you set original intentions in your relationship with the other person? What kind of person did you want to be in the relationship?

2. What distracted you from your original intentions? Were you distracted by specific thoughts or emotions or both? Can you be kind to yourself as you identify the distractions?

3. Would you like to return to your original intentions or set new ones?

Demonstrating acceptance. Acceptance is a critical element in our clients' relationships with others. In a contemplative approach to counseling, counselors are curious about their clients' abilities to abandon judgment in order to truly empathize with the experience of others. Once this domain is assessed, the contemplative counselor will attempt to enhance this area of their clients' lives.

Some of the questions that contemplative counselors may want to pose as they assess clients in this area are as follows:

1. Are you able to stop yourself before you express judgment and blame?

2. Can you shift to a position of acceptance? That is, are you able to listen with curiosity to the other person's point of view?

3. Can you tune in to the other person's pain and be touched by that person's emotions?

4. Are you able to extend kindness to others in their shortcomings and when they are different from you?

Relationship with God. A client's relationship with God is the centerpiece of our new paradigm of counseling. Clients cannot not have a relationship with God. They are either moving away from or toward God. Thus, our clients will benefit from discussions about their connections (or lack thereof) with God. This may not be the first area that we assess, but by showing curiosity in this domain, we open the door to important issues. Ultimately, as we explore their love (or lack of love) for God, we gain an opportunity to explore deep issues of the heart. After the assessment, the contemplative counselor will continue to explore ways to help the client build a stronger relationship with God.

Below are useful questions that contemplative-oriented counselors might ask as they explore this area:

1. Do you believe there is a God? If so, what is your view of God?

2. Do you believe that God is present in your life? If so, in what ways?

3. Do you take time to be present with God? In what ways?

4. What is the connection between your body and spiritual life?

5. What is the connection between your mind (both thoughts and emotions) and your spiritual life?

6. Do you love God? Can you describe what that experience is like?

7. What is the connection between loving God and loving yourself/others?

8. Is there a reason to be kind to yourself? To others?

CONCLUSION: ASSESSMENT OF ADAM

This final section offers us a chance to observe the dialogue between a contemplative-informed counselor and a client. The scenario below gives us access to both the conversation and the thinking of a counselor who is informed by a contemplative view of human nature. The script is an attempt to demonstrate some of the concepts examined in this chapter. The client is Adam, and he has arrived for his initial appointment. Using a contemplative perspective, the counselor is assessing Adam's situation. The counselor is looking at Adam in a certain way—a contemplative-informed way—in hopes of laying a foundation for their future work together. This is how their session might sound.

> **Therapist:** I am so glad that you have come in to talk with me. What do you want to talk about?
>
> **Adam**: Something really terrible happened to me recently.
>
> **Therapist**: Do you want to tell me about it?

Adam: Okay. Eve and I were supposed to meet God in the garden the other day, but it didn't go very well.

Therapist: Now Eve . . . that's your wife?

Adam: Yes.

Therapist: You said that you were supposed to meet with God. Can you tell me about your relationship with him?

The counselor is exploring Adam's relationship with God. The counselor is examining the heart dimension.

Adam: Well, we've always had a good relationship . . . that is, until recently. In the past, we would always meet in the garden and go on walks together. That's not going to happen anymore.

Therapist: What happened to change things?

Adam: He told us not to eat fruit from a particular tree in the garden. But we went ahead and ate from it anyway. When God came to the garden, he asked me if I had eaten from the tree. What was I supposed to say?

Therapist: So, what did you say?

The counselor is gathering information about Adam's relationship with his wife. The counselor doesn't condone Adam's actions but doesn't judge him either.

Adam: I told him the truth. I told him that Eve was the one who gave me fruit from the tree.

Therapist: Were you and God talking face-to-face?

The counselor continues to learn about Adam's relationship with God.

Adam: No, I was hiding behind one of the trees in the park.

Therapist: You must have been feeling very afraid if you were hiding. Is that right?

Here, the counselor is gathering information about the mental dimension. What was he feeling? (Adam seems self-aware in this area.)

Adam: Yes, I suppose so.

Therapist: What do you suppose you were thinking when you hid behind the tree?

The counselor wants to know if Adam is also aware of his thought processes. (Adam seems out-of-touch in this area.)

Adam: I don't know what I was thinking. I was just afraid of God. I didn't want him to be mad at me.

Therapist: Let me make sure that I'm getting this. After eating the forbidden fruit, you went to the garden. When you heard God coming, you felt afraid and hid behind a tree. Did I get that right?

The counselor is drawing a connection for Adam between his emotions and his actions.

Adam: Yes, you're getting it.

Therapist: As you're telling me this story, what are you feeling in your body? Can you describe it to me?

The counselor is interested in the physical dimension. Is Adam aware of his body? (He seems to be.)

Adam: Yeah, I can feel my heart racing, and I'm feeling kind of sweaty.

Therapist: It must have been so scary for you because your relationship with God is so important.

The counselor is showing acceptance for Adam by reframing his fear in terms of how he values his relationship with God.

Adam: (nods)

Therapist: When you were hiding, what do you think was going through your mind?

Once again, the counselor is checking out Adam's awareness of his thinking—the mental dimension. (He shows more awareness this time.)

Adam: I was thinking that I had really messed up my relationship with God. He probably wouldn't want to have anything to do with me.

Therapist: You were saying to yourself: I have done something really bad. There is no way that God could love me now. I have become unlovable. God is not going to want to have anything to do with me now. Is that right?

Here, the counselor is focusing on Adam's relationship with himself. Adam is feeling very unlovable.

Adam: That sounds about right.

Therapist: What are you hoping will happen between you and God now?

The counselor is returning to Adam's relationship with God—the heart dimension.

Adam: God has told me that we have to leave the garden and that we can't come back. I don't know what we're going to do now. We've lost everything.

Therapist: You look like you are feeling afraid again. Is that right?

The counselor is revisiting the emotional side of the mental dimension.

Adam: Yeah, I'm pretty worried about our future.

Therapist: Well, it makes sense that you are worried. You have had some major changes happen in your life.

The counselor continues to extend acceptance to Adam.

Therapist: Would you like to make another appointment with me? We can set some goals for how you want your life to be in the future. You and Eve have a lot to sort out. There's your relationship with God. Also, you have to figure out where you're going to live and how you're going to make ends meet.

Here, the counselor is trying to build upon the initial assessment and set the stage for future counseling.

Adam: Yes, I think that coming back would be a good idea.

Therapist: Okay, I will look forward to seeing you next time.

HOW PEOPLE CHANGE

WE ARE USING contemplative prayer as a lens through which we view our clients' situations. In chapter three, we began our discussion of how we look at or conceptualize our clients' issues by examining the human condition. To enhance our perspective of clients, in this chapter we will move on to the psychological and relational issues that are most likely contributing to a client's presenting problem.

Presenting problems typically fall into three categories (Cozolino, 2016). First, clients may present with problematic symptoms such as depression or anxiety. Next, they complain of troubling behaviors like self-harm, gambling, or drinking. Finally, concerns about relationships—conflicts, separations, or loneliness—are common. We are tempted to focus our treatment on these presenting concerns. However, they are most often just the tip of the iceberg. It is important for counselors to address the primary issues hidden below the surface.

In the first part of this chapter, using the perspective of interpersonal neurobiology (IPNB), we will identify six primary issues that underlie our client's presenting problem. We will also visit the original experiences of humankind to discover that the modern findings of neurobiology are captured in the Genesis account of Adam and Eve. The six issues are as follows:

- threat response system
- fear

- avoidance
- limited self
- shame
- hidden functions

In case conceptualization, we not only identify the key dynamics that are targeted for change, but we also propose clear ideas about the mechanisms that can bring about change. In part two of this chapter, we utilize Christian contemplative thought to illuminate six mechanisms of change. They are as follows:

- rest (safety)
- love
- approach
- true self
- vulnerability
- resting in darkness

PRIMARY ISSUES

THREAT RESPONSE SYSTEM

> *You have made us for yourself, and our heart*
> *is restless until it rests in you.*
> **AUGUSTINE**

It is undeniable that we are social creatures. We are born into significant relationships, and we are primarily interested in maintaining safety within the context of these basic connections. As long as we are unharmed in our affiliations, we remain relaxed, secure, and balanced. However, once our sense of safety in these relationships comes into question, a complex, comprehensive system is activated. It is called the threat response system, and it has the power to alter our behavior, thoughts, bodies, and feelings.

From an IPNB perspective, the threat response system moves through three critical stages: (1) red alert, (2) ready the troops, and (3) all-out war (Tatkin, 2011). The first line of defense is the detection stage. This function is carried

out by the amygdalae, almond-shaped structures located in the limbic area—
or central region—of the brain. (Since the brain is divided into two hemi-
spheres, there are two amygdalae, one in the right brain and one in the left.)

Neuroscience informs us that the amygdalae are mature at birth, whereas
the systems that regulate them and inhibit them take many years to develop
and mature (Cozolino, 2016). This means that we enter the world totally prepared to detect threats to our safety while we have absolutely no ability to
protect ourselves from these dangers. At the same time, we do have the capacity to attach ourselves to caretakers who have the potential to protect and
calm us. This is why we stay in close proximity to our parents during our
early years.

From birth to death, the amygdalae are continually scanning the environment, looking for signs of danger. Within the context of our all-important
relationships, the right-side amygdala makes note of dangerous nonverbal
messages such as movements, postures, voices, and facial expressions, whereas
the left-side amygdala notices threatening words. Once danger is perceived or
detected, the amygdalae send out an alarm: "Danger, danger!"

According to neuroscience, the amygdalae receive information about
threats through two different circuits: one fast, the other slow. If the slow
system is used, data travel through the cortex, where thinking occurs, before
they reach the amygdalae. However, when the fast route is activated, facts
about the experience bypass the cortex and go directly to the amygdalae, a half
second faster than the slow route.

The red-alert stage of the threat response system can be likened to the
school fire-alarm system (Jennings, 2013). When the fire alarm is activated at
the school, it has a twofold purpose: to signal the 911 operator and to warn
everyone in the building. (In this analogy, the 911 operator is the hypothalamus,
and the occupants of the building are the brain, mind, and body.) Like the
alarm, the amygdalae alert the 911 operator—the hypothalamus—to send out
an urgent call.

Once the hypothalamus is alerted, the threat response system has entered
the second stage: ready the troops. The hypothalamus, also located in the
limbic region, acts as the master of the endocrine control system. Working
with the endocrine system, especially the pituitary and adrenal glands, it is
primarily responsible for getting our minds and bodies ready for action.

Under the command of the hypothalamus, the pituitary and adrenal glands release hormones, adrenaline and cortisol, that prepare us for motion. Together, these structures and hormones form our stress response system.

Finally, we enter stage three of the threat response system: all-out war. We now move into the action for which stage two has prepared us. If our brains assess that we can handle the danger, the sympathetic branch of the autonomic nervous system is activated. Our metabolism increases as we prepare for the energy demands that lie ahead. We are ready to fight or run away. On the other hand, if we determine that we cannot escape from the danger, the parasympathetic system takes control and puts the body into freeze mode (Schore, 2012).

While the threat response system energizes the body, it also activates other important systems: emotional and behavioral. Emotions are integrally connected to and receive information from the body. As our bodies are triggered during the threat response, so too are our emotions. The two most powerful threat-based emotions are anger and fear. In some situations, anger may emerge as a protective response that moves us toward and against the threatening situation. However, at other times, fear may provide us with safety by prompting us to move away from the threat or to shut down in the face of danger.

Finally, the threat response system affects one other operation of our being, our cognition. We see that the behaviors of fight, flee, or freeze are manifestations of the threat response system. But what about our thinking? In addition to reaching down into the deeper, limbic regions of our brains, the threat response system reaches up to the higher, frontal cortex of our brains to change our thinking (Haidt, 2006). It shifts the mind into a specific orientation, one that is pessimistic. Our minds generate negative thoughts about others, the self, and the situation, focusing on the faults of the world, the people in our lives, and ourselves. As a result of an unregulated threat response system, we are "rarely if ever at ease" (Langshur & Klemp, 2016, p. 20).

The Genesis story of Adam and Eve reveals people who were painfully familiar with what modern neuroscience calls the threat response system. Their very survival was at stake when they ate from the tree of the knowledge of good and evil because God had warned them, "When you eat from it you will certainly die" (Gen 2:17). We don't know how Adam and Eve interpreted this word *die*, but the warning from God must have represented a real danger to them.

Two Christian psychiatrists propose that Adam and Eve's interest in the fruit from this tree indicates an activated threat response system (Jennings, 2013; Thompson, 2015). They suggest that Adam and Eve had already detected something that led them to think God couldn't be trusted. Anderson and Granados (2009) posit that they may have perceived God as mean and dictatorial since God had warned them against eating from the tree. Their faulty thinking may have been, "Can we trust God if he is withholding something good from us?" These experiences of doubt and distrust could certainly have set the threat response system in motion. As a result, for Adam and Eve, "the world became a threat instead of a home" (Anderson & Granados, 2009, p. 109).

FEAR

Fear shrinks back at sudden and unusual things threatening
what it loves, and is on watch for its own safety.
AUGUSTINE

Human beings have an innate drive for safety. Most importantly, we want to feel protected and secure within the context of our primary relationships. We want to feel connected to the ones we love. From our previous discussion of the threat response system, you will recall that the amygdalae are constantly scanning the environment for any threat to our safety. When danger is detected by the amygdalae, an alarm is sounded.

What is this alarm signal that blasts out from the right-side amygdala? Fear. Fear screams out: "Be afraid! Be very afraid!" Fear is the intense cry we hear and feel when danger, either real or perceived, is detected. Its sound is fast, strong, and loud. We can't miss it. It jangles all our senses, bringing all our resources to attention. In desperation, it can quickly and automatically take over our bodies, minds, emotions, and behavior.

Fear is housed in and generated from the right-side amygdala. From this limbic region of the brain, fear links and orchestrates all our physical and mental responses to the perceived danger. Fear arouses the autonomic nervous system, modifies our thinking, and moves us to fight, flight, or freeze. All these fear-generated reactions are aimed at one purpose: to regulate the threat. Fear wants to protect us and bring us back to a state of safety.

Fear changes both our emotions and our thinking. As long as we perceive that our safety is in jeopardy, we may be overwhelmed and flooded by feelings of anxiety. In addition, as threat-generated signals of fear reach up to the frontal cortex, our thinking is altered (Cozolino, 2016). Fear and cognition act as a two-way street. Thoughts can arouse intense emotions, but anxiety can also shape our thinking. Fear, acting as a mental filter, can cause us to see events as dangerous. Through a fearful lens, the actions of others may be perceived as threats and attacks.

From an IPNB perspective, we can sometimes see our fear, but just as likely, it may be acting outside of our awareness. In other words, we may be able to identify it for what it is and say, "I am afraid." But at other times, we may adamantly deny the presence of fear. To ourselves, the fear is unseen. If others ask us if we are scared, our quick reply may be, "No, but I sure am frustrated!"

From the beginning, human beings have been flooded and overwhelmed with the power of fear. We discover in the Genesis account that Adam and Eve were afraid of losing their connection with God. So they hid from God. When God called out to Adam, Adam replied, "I was afraid . . . so I hid" (Gen 3:10).

This narrative illustrates an ironic side of fear. In our eagerness to find protection from the threat of disconnection, fear can move us away from those we love the most. Without our realizing it, fear can take over our emotions and minds, causing actions that we later regret.

AVOIDANCE

Farther and farther I went from you.
AUGUSTINE

Human behavior is governed by two motivational systems: approach and withdrawal (Haidt, 2006). The approach system motivates us to move toward certain things while the withdrawal system prompts us to pull back and avoid specific situations. As previously discussed, when a threat is detected, we might move against something with anger in what we call a fight response. On the other hand, danger can elicit fear and withdrawal, which we have termed the flight and freeze responses. In this section, we are looking at the withdrawal response.

Avoidance serves an important function. It is an attempt by the threat response system to protect us from perceived danger. Withdrawing from the threatening situation and limiting our contact with the world is the system's method of bringing us to safety (Cozolino, 2016). Sometimes we are aware of withdrawing tendencies, but at times, outside of our awareness, we quickly and automatically engage in avoidant behaviors (Ginot, 2015).

Avoidance shows itself in two specific ways: flight and freeze. In a situation that is perceived as dangerous, the threat response system will initially activate the sympathetic branch of the autonomic nervous system, causing a high state of physical and emotional arousal. Once energized, in order to protect ourselves, we may try to avoid or run away from the situation.

However, there is a second response that is decidedly different from the initial hyperaroused reaction (Schore, 2012). In this situation, we discern that there is no escape from the perceived threat. It is as if we resign ourselves to the inevitability of overwhelming danger, so we resort to our last form of defense. At this point, our parasympathetic system kicks in, affecting our bodies, emotions, and behavior. In the physical arena, we experience a shutdown of metabolic activity, accompanied by a decreased heart rate and blood pressure. As our metabolism decreases, our emotions turn to hopelessness and helplessness. These physical and emotional responses culminate in behavior that looks like hiding. At this point, we are motivated to avoid the attention of others. It is as if we want to be unseen.

Children often find themselves in situations that provoke a hiding response (Schore, 2012). Perhaps the child wants to turn to a loved one for protection, but at the same time the child is fearful of this same person. A child caught in this untenable and unbearable situation is easy to spot. Moving into a parasympathetic state, the child will avoid eye contact with the parent or caregiver. Trying to cope with danger, the child will, in verbal and nonverbal ways, send the message to stay away. In hopes of calming fear, the child will communicate an intention to disconnect. For scared children, disconnecting becomes the final means of escape.

Hiding, a primitive way of coping with danger, is a way of cutting off attention from "both the outer and inner worlds" (Schore, 2012, p. 277). When we become withdrawn in this way, we detach from the environment; that is, we stop interacting with others. But in addition, in this parasympathetic state, we unhook from ourselves. What does this mean? It means that we lose touch with our bodies, our actions, and our own identity. We seem to lose touch with how we normally see ourselves and interact with the world. In this state, my clients will sometimes remark: "I don't feel comfortable in my own skin."

In the Genesis story of Adam and Eve, we see signs of this primitive coping strategy. Adam and Eve found themselves in an impossible situation. After disobeying God, they felt the danger of being disconnected from God, their source of life. Being unable to escape from God, they undoubtedly experienced the parasympathetic state described in this section. In great fear, what could they do? They resorted to the last thing they could think of: hiding. The story tells us, "They hid from the LORD God among the trees of the garden" (Gen 3:8).

LIMITED SELF

I had no clear idea even of my own self.

AUGUSTINE

There is a question we cannot shake: Who am I? Somehow, we are driven to respond to this question of identity. The answer takes shape and is threatened within the same context, that is, inside relationships. We desperately want to hold on to our sense of self, but it seems to slip from our fingers when our threat response system becomes activated. In a threatened state of mind, it is as if our sense of who we are morphs into something completely different.

From an IPNB perspective, our sense of identity is inseparable from the threat response system. When we feel that our safety is in jeopardy, a predictable cascade of events happens: our bodies become energized, our emotions become aroused, our actions become self-protective, and our sense of identity turns negative (Ginot, 2015). In an unregulated state of threat, our view of self turns dark. We become negative toward ourselves, engaging in self-critical and self-denigrating thoughts. And it seems to us that others must be thinking ill of us as well.

We make sense of who we are by creating stories (D. Siegel, 2010b). As our bodies and emotions become dysregulated, the words that we select to form a narrative about self can turn negative. Outside of our awareness, a dangerous event may be activating memories from our past, exposing us to memories of significant others who demonstrated mean, negative, or indifferent attitudes toward us when we were young (Cozolino, 2016). These painful memories can infiltrate our narrative, casting a dark shadow on who we think we are. It is often these negative stories that bring our clients to therapy.

There are several prominent characteristics in a narrative that answers the question, Who am I? First, it has an author: myself. This brings an important element into focus—that the story is being told from one perspective, my own. With only one "legitimate" perspective to draw on, I arrive at the conclusion that my account is true. This is the second element. Since it is *my* story, this creates a feeling of ownership, evoking a feeling of truth (Damásio, 1999). I wind up thinking and sounding this way: "The way I see it is correct." Finally, narratives are selective. This means that the mind makes up a story based upon minimal information. The account contains only a small portion of details, excluding other important particulars.

It seems that we become attached to the narratives we tell about ourselves. The problem, though, is that our stories about our identities are distorted and insufficient. In the end, our narratives trap us in a limited sense of self (Gehart, 2012). As Daniel Siegel (2010b) teaches us, in a threatened state of mind we develop "narrow definitions of self" (p. 257). To counteract this problem, Siegel (2010b) establishes one of the primary goals of counseling: "to clear us of these restrictive definitions of ourselves" (p. 260).

The Bible sheds light on the essential question of identity. From the beginning, we see signs that the human experience is based on a foundation of knowing who we are. Returning to the Genesis account of Adam and Eve, we observe that identity was a gift received in the context of their relationship with God (Anderson & Granados, 2009). They were secure in who they were: children of God, made in his image (Gen 1:27). As long as they continued in dialogue with God, walking with God in the garden (Gen 3:8), their identities remained secure. They knew who they were.

However, after the fall, Adam and Eve forgot who they were. They left the garden, not only in search of a new home but in search of an identity apart from the Creator (Anderson & Granados, 2009). Their story of lost identity is repeated in the story of the lost son (Lk 15:11-24). Like Adam and Eve, he "set off for a distant country" (Lk 15:13). There, he tried to "un-son" himself with a change of identity (Volf, 1996). He began to think of himself as "no longer worthy to be called" his father's son (Lk 15:19). He had clearly forgotten who he was.

These two narratives—the stories of Adam and Eve as well as that of the lost son—reveal the challenges we face as we attempt to answer the question, Who am I? According to Christian psychologist David Benner (2004), we are not who we think we are. The real self is not the narrative that we have created about ourselves. Our narrative is a self-made image, a false portrayal of who we really are. Christian psychologist Gary Moon (2004) advances the belief that fear causes us to hide our real identity—or true face—"behind the veil" (p. 57).

Was Moon (2004) referring to the main character, Orual, in C. S. Lewis's novel, *Till We Have Faces* (1956b)? Orual, the king's daughter, afraid that she was too ugly, grew up with her face hidden behind a veil. Eventually, upon her father's death, she became the queen, still wearing a veil. More and more, Orual identified with her role as queen, losing sight of her real self. Orual said, "The Queen of Glome had more and more part in me and Orual had less and less. I locked Orual up. . . . The thing I carried in me grew slowly smaller and less alive" (p. 226).

Like Orual, our clients find themselves imprisoned in a restricted sense of self. Like her, their true identity—or the "thing" they carry around inside—becomes smaller and less alive. Out of fear of what others might think of them, they hide their faces behind a veil, as "a means to be unknown" (Lewis, 1956b, p. 278).

Entering old age, a scary question began to prod at Orual's mind: What if she removed the veil? Knowing that no one would recognize her real face, one day she "went out bareface; showed that face which many had said . . . was too dreadful to be seen" (Lewis, 1956b, p. 278). Finally, she dared, for only a brief period, to show her true face.

This experiment led Orual to a great discovery: it takes great courage to show your real face, your true identity. Most of us go our entire lives afraid to remove the veils behind which we hide. We wind up thinking that we are the masks we wear. Regrettably, we don't find the eyes to see or the words to describe who we really are. No wonder God's face seems cloudy and unclear to our eyes. How can we see God's face from behind a veil? Nearing death, Orual remembered the words of her beloved teacher, "Child, to say the very thing you really mean, the whole of it, nothing more or less or other than what you really mean; that's the whole art and joy of words" (Lewis, 1956b, p. 294). Pondering his words, Orual concluded, "Till that word can be dug out of us, why would they [the gods] hear the babble that we think we mean? How can they meet us face to face till we have faces?" (p. 294).

SHAME

> *I was sick and tormented. . . . I twisted and turned in my chain. . . .*
> *By an austere mercy you redoubled the scourges of fear and shame.*
> **AUGUSTINE**

From an IPNB perspective, shame happens between people. Because we are social creatures, we need to be seen and understood by others. We seek connection (D. Siegel, 2010b). But when we feel ignored, misunderstood, and disconnected from the primary people in our lives, we feel threatened. The prospect of being abandoned or cut off from the ones we love sets off the threat response system.

As I have shown, the threat response system is an intertwined set of physical, behavioral, emotional, and cognitive functions. When the fear of disconnection—we call this *shame*—is activated, we immediately feel it in our bodies. Our fear and shame are experienced as a shutting down of the parasympathetic system. It is as if someone has slammed the brakes on our autonomic nervous systems. For some people, this physiological response may be experienced as heaviness in their chests, while for others it is felt as nausea in their stomachs.

Once activated, shame alters our sense of identity. This happens because of our attempt to answer the question, "Why has my loved one withdrawn from me?" The voice of shame offers a decidedly negative answer. According to IPNB, shame harshly says, "They have left you because you are unlovable" (Cozolino, 2016). Shame carries with it a sense of worthlessness: "I am not worthy of connection." Shame shapes a narrative about there being something deeply wrong with us. The story of shame is, "I am not enough; I am bad; or I don't matter" (Thompson, 2015, p. 24).

Shame fills us with fear. We are terrified that others will find out there is something wrong with us. We are scared of what our loved ones will think when they see our flaws. We are afraid that others will find us unworthy of their love. And then we experience the greatest fear of all, that our loved ones will not want us and that they will abandon us. The emotional pain of shame can be unbearable. The fear of being left robs us of our sense of safety.

What do we do to protect ourselves? Thompson (2015) writes, "Hiding is the natural response to shame" (p. 108). We turn away from others in an effort to reduce the awful emotional pain that we feel. Paradoxically, out of fear of disconnection, that is, that our loved ones will not want us, we move away from the ones we love. One of the first things we hide is our face. We turn our eyes away from others, thinking, *Don't look at me.* Schore (2012) puts it this way, "We hide our shame . . . from others because we want others to be blind to what we cannot tolerate seeing" (p. 98).

The discoveries of neurobiology were foretold in the early pages of the Bible. Shame was active from the very beginning of humankind. Of course before the fall, "Adam and his wife were both naked, and they felt no shame" (Gen 2:25). Secure in their identities, they felt loved and wanted by God. Unafraid of being seen by God, they walked naked with God in the garden. But this all changed after they ate from the forbidden tree.

After the fall, Adam and Eve experienced the reactions identified by neuroscience. New questions popped into their heads: *Would God continue to love them? Were they worthy of his love? Would God still want them?* The fear of being abandoned by God was terrifying. So what did they do? They hid from God's presence, desperately seeking protection. They felt overwhelmed with the fear of disconnection and the discomfort of nakedness. Not wanting God to see them, they covered themselves for the first time.

Augustine was familiar with shame. Identifying with Adam and Eve's state of shame, Augustine (1960/2014) wrote, "I was Adam's son" (p. 160). Capturing the pain of shame that he shared with Adam, Augustine proclaimed, "I was sick and tormented. . . . I twisted and turned in my chain. . . . By an austere mercy you redoubled the scourges of fear and shame" (p. 162). We are all children of Adam. We all experience shame.

HIDDEN FUNCTIONS

*You took me from behind my back, where I had placed myself
because I did not wish to look upon myself.*

AUGUSTINE

There are many ways of thinking about the mind. It can be divided in four ways: mind versus body, left versus right, new versus old, and controlled versus automatic (Haidt, 2006). For our purposes here, we are going to focus on the last comparison—controlled versus automatic processes. These two processes are also referred to as the conscious and unconscious systems.

The conscious and unconscious systems are two parallel tracks for handling information (Cozolino, 2016). The conscious, controlled system employs processes of which we are aware: words, thoughts, memories, emotions, behavior, and physical operations. On the other hand, when the unconscious, automatic system is in charge, physical sensations, memories, feelings, actions, and cognitions can be hidden functions. This means that these operations are totally outside of our awareness.

It is significant that the conscious and unconscious systems process information at different rates of speed (Cozolino, 2016). The unconscious system processes sensory, motor, and emotional information in ten to fifty milliseconds (approximately 1/20th of a second). In contrast, it takes five to six hundred milliseconds for brain activity to register in conscious awareness. The difference in processing speed between the fast system—the unconscious—and the slow system—consciousness—is approximately one half second. This half second may seem insignificant, but for the brain it is a long time. By the time we are consciously aware of an experience, the unconscious system may have processed the information many times and led us to think, feel, and act in ways of which we are unaware.

Let's compare these two tracks in terms of the threat response system. Picking up on some incoming danger, the slow, conscious system relays information to the cortex. On the other hand, outside of our awareness, the amygdalae observe this same threat and send out the alarm: "Danger, danger!" Bypassing the slow system, the fast system arouses fear, activates the autonomic system, utilizes memories, and sets the fight-or-flight reaction into motion.

All these bodily, emotional, cognitive, and behavioral functions are orchestrated by the unconscious system outside of our awareness; they are hidden. By the time the slow system has processed the situation, the fast system has already acted.

From an IPNB perspective, counselors have historically placed far too much importance on the conscious system (Ginot, 2015). We have assumed that people are in control of and entirely conscious of their cognitive, physical, emotional, and behavioral processes. But, according to modern neuroscience, we have ignored a system that is larger, quicker, and more comprehensive—the unconscious.

Perhaps a metaphor can help us understand the relationship between these two systems. Haidt (2006) suggests that the relationship between the unconscious and conscious systems is like that of the elephant and its rider. The elephant—or unconscious—includes the gut feelings, visceral reactions, emotions, hidden memories, and intuitions of the automatic system whereas the rider—or consciousness—includes the thoughts, emotions, bodily reactions, and behaviors that we can express through words. The rider, sitting atop the elephant, can see what lies ahead and can gently coax the unconscious in the right direction. However, the rider is misled if he thinks he can control and order the elephant around. Spotting a beehive in the tree, the elephant is going to change its course despite the rider's best efforts to get it to walk under the tree.

For too long, we have not only ignored but misunderstood the unconscious. Much of the confusion is due to Freud's depiction of the unconscious as the container for fantasies and forbidden impulses (Ginot, 2015). Freud associated the unconscious with repressed memories. In his model, the unconscious system is willfully attempting to remain unaware of intolerable experiences.

According to modern neuroscience, Freud's model has been disproven (Ginot, 2015). His old beliefs about the unconscious can no longer be accepted. Instead, an updated understanding of the unconscious—one that contains recent findings from neurobiology—must be incorporated into our work with clients. We need a new model of the unconscious.

This new model, incorporated by IPNB, offers a newer understanding of the unconscious (Ginot, 2015). Far from being just a container of rejected memories, the unconscious processes are recognized by the new paradigm as the force behind most of our mental, emotional, and behavioral functions.

Even though it may appear as if our thoughts and actions are willfully and consciously enacted—that is, it seems as if we are under the control of the rider—in actuality, most of our cognitive, emotional, and behavioral functions are being executed outside of our awareness.

The unconscious is hidden, but it is not inaccessible. It is important for us to realize that consciousness occurs on a continuum (Levine, 2017). We are not simply dealing with a black or white mechanism. Instead, consciousness can be a multitude of shades from white, through many shades of gray, to black. Our clients can move among unconscious, less conscious, and fully conscious states. Of course, we cannot ask clients to verbally describe the contents of their unconscious. However, by paying close attention to subtle, nonverbal cues, we help clients move information from the "dark and dusty nooks and crannies of the mind" (Schore, 2012, p. 121) into conscious awareness. As counselors, we must be attuned to bodily based, emotion-based unconscious communications. We must observe the messages that clients send through movement, posture, facial expressions, and tone of voice. Beneath their words, clients are communicating with us through their bodies, behaviors, and emotions.

From an IPNB perspective, it is time to "recognize the unknown" (Ginot, 2015, p. 73) and embrace the unconscious system with less fear. We do this by paying more attention to the wordless messages that our clients are expressing through their bodies, emotions, and behaviors. We access the unconscious by asking ourselves, "How have hidden threats, fears, shame, and emotions been driving my client's behavior?" Our goal is to notice and slow down quick, automatic functions—bodily sensations, strong emotions, and reactive behaviors—that show up during the sessions so that clients can verbally express them and bring them under conscious control.

How do we apply the neurobiology of the unconscious to the narrative of Adam and Eve? We usually assume that Adam and Eve were conscious of and in control of their behavior. We conclude that they consciously chose to disobey and hide from God, that they were aware of their fear and of their behavior. But is that actually the case?

Have we unknowingly superimposed our Western bias for the conscious system onto the story of Adam and Eve? Of course the writer of Genesis was aware of Adam and Eve's thoughts, feelings, and actions. But were these same physical, emotional, cognitive, and behavioral operations kept secret from Adam and Eve? In real time, were they aware of their negative thoughts, their fear and shame, and their avoidance of God?

The writer's account of the story doesn't offer definitive answers to our questions, but, from a modern neurobiological perspective, we might conclude that all the operations that we have described were concealed and unknown to Adam and Eve. If they were our clients, wouldn't we want to access their hidden functions—physical, emotional, and behavioral—and reflect upon them within the context of a loving, safe relationship?

DYNAMICS OF CHANGE

Rest (safety). Contemplative prayer offers us a reasonable reply to the first underlying issue: the threat response system. The impact we achieve by turning our loving attention to God is one of rest and safety. For many of us, contemplative prayer is an introduction to rest. This rest comes as we learn— maybe for the first time—how to calm our bodies. In centering prayer, we learn how to soothe our bodies through three practices. First, learning to pay better attention to our bodies has a peaceful effect. Next, practicing the art of letting go of physical sensations and tension is quieting. Third, proper breathing brings calmness. Breathing is essential to finding rest and peace.

Once we bring the body to a resting state, we turn to the mind. Slowing down the mind is more difficult. In silent prayer, I can be sitting in my favorite spot on the sofa, but my mind can still be racing. Even though my body is still, I may still be "carrying" a heavy emotional load. The mind is only at rest when it ceases to be unsettled and disturbed. In contemplative prayer, we respond to Jesus' invitation, "Come to me, all you who are weary and burdened, and I will give you rest" (Mt 11:28).

Rest is found in God. Early Christians often referred to contemplation as resting in God (Frenette, 2012). More recently, Thomas Keating (1999) has referred to contemplative prayer as resting in God's arms. I like the thought of resting in God's arms while I am practicing God's presence without words. Aren't open arms the universal sign of a parent's love for a child?

Jesus, who reveals to us the Father's love, employed the image of open arms in two stories: an analogy about a hen and the parable of the lost sheep. In a conversation with the Pharisees, Jesus used a surprising metaphor. He compared himself to a hen. He said, "How often I have longed to gather your children together, as a hen gathers her chicks under her wings" (Lk 13:34). This must be where young chicks find the greatest safety and rest.

On another occasion, Jesus told a story about a lost sheep (Lk 15:3-6). In this parable, the shepherd (representing Jesus) goes in search of a missing sheep. When he finds it, "he joyfully puts it on his shoulders and goes home" (Lk 15:5-6). Notice how Jesus feels when we rest on him: joyful. Observe where he takes us: home. Home refers to a state of safety. Being at home refers to the original experience that Adam and Eve had in the garden, before encountering fear and danger. Returning home and achieving a state of rest is the experience we enter during contemplative prayer.

The Bible offers us a wonderful contrast between a person caught in the threat response and a person at rest. This is the story of Mary and Martha (Lk 10:39-42). Martha shows many of the signs of a dysregulated person—distracted, worried and upset, with negative thoughts about both Jesus and Mary. On the other hand, Mary, sitting at Jesus' feet, is a picture of calmness. I imagine her, in a state of rest, turning her loving eyes toward his face. Jesus says, "Mary has chosen what is better" (Lk 10:42). Encouraging our clients to emulate Mary and engage in contemplative prayer plays an essential part in bringing our clients to a state of safety and rest.

Finally, let's examine the neurobiology of contemplation and safety. How does a contemplative practice settle a dysregulated threat response system? Daniel Siegel (2007) asserts that contemplative practices alter the connections between the prefrontal cortex and limbic zones of the brain—home of the amygdalae and hypothalamus. As we engage in contemplative prayer, the neurotransmitter GABA is released from the middle prefrontal cortex to the amygdalae, thus soothing upset emotions. Our intense, negative emotions are calmed as axonal fibers carry GABA from the middle prefrontal region to the fear-encoding neurons of the amygdalae (Badenoch, 2008). Expressing this view in a different way, Davidson and Begley (2012) argue that contemplation activates circuits in the prefrontal cortex, thus sending signals to the amygdalae to calm down.

Love. The antidote to fear, the second issue, is found in contemplative prayer. Letting go of all distractions, we want to connect with God, but a formidable factor—fear—can be hard at work, blocking our view of God's face.

Why does fear appear when we sit down to be alone with God? According to Gary Moon (2004), fear can indicate that we are approaching God in the wrong way, a religious way. Religion is about doing something in order to get God to love us more than we think he is inclined to do. Out of fear that we can't control God or get him to love us, we keep him at a distance.

In contrast, Moon (2004) suggests another approach to God, the way of righteousness. *Righteousness* is "a relationship characterized by mutual delight" (p. 54). Righteousness is about love and surrender. When we move toward God in this way, intent on enjoying his presence, we feel safe.

Whenever fear slips into contemplative prayer, it reveals our misunderstanding of God. If our mind sees God as in some way unkind, untrustworthy, and threatening, then we will surely be afraid. However, as we learn to approach God as Jesus taught us—as "Our Father" (Mt 6:9) or as "*Abba*, Father" (Mk 14:36)—we find a relationship that is kind, gentle, and embracing.

Contemplative prayer confronts us with the true nature of God, that is, love (see 1 Jn 4:16). When we approach God, the Spirit makes God's love known to us. We read in Romans 5:5, "God's love has been poured out into our hearts through the Holy Spirit." This is an important image. In this verse, we are described as vessels of love (May, 1991). God wants to fill us to capacity with his love.

In contemplative prayer, we come to realize that God loves us the way he loved his Son, Jesus (Pennington, 2001). We learn a great deal about the relationship between the Father and Son in the story of Jesus' baptism. Matthew tells us that a voice from heaven said, "This is my Son, whom I love; with him I am well pleased" (Mt 3:17). As we wait in rest in God's presence, we enter this same relationship with God. The look on God's face is one of love and approval, telling us that he is pleased with what he sees. Why is that? Not because we are good or have behaved in a proper way. No, it is because we are his children and he sees us as "in Christ."

God's love invites us to contemplative prayer, and then contemplation leads us to even greater love. Through time alone with God in silence, we continue to mature in love. This is the purpose of contemplative prayer—to grow in love toward God, others, and self. And as we mature in love, we discover the truth of 1 John 4:18: "There is no fear in love. But perfect love drives out fear, because fear has to do with punishment."

Contemplative prayer and neuroscience lead us to the same conclusion: love is the antidote to fear. From an IPNB perspective, love is the destination of our work with clients. In one of his earlier works, Daniel Siegel (2007) observed that contemplative practices activate a system that is similar to "love without fear" (p. 130).

Approach. Contemplative prayer offers us a remedy to the third issue of avoidance. The proper response is to approach. Instead of hiding in isolation, in contemplative prayer, we can turn toward God. Instead of hiding from God's presence, we can open ourselves to his love for us. When we have a faulty view of God, we fearfully distance ourselves from him, but a proper understanding of God's love causes us to turn our faces toward him.

In contemplative prayer, we learn a lot about sitting. In his famous line, "All of humanity's problems stem from man's inability to sit quietly in a room alone," Blaise Pascal implies that a special kind of sitting can change the world. I think this type of sitting happens during our contemplative practice. It is a kind of sitting that requires intentionally turning toward the face of God.

Learning to sit is difficult. Before long, we become restless, bored, or distracted. And what do we do? We go away. Perhaps we don't leave our seats, but we still abandon our original intention. We lose our focus. We turn our attention away from God to other things. We forget our divine companion. Instead, we concentrate on mental visitors who demand our attention. We become preoccupied with memories of the past, fears for today, and worries about the future. Other things seem so much more important at that moment than God.

In sitting, we learn to turn toward God and not go away. In the New Testament, this waiting on God is called patience. In centering prayer, the practice is to sit patiently for twenty minutes. For twenty minutes we simply sit in the presence of God. We are not expecting anything in particular to happen. Our only desire is simply to turn our attention to the indwelling Spirit of Christ.

There are many examples in Scripture of people moving from avoidance to approach, but my favorite is Jesus' parable of the lost son (Lk 15:11-24). In this story, the younger son separated himself from his father. Like Adam and Eve, he wanted to do his own thing. But eventually he decided to return home. He turned back to his father. As he approached his father, "his father saw him and was filled with compassion for him; he ran to his son, threw his arms around him and kissed him" (Lk 15:20). Continuing to speak, the father says, "This son of mine was dead and is alive again" (Lk 15:24).

What a wonderful image of approaching God. When we turn to him in contemplative prayer, he is already there waiting. During our time of prayer, God is not only compassionate . . . but affectionate. During our time of opening ourselves to the Spirit of Christ, we come alive. Finding an interior place of quiet, we engage in worship of God. Christian psychologists Siang-Yang Tan and Douglas Gregg (1997) inform us that the most common New Testament word for worship—the Greek word *proskyneō*—means to "step toward a kiss" (p. 142).

True self. How can contemplation help us with the fourth issue—the dilemma of a limited self? As we spend time in silence with God, we rediscover our true identities. The precondition for unearthing our real selves is letting go of the narratives that we have fabricated about ourselves. We must first release the language and words we use to define who we are.

Contemplative prayer is an exercise in letting go. In centering prayer, we release attention to any thoughts that our minds want to offer about our selves. We let go of any words that can be used to construct an identity. It doesn't matter if the words are positive or negative. We simply turn our attention away from them. In contemplative prayer, we find ourselves letting go of our "old" identities so that we can open ourselves to "new" ones.

Contemplative prayer is about openness. Letting go of words, we open ourselves to how God wants to define us. In openness to God, we cease our efforts at shaping ourselves into any particular image. We find that we cannot make ourselves. Instead, we discover that each true identity is a gift of God (Benner, 2004). In contemplative prayer, we are like wax waiting for a seal (Merton, 1962). We are being softened and prepared to become our true selves. Like soft wax that receives the seal, we take on the configuration of the seal. We take on the shape—or identity—of Jesus.

When we open ourselves to God in contemplative prayer, we receive God's love. God's love is the basis of our identities. It is his love that transforms us. In God's love, we discover that we are not who we thought we were. We find our real selves hidden in Jesus. We receive the gift of being ourselves in Jesus. When we leave behind our self-made identities and openly receive who we are, "we are essentially prayer—response to God" (Pennington, 2001).

The adoption of a new identity is often portrayed in Scripture as a change in clothing. The apostle Paul used this analogy effectively: "Do not lie to each other, since you have taken off your old self with its practices and have put on the new self . . . in the image of its Creator" (Col 3:9-10). In another passage, referring to our new identities, Paul adds, "Clothe yourselves with the Lord Jesus Christ" (Rom 13:14). Employing this same metaphor, Jesus concludes the story of the lost son with the father replacing the son's worn-out rags for "the best robe" (Lk 15:22). His old tattered identity was replaced with a regal garment, the gift of sonship, the gift of a new identity. Because he now had a face—a true identity—he could meet his father "face to face" (1 Cor 13:12).

Vulnerability. In contemplation, we discover an alternative to the fifth issue: shame. As we spend time with God, several key changes happen. First, we understand how to recognize and accept our condition. Next, we learn to stop hiding our faces. Finally, we discover how to accept God's healing.

Contemplative prayer exposes us to our true condition. Embedded in our nature is a desire for connection; we long for love. But this yearning opens us up to suffering. The truth is obvious: if we want someone's love, that person can reject us. How risky! Our desire for love makes us vulnerable. Christian philosopher Peter Kreeft (1989) writes, "If you love, you will suffer" (p. 113).

Not only does love bring suffering but so do our shortcomings. When we face the truth about ourselves, when we see our deficiencies, it is painful. Like Adam and Eve, we are distrusting and disobedient. As imitators of Martha (Lk 10), we can be demanding and easily upset. We can be negative and hard to convince, like Thomas (Jn 20:24-29). Following the example of James and John (Lk 9; Mt 20), we can be harsh, vindictive, and concerned about status and position. The truth is that we are broken.

In contemplative prayer, we admit our brokenness to God. We acknowledge that we are fellow sufferers with people in the Bible, characters who were blind, sick, hungry, lost, and wounded. We confront the painful truth about our failings and shortcomings. We admit that we are weak and deficient. Instead of avoiding our pain, we accept it: "I hurt; I suffer."

In contemplative prayer, we resist the tendency to hide from God's presence. Instead, we dare to turn toward his face. Courageously, we let down our masks and reveal our faces with all their blemishes. We don't hide them or cover them with makeup. We confront our scary questions: What will God do when he sees my face? Will he reject me? Will he still want me? Contemplative prayer requires us to confront our deepest fears of criticism, judgment, and abandonment.

The frightening journey of contemplation brings us to a wonderful truth: God loves us. When we acknowledge our brokenness, God does not judge us. Instead, he welcomes us with open arms. He sees us as his children. He sees us as in Jesus. In contemplative prayer, the belief that we cannot show up before God in tattered rags is revealed as a lie. Our fears of rejection melt away. In contemplative prayer, "we do not have to do anything, except let our unworthy, ungrateful selves be loved as we are" (Manning, 2000, p. 178).

"Love and belonging are impossible to experience without vulnerability," observes Brené Brown (2012, p. 156). We discover this truth in contemplative prayer—as we stand naked before God, we experience his love for us. Vulnerability is about being naked. Being naked is the human condition. There is no doubt but that we are going to be naked at some time. The question can only be, When am I going to be naked? (Thompson, 2015). In contemplative prayer, the response is: "God, I am going to be unclothed now. I am willing to be seen." Yes, this is vulnerability. It is scary, but it does offer us hope from the scourge of shame. As Curt Thompson (2015) asserts, "Honest vulnerability is the key to healing shame" (p. 104).

Resting in darkness. How do we respond to the sixth dilemma—that many of our functions (e.g., physical, emotional, cognitive, behavioral) are hidden outside of our awareness? The school of contemplative prayer teaches us about the unconscious system by helping us recognize it, dissolve our fear of it, and rest in it. This last dynamic of change returns us full circle to the first dynamic: rest.

Centuries before Freud used the term *unconscious*, Christian contemplatives were familiar and grappling with this same phenomenon. However, they called it by another name: *darkness*. When John of the Cross—from sixteenth-century Spain—used the image of darkness, he was suggesting that something outside of our normal awareness was happening in the context of contemplative prayer (May, 2004). The author of the fourteenth-century classic *The Cloud of Unknowing*, the inspiration for centering prayer, frequently employed the same image of darkness.

Quoting from *Cloud of Unknowing*, Cynthia Bourgeault (2016) writes, "Prepare to abide in this darkness as long as you may, evermore crying out after him that you love. For if ever you shall feel him or see him as it may be here, it behooves you always to be in this cloud and this darkness" (p. 144). The author is preparing the practitioner of contemplative prayer for the experience of darkness. This is an event with which we will become familiar. It is a state in which we will learn to reside. These early contemplatives were teaching us to settle into the darkness of contemplative prayer.

The apostle Paul made use of the metaphor of darkness. He told the Christians in Corinth, "He will bring to light what is hidden in darkness and will expose the motives of the heart" (1 Cor 4:5). Paul points out that certain things, the motives of the heart, can remain unseen because they are hidden in the dark.

In a verse often associated with contemplative prayer, Jesus said, "When you pray, go into your room, close the door and pray to your Father, who is unseen" (Mt 6:6). Was Jesus employing an image of darkness in this teaching? After closing the door to the closet, was it dark inside? Was it because of darkness that the person in prayer could not see God?

One of my favorite pastimes as a child was playing hide-and-seek. Hiding in Mom's closet was a wonderful experience. I would press up in the corner, hiding behind her large, heavy coats. It was dark, but I loved it. Sitting there in the dark, alone, quiet, smelling the perfume on her clothes, there was nothing more for me to do. I simply waited to be found.

The instructions of Jesus, and to a lesser extent, my story of hide-and-seek, capture some of the elements of contemplative prayer. Sitting in the dark, we settle into it until we are found. There is nothing to fear within the room. It is a safe place. The scent of God, from our last visit in the closet, is a welcome aroma. Waiting to be met by God, we cease all our efforts. We just rest.

One of the behaviors we relinquish in contemplative prayer is talking. Don't we become quieter in the dark? We may stop talking, but we don't stop communicating. We just communicate on another level, a spiritual one. Speaking about this unconscious level of communicating, Paul wrote, "The Spirit himself testifies with our spirit that we are God's children" (Rom 8:16). A few verses later, Paul adds, "We do not know what we ought to pray for, but the Spirit himself intercedes for us through wordless groans. And he who searches our hearts knows the mind of the Spirit, because the Spirit intercedes for God's people in accordance with the will of God" (Rom 8:26-27). Unlike verbal interactions, this communication takes place at a level that is hidden from the conscious mind.

It takes practice to become comfortable with darkness. We prefer the light to the dark. In the light, we can see and know the events going on around us. This seeing gives us a sense of control. We have confidence that we can take certain actions if the need arises. However, in darkness we lose that sense of control. We can only sit, waiting for God to find us.

Contemplative prayer is like learning to see in the dark (Bourgeault, 2016). Isn't it amazing that our eyes have the ability to adjust from light to darkness? During the daytime our vision relies primarily upon photoreceptor cells called cones, but as daylight fades we increasingly rely upon other cells called rods. Studies show that the normal length of time that it takes for day vision to give way to night vision is twenty minutes. Isn't it uncanny that this is the exact length of time recommended for centering prayer?

As we enter into our room to pray silently, we are tempted to leave on the lights. We resort to something familiar—light—to illuminate our thoughts and feelings. But contemplative prayer is about adjusting to the dark. That is, we stop relying upon the light of conscious processes. We shift our attention away from any sensation, idea, or emotion that captures our attention. Instead, letting go of conscious processes, we adjust to the dark.

When we pray in the dark, unconscious processes inevitably emerge into conscious awareness. Painful material begins to surface during our time of silent prayer. This material may take the form of painful memories, the appearance of emotionally charged thoughts, or the presence of physical pain. What are we to do? We simply let go of these operations that have appeared in conscious awareness. Letting go of these thoughts, we return to the darkness. Thomas Keating (1999) calls this process the "unloading of the unconscious" (p. 95).

Referring to the unloading of the unconscious, Keating (1999) writes, "The emotional junk in our unconscious emerges during prayer in the form of thoughts that have a certain urgency, energy, and emotional charge to them. There is ordinarily just a jumble of thoughts and a vague or acute sense of uneasiness. Simply putting up with them and not fighting them is the best way to release them" (p. 93). Here, Keating teaches us what to do in order to "unload" the unconscious. Don't resist the thought, don't hang onto the thought, and don't react to the thought. Simply notice it, then let it go.

Unloading the unconscious is a byproduct, not the intention, of centering prayer. Unlike counseling, where our aim is to bring the unconscious into consciousness, this is not the purpose of silently spending time in God's presence. To do so would put us in charge of the method and consequences of contemplative prayer. No, in centering prayer we leave the process and outcome up to God. We just want to be present in love to the One who is present in love to us.

CONCLUSION

In the first part of this chapter, we identified six issues that are underneath the problems that clients bring to counseling. Relying upon Christian contemplative thought, in the second part, we have offered six mechanisms of change. These mechanisms are at the hub of positive change. In concluding this chapter, we will offer some ways in which these mechanisms can point us in the direction of successful outcomes for counseling.

1. *Rest.* A theme of our work will be safety. Is the client feeling safe with us at this moment? We will want to help them lessen their sense of distress during the session.

2. *Love.* A key to therapeutic success will be helping our clients approach, face, and process their fears. It will be important for us to help them put their emotions into words. Another key will be the presence of our love for them. This love manifests itself in the form of curiosity, openness, and attentiveness.

3. *Approach.* A sign that our clients are making progress will be a decrease in avoidance. Are they taking risks and engaging in new thoughts and behaviors?

4. *True self.* One of our aims will be to identify the stories that our clients tell about themselves. As we make progress in counseling, they will release their grip on these old narratives and show a willingness to create new stories about themselves.

5. *Vulnerability.* We will help our clients face and name their sense of shame. Our goal is to be trustworthy as they risk being vulnerable.

6. *Resting in darkness.* A key to success will be our clients' willingness to recognize, embrace, and not be afraid of hidden functions. In counseling, we will want to reflect upon physical sensations, nonverbal messages, and strong emotions that arise in real time during the session.

5

THE COUNSELOR'S PRESENCE

THIS CHAPTER BRINGS us to the primary catalyst for change—relationships. At its core, Christian contemplative prayer is a human-divine encounter. And the fundamental nature of this relationship between God and human beings is one of love. At the center of counseling is another engagement, one between counselor and client. In this chapter, our contemplative-oriented model of counseling will set forth the essential qualities of this therapeutic relationship.

The discipline of counseling has answered some important questions about the therapeutic relationship. First, one might ask, Is the relationship between counselor and client a critical ingredient of counseling? Counseling literature makes it clear that the quality of the counselor-client relationship is a principal component in counseling. Lambert (1992), for example, suggests that 30% of the positive change that occurs in counseling is a result of the relationship between the counselor and client. After decades of research, mental health professionals are in agreement that the therapeutic relationship is a better predictor of outcome than any specific model of counseling (Lambert & Simon, 2008; Miller, Duncan, & Hubble, 1997).

Second, one could ask, What counselor qualities correlate highly with positive client outcomes? Carl Rogers (1961), who has the most famous response to this question, identifies empathy, genuineness, and positive regard as the key elements needed by counselors. Recent studies indicate that the most successful counselors are more understanding, accepting, empathic, warm, and supportive (Lambert & Simon, 2008).

In review, we know without a doubt that the counseling relationship is critical to the outcome of counseling, and we are certain that specific counselor traits make a difference. Supporting these conclusions, Gerald Corey (2013) says, "The single most important element in becoming a competent counselor is your way of being." And he adds, "More important than the techniques you use are the attitudes you have toward clients" (p. 29).

These conclusions then raise the question, How do we go about helping counselors develop these necessary and appropriate attitudes? We know that graduate schools are successful at teaching counseling techniques, but can they construct a counselor's "way of being" (Lambert & Simon, 2008)? Specific skills and abilities—for example, reflective listening, forming a working relationship, or summarizing (Young, 2005)—can be defined, measured, and taught, but can the same be done with counselor demeanor and qualities?

What are training programs supposed to do? Will they focus on specific clinical interventions while ignoring the counselor who employs these techniques (Sprenkle, Davis, & Lebow, 2009)? Will they treat counseling as if it were some kind of pill, in no way affected by the person supplying the medicine? Will they relegate the self of the therapist to the counselor's own personal psychotherapy and clinical supervision? The critical question for the discipline of counseling is, Can we find effective means for cultivating qualities associated with a strong treatment relationship?

This is where training in and the practice of contemplative prayer come in. To fill the gap, our contemplative-oriented approach to counseling first names and describes the personal attitudes or dispositions that are basic to the therapeutic relationship. Second, this new paradigm for counseling reveals a way to develop these identified traits—through consistent and ongoing contemplative prayer

In the first section of this chapter, based upon a dialogue among theology, interpersonal neurobiology (IPNB), and contemplative prayer, we will arrive at seven qualities that are needed of counselors:

- presence

- openness

- attention

- acceptance

- compassion

- resonance

- love

NECESSARY COUNSELOR QUALITIES

Presence. The presence of God is the central fact of Christianity, asserts A. W. Tozer (1948). Describing God's presence, theologian Evan Howard (2008) portrays it as "free, actively involved, self-communicating, welcoming, transforming" (p. 208). We could also add that God's presence is *here*. When Jesus instructed us to pray—"Our Father in heaven" (Mt 6:9)—he was not depicting a God who was far off. Heaven is not in the distance. Instead, heaven is right here. Heaven is the space immediately around us. Dallas Willard (1998) tells us that God is "constantly available here" (p. 69).

God's presence is also at the heart of contemplative practice. Howard (2008) refers to contemplative prayer as "the recognition of the presence of God" (p. 325). In the first guideline of centering prayer, Keating (1999) teaches us to "consent to God's presence" (p. 139). As we open our hearts to attend to Jesus and the indwelling Spirit, we are bringing ourselves into God's presence. We are responding to God's nearness by making ourselves present. Just as Adam and Eve were alert to God's companionship in the garden, in contemplative prayer we are cultivating an awareness of God's constant presence.

Contemplative prayer is about sitting with God. God is here, and it is important for us to also be here. As Richard Foster (2008) points out, "There is a big difference between simply being in the same room with others versus truly being present to them" (p. 68). Our problem is that we are often in another location. We must often recollect ourselves—body, heart, soul, and mind—in order to come more fully into the room with God. We must be in God's presence not only *here* but also *now*. Peter Kreeft (1989), the Christian philosopher, reminds us, "God lives in the present and enters the present only" (p. 135).

God's presence and our receptivity of his presence transform us. Contemplative prayer is not a self-improvement project. Yes, it requires some activity on our part, but becoming like Jesus is not the result of our own effort. As we sit with God, we are not altering ourselves. Instead, we are receiving change—called transformation—that happens by the Spirit of Christ.

Just as contemplative prayer is about coming into God's presence, counseling is about clients coming into our presence. From an IPNB perspective, the counselor's presence is "the most important element of helping others heal" (D. Siegel, 2010a, p. 1). This kind of presence is the ability to live fully in the present moment. Presence occurs not yesterday or tomorrow but right now. But it is hard to stay in the present moment. Our minds have a tendency either to pull us into the past or to push us into the future, avoiding the present. As we develop the quality of presence, we learn to return again and again to the present moment.

Being present can be challenging for counselors. All too often, we get in our own way. We are full of ourselves. We think we know what to do. We get boxed into our own opinions, perceptions, and preconceived ideas. We are dominated by our own feelings and beliefs about how things should operate. We have already decided how things must be. What is the answer to this challenge? According to Christian psychologist David Benner (2011), "Emptying ourselves must precede any genuine presence" (p. 152).

Openness. How are we to reply to God's invitation to enter into his loving presence? Our response is a positive one, one of openness. When Keating (1999) instructs us in centering prayer to "consent to the God's presence" (p. 139), he is telling us to be open. What is openness? How do we open up to God?

A wonderful image, capturing the nature of the relationship between humans and God appears in Scripture: "Here I am! I stand at the door and knock. If anyone hears my voice and opens the door, I will come in and eat with that person, and they with me" (Rev 3:20). This verse, with the concept of openness, opening a door, situated in the middle, attends to our questions.

This verse contains some valuable lessons about opening to God. First, notice what precedes openness: God must knock. Next, we must pay attention to, or be aware of, the sound of God knocking at the door of our heart. Then comes our action of opening. All along, we thought that opening the door would require hard labor, but it doesn't. The work is actually up to God. Yes, there are things we must do to open the door—listen, approach, unlock, turn the handle, pull on it ever so slightly—but it doesn't require much effort.

Contemplative prayer is about opening to God. Yes, there are things we do when we sit with God, but it is not painful work. We are making important choices, but selecting hard labor is not one of them. Addressing this issue, Keating (1999) observes, "The chief act of the will is not effort but consent" (p. 71). Contemplative prayer is primarily about consent, not effort.

Let's think about this word for openness: *consent*. When we consent, we are granting someone permission to do something. From the verse in Revelation 3:20, we notice that we are allowing God to take action. What is that? First, we are granting God access to the "room" of our lives. We are no longer distant from God, but close. Next, we are authorizing God to rearrange the "furniture"—emotions, beliefs, attitudes, etc.—in our lives. As we open up to God, new possibilities present themselves. Now, anything can happen.

Keating (1999) offers us another term for openness: *receptivity*. This is our response to God's knock at the door. We could resist his request to come in. We could shut down and become unresponsive. We could shut off the light and pretend that no one is at home. Instead, with receptivity, we welcome God with enthusiasm. Rather than being guarded, we make ourselves vulnerable. Instead of holding back, we now entrust ourselves into his care.

This affirmative reply to God is captured best by one word: "Yes. Yes, come in." This faithful yes is demonstrated in the story of Zacchaeus (Lk 19:1-6). Jesus, seeing Zacchaeus in the tree, asks if he can come to Zacchaeus's house. The passage reveals that Zacchaeus "welcomed him gladly" (Lk 19:6). This is the way we receive God—gladly.

From an IPNB perspective, presence is defined as the state of being open (D. Siegel, 2010a, p. 35). Yes, there is also a "door" between the counselor and the client. But are we willing to open that door? Are we willing to be open, now, to whatever is?

The process of openness begins with ourselves as counselors. Am I willing to be open to myself? Perhaps my threat response system is activated. I may be anxious and fearful. I may fret: "Does the client trust me and have confidence in me? Do I know what I'm doing? What do I do next?" My own body may be activated and hyperaroused. I may be feeling self-protective. Openness means that I am aware of all these processes—physical sensations, thoughts, behavioral tendencies, emotions—"knocking" around inside.

The opposite of openness (or receptivity) is reactivity. Reactivity occurs when we fail to notice our own threatened state of mind. Unbeknownst to us, we reactively engage in self-protective behaviors. One common method that counselors use for "hiding" from clients is the use of words. We conceal ourselves behind academic concepts and technical language. We disappear behind the thoughts we are having about what to do or say next. Sometimes openness means attending to the physical and emotional functions going on inside instead of holding onto words. Daniel Siegel (2010a) reminds us, "Being open may require we let go of the tendency of words to dominate our present awareness" (p. 106).

Being open to ourselves is a prerequisite for being open to our clients. Can we be open to whatever they bring us at this moment? What are they sensing, feeling, and thinking right now? Can we consent to it? Can we receive it? Can we be present to what the client is undergoing at this point in time? What they bring may not fit with our agenda or expectations. Their experience may be unexpected, and it may catch us by surprise. But, with presence of mind, our aim is to welcome our clients, as they are right now, with open arms.

Attention. Attentiveness—not talking—is at the heart of contemplative prayer. Foster (1992) writes, "Contemplative prayer is a loving attentiveness to God. In contemplative prayer talk recedes to the background" (p. 158). Howard (2008) adds, "Without attention there is no prayer" (p. 311). What is attention? How is it related to contemplative prayer?

Let's turn to three Gospel stories in order to gain a better understanding of attentiveness. In the first parable, Jesus tells us about several attentive servants (Lk 12:35-38). In the story, the master returns home and finds his servants waiting for him. He knocks on the door, and they "immediately open the door for him" (Lk 12:36). Jesus describes the servants as "watching" (Lk 12:37).

The next two stories are also revealing. In one narrative, Martha invites Jesus to her house (Lk 10:38-42). In this account, a clear contrast is developed between Martha—who is described as "distracted" (Lk 10:40)—and her sister Mary. On the other hand, Mary "sat at the Lord's feet listening to what he said" (Lk 10:39). The final account is a story about Jesus (Mk 12:41-42). In this narrative, we find Jesus sitting and watching people as they bring money to the temple. The rich people give large contributions while a poor widow offers "two very small copper coins" (Mk 12:42).

We learn four important lessons about attentiveness from these stories. First, an attentive person is oriented to the present. Notice in the first story how the servants "immediately" opened the door. Next, an attentive person is a good listener. In the first parable the servants were listening for the sound of his knock. In the story of Mary, she was "listening" to Jesus. Third, an attentive person is focused on something. Observe in the first narrative how the servants were centered on their master. In the story of Mary, her attention was concentrated on Jesus. Finally, an attentive person is tuned into fine details. In the story about Jesus, we observe his attention to particulars: "two very small copper coins."

Attention refers to how we process information. We cannot focus on everything, so attention helps us filter out unimportant data. Attention is selective, helping us concentrate on one thing. In all three stories, the leading characters were tuned in to one thing. The servants were attentive to their master, Mary was focused on Jesus, and Jesus was considering the poor widow. Attention allows us to withdraw our concentration from distracting information so that we can narrow our focus on something more important.

Let's apply the lessons that we have learned from Scripture to contemplative prayer. In contemplative prayer, we concentrate on one thing: God. We remember to pay attention to him *now*. And when we notice that our attention has wandered to a thought, something less important than God, we refocus our minds on God.

Contemplative practices are central to a contemplative-oriented approach to counseling. They are necessary because these practices support our ability to pay attention and increase our capacity to notice when our attention has wandered (D. Siegel, 2007). As we engage in contemplative practices, we learn to "pay attention in the present moment, on purpose" (D. Siegel, 2007, p. 132).

When the contemplative skill of attention is applied to the attitudes of the counselor, it is called "attunement" (D. Siegel, 2010a). From an IPNB perspective, the counselor demonstrates two types of attunement: intrapersonal and interpersonal. The first type—intrapersonal—refers to the counselor's ability to pay attention to his or her own internal world. What are the signals coming from my own experience right now? Is my body sending me important information? Are messages being transmitted by my emotions?

Our ability to be attuned to ourselves is a prerequisite for interpersonal attunement. This is the capacity to tune in to the signals that are being transmitted by our clients, meaning that we are open and attentive to the messages that they are sending. Some of their messages—usually in the form of words— are conscious. However, other signals—most of which are nonverbal—are being communicated unconsciously. The attuned counselor tracks both verbal content and nonverbal messages. According to Ginot (2015), the skillful counselor is "focused on barely perceptible cues that signal a change in state, and on nonverbal behaviors and shifts in affect" (p. xvii). These cues can show up as slight changes in facial expression, as a small shift in posture, or in a moderate change in tone of voice.

Acceptance. One does not have to practice contemplative prayer for an extended period of time before observing a glaring trait of the mind—it is prone to wander. Even though our intention is to be open to and to concentrate on God, before long our attention is captured by something else. In contemplative prayer, our objective is to notice that our attention has wandered and bring it back to its focus on God.

However, an important question is, With what attitude will I bring back my wandering mind? For many of us, that attitude can be one of judgment. Our minds point out our shortcomings in being present with God. In self-condemnation, we declare to ourselves that our loss of focus is "wrong." Judgment rules that we are "bad" at controlling our thought processes. We say to ourselves, "What is your problem? Can't you stay focused? You are no good at this. Others are better at this than you are. You are pathetic."

Where does judgment originate? It is directly related to the faulty belief that prayer is a technique (Frenette, 2012). This misunderstanding leads us to consider contemplative prayer as something that we do to produce certain results. This mistake in thinking puts us at the center of the process. The prayer becomes about me: "Am *I* doing everything correctly? Am *I* getting it right? Am *I* putting forth enough effort?"

Jesus confronts the mental error of judgment. In his Sermon on the Mount, Jesus said, "Do not judge" (Mt 7:1). In the context of this sermon, Jesus was teaching his followers how to interact with one another, that is, without judgment. However, Scripture teaches us not only to treat others well but also to love ourselves (see Mt 22:39). We are to avoid harsh self-judgment. Look at the example set by Paul, who said, "I do not even judge myself" (1 Cor 4:3).

There is an alternative to judgment: acceptance. Notice how judgment and acceptance are contrasted in this passage: "Accept the one who is weak in faith, but not for the purpose of passing judgment . . . , for God has accepted him" (Rom 14:1-3 NASB). Please bear with me as I change the wording ever so slightly in order to personalize it: Accept your weak mind, without passing judgment on yourself. God has accepted you. Who are you to judge yourself?

We discover the attitude of acceptance right at the center of contemplative prayer. Keating (1999) introduces it in the third guideline of centering prayer: "When you become aware of thoughts, return ever-so-gently to the sacred word" (p. 139). How do we lead our minds back to Christ? Not with harsh judgment but with gentle acceptance.

Contemplative prayer is training in acceptance. As we practice God's presence without words, acceptance becomes as common as distractions. Each time our mind wanders away, we return with gentle acceptance. If our attention drifts away from God fifteen times, then fifteen times we return it to its focus with acceptance. When the mind shifts its concentration to something new, with gentle acceptance we respond, "Oh yeah, you are thinking about something else now. I expected that. That's what you do." There is no blaming or faultfinding. There is no anger. There is only acceptance.

From an IPNB perspective, presence is imbued with acceptance (D. Siegel, 2010a). Acceptance is about receiving things as they are this moment. Acceptance says, "I don't have to change, remove, or judge what is happening right now." Acceptance is about seeing things as they are at this moment. So often our minds carry us into some imaginary future where circumstances are the way we want them to be, where everything meets our expectations. Acceptance frees us from this narrative in our heads that says things have to be a certain way, a different way. Instead, acceptance says, "At this moment, the situation is the way it is. Be open to it. Pay attention to it. Receive it."

Compassion. When we enroll in the school of contemplative prayer, there is one thing that we soon discover. We are just like everyone else who intends to listen to God's presence. No one "succeeds" in maintaining concentration in this endeavor. We all struggle to withdraw our attention from everything but God. All practitioners fall down in their attempts to keep their minds on God. We soon realize our own frailty and weakness. We suffer just like everyone else.

According to Christian philosopher Robert Roberts (2007), this realization is called *compassion*, a trait that allows us to see ourselves as having deficiencies, just as others do. As Roberts (2007) says, we are "fellow-sufferers" (p. 180). We see that we are vulnerable to suffering just like every other human being. I too am weak and wanting.

Compassion has another quality. It draws us in close to our fellow sufferers. We take a kind interest in what they are experiencing. In the Gospels, Jesus told several stories of compassion. In one story, coming upon two blind men, Jesus "had compassion on them and touched their eyes" (Mt 20:34). In the parable of the good Samaritan, who had compassion on the man who was attacked by robbers, "He went to him and bandaged his wounds, pouring on oil and wine" (Lk 10:34). And in the parable of the lost son, "His father saw him and was filled with compassion for him; he ran to his son, threw his arms around him and kissed him" (Lk 15:20). In these three stories, the compassionate figure leaned into the suffering person.

The opposite of compassion is aloofness (Roberts, 2007). Aloofness sends the message that we share little in common with the person who is suffering. Dwelling on our differences, we create a distance between ourselves and others. Jesus captures the essence of aloofness in the parable of the Pharisee and the tax collector (Lk 18). Both of these men were at the same place (i.e., the temple), at the same time, to do the same thing: pray. "The Pharisee stood by himself and prayed: 'God, I thank you that I am not like other people—robbers, evildoers, adulterers—or even like this tax collector'" (Lk 18:11), distancing himself both physically and socially from another man at prayer.

We learn that in contemplative prayer compassion encompasses two qualities. First, it is a type of love that says, "I have much in common with you. I'm not good at paying attention either, but that's okay. My mind wanders, just like yours, but there's nothing wrong with that. I struggle at this too, but we will keep trying." Second, compassion draws us in close to others. Instead of distancing ourselves, we lean in toward a fellow contemplative who is talking about his experience and say, "Tell me your story. I care. I'm interested. I will pay close attention. I will see you and hear you."

From an IPNB perspective, compassion is a vital element of attentiveness (D. Siegel, 2010a). If we pay attention to our clients without compassion, it leaves them feeling empty and disconnected. The way we respond—once we have paid attention—makes all the difference. Do we respond with kindness—which is compassion—or with judgment and distance? The counselor's compassionate concern emerges from a threat response system that has been calmed. We are not afraid, and we don't hide. Instead, with love, kindness, and interest we approach the one who is suffering.

Resonance. Contemplative prayer can take us to a form of communication that is deeper than words. This form of communication is called communion—"in which no overt word is needed or wanted" (Willard, 2012a, p. 151). Dallas Willard (2012a) uses another word for communion: *union.* For Foster (1992), union with God is the goal of contemplative prayer.

When we identify union as the goal of contemplative prayer, we must carefully consider the complex nature of union. Paradoxically, union speaks of both togetherness and separateness. Referring to togetherness, Jesus said, "My prayer is . . . that all of them may be one, Father, just as you are in me and I am in you . . . that they may be one as we are one—I in them and you in me—so that they may be brought to complete unity" (Jn 17:20-23). Union is about being one.

We see this concept of oneness in the Trinity. Each person in the Trinity—Father, Son, and Spirit—is interrelated. Each divine person is "in" the other divine persons. (This is the Christian doctrine of *perichoresis.*) Divine math looks like this: $1 + 1 + 1 = 1$.

At the same time, union speaks of separateness. Each person of the Trinity has a unique role or responsibility. Each divine person is distinct. According to theologian Stan Grenz (2006), the divine pattern is "plurality-in-unity" (p. 290). Using the body as an example, the apostle Paul provides us with a good analogy of plurality in unity (1 Cor 12:15-26). Paul points out that the body has many parts: feet, hands, ears, eyes, and nose. Each component is distinct and necessary, deserving special attention. Paul writes, "There are many parts, but one body" (1 Cor 12:20).

These two experiences of togetherness and separateness occur within the context of contemplative prayer. Sometimes I can feel very close to God. There have been moments when I have lost all sense of time, space, and identity. It is as if time stops and I am simply lost in God. But, after a brief period of oneness, I return to my normal way of doing things. I begin to think about my day and about the ordinary events that lie ahead of me. On the other hand, contemplative prayer can come with a sense of separateness. Sometimes I may be absent from God. At other times God may "seem" absent from me.

IPNB replaces the term *union* with a nonreligious term: *resonance* (D. Siegel, 2010a). *Resonance* refers to a sense of connection between two people. Siegel (2010a) defines *resonance* as "the coupling of two autonomous entities into a functional whole . . . two literally become linked as one" (p. 54). (This is starting to sound more like the Bible.) There is both separateness and togetherness.

When two people are in resonance, each is attuned to the other and each is changed. The analogy of tuning and playing the guitar may be a useful illustration of resonance. When the guitar is properly tuned, each string vibrates at a certain frequency. The next step in playing the guitar is learning how to play chords, that is, playing several notes together. If the guitar is properly tuned, the different notes being played together create a pleasant sound. The notes are in harmony. We could say that the notes have resonance.

In a state of resonance, the counselor and client are actually picking up on the "vibrations" of the other person. Each is being affected by the other person's internal state, their physiological and emotional processes. The counselor is simply present and soaking in the internal state of the client. As a result, the client begins to feel close to, heard by, and seen by the counselor, producing the client's own experience of resonance. The client feels at one with the counselor for a brief period of time.

Ginot (2015) captures the meaning of resonance well: "My mental posture is one of leaning back to let the mood, the atmosphere, come to me—to hear the meaning between the lines, to listen to the music behind the words. The therapist listens and interacts on an unconscious level, a level that processes communications at levels beneath awareness" (p. xvii). The union of contemplative prayer, like the resonance of counseling, is not something that we consciously try to achieve. Instead, we simply open ourselves to a level that is beneath words. We enter into darkness (or the unconscious) without effort and without fear. In this state, we pick up on messages that are sent without words, allowing ourselves to be changed by the other. We bask in the experience of oneness.

Love. Ultimately, to help us understand the nature of presence, Daniel Siegel (2010a) brings us to the subject of love. For too long, because of its uncomfortable association with romance or sexuality, we have kept the language of love out of counseling. But Siegel (2010a) dares to speak of a "professional form of love" (p. 245), and he declares that this love is an essential part of healing.

To unpack the meaning of love, Siegel has developed an acronym: COAL (i.e., curiosity, openness, acceptance, love). Siegel (2010a) writes, "This experience of caring for others with curiosity, openness, and acceptance can be seen as the core of what we experience as love" (p. 246). We are familiar with openness and acceptance, but what about curiosity? What is it?

Curiosity is the key to paying attention. Without it, we can fall into thinking that we know our clients. Once we accept the mistaken notion that we know our clients, we stop learning and the client becomes an unchanging object—like a chair.

Curiosity pushes us to wander, ponder, and ask why (Baer, 2015). The curious counselor is full of questions: What is the longing that drives your behavior? What is it about your past that informs this pattern of behavior? How do you make meaning of the events of your life? What hidden emotions lie beneath the ones you show so readily? What physical sensations do you experience as that sad look spreads across your face?

Curiosity prompts us to explore for a deeper understanding. Curiosity recognizes the mystery of our clients. There are things we will never come to understand about them. But, with curious attention, we continue to listen and to be present.

As we approach our clients with love—curiosity, openness, and acceptance—they begin to feel safe and connected. They begin to experience a sense of "we": "I am not alone. My counselor gets me. We are in this together." Siegel (2010a) observes, "This sense of 'we' . . . may be the simplest way of describing love" (p. 245).

Not only is love at the center of counseling, but it is also at the heart of contemplative prayer. Contemplative prayer is schooling in love. Contemplative prayer begins in love, continues in love, and leads to love.

Contemplative prayer begins with God's love for us. As John writes, "We love because he first loved us" (1 Jn 4:19). In contemplative prayer, we are invited into God's loving presence. As we turn toward him, we notice that he has been waiting for us. We look up at God only to see that he is already gazing at us. The table is set; the food is prepared.

Contemplative prayer is simply a time of receiving God's love. God shares his love with us, and we accept it. We read in Romans 5:5, "God's love has been poured out into our hearts through the Holy Spirit." We become vessels of God's love. We are filled with his love. His love is poured into us.

Love is a mystery. Love is in us, but we are also "in" love. We read in 1 John 4:16, "God is love. Whoever lives in love lives in God, and God in them." What an astonishing truth: We are in God, and God is in us. Love is in us, but we are also in love. The word *in* points to a location. Where are we located? In love, says Kreeft (1989).

David Benner (2003) offers us a view of *how* to respond to God's love: in surrender. Surrender is about turning ourselves over to another person. We put ourselves in their hands. We usually react negatively to the idea of handing ourselves over to someone. But what if that person loves us? God's love for us changes everything. In contemplative prayer, we are surrendering ourselves into God's loving hands.

Surrender has another meaning: to put your full weight on someone (Benner, 2003). In contemplative prayer, we shift the burden of our lives over to One who loves us. In my own times of contemplative prayer, I am discovering how to take small breaks from my life. For twenty minutes, I turn over control of the time to God. I try to let go of all my worries. He is in charge. As I am learning to surrender to his love, I am finding God to be a loving companion and coworker.

As we receive God's love, reside in God's love, and surrender to God's love, something amazing happens. We become instruments of God's love. We begin to dispense the love that has been poured into us. The lesson we take away from the school of contemplative prayer is that love does not originate with us. It is not some kind of skill that we cultivate. Instead, it is a matter of character. Love is a quality of being that exists before and beneath all our activities (May, 1991). Willard (1998) says that love "is at the very core of what we are . . . not something that we do" (p. 184).

The movement of love goes like this: We are loved by God, and then we love others through him (Willard, 2012b). God first loves us, and then we love others. In contemplative prayer, we sit in God's loving presence, and then we become a loving presence to others.

SIGNS OF THE COUNSELOR'S PRESENCE

When someone appears at an event with a pleasant-smelling cologne, we can tell. The same thing is true when the counselor shows up for a session with presence. There is something qualitatively different about that counselor. Of course the client cannot see the counselor's character, but there are indicators. The counselor's actions and words can signal a loving presence. The following verbal and nonverbal messages sent by the counselor may be signs of the qualities we have identified:

- Place a hand on his or her own chest when the client refers to a heavy heart.
- Ask, "Can we get back to where we were a minute ago?"
- Pay attention to the present moment: "What is happening right now?"
- Use simple, common (versus academic-sounding) words.
- Place emphasis on the client, not on the counselor: "How do you make sense of this?"
- Focus on where the client is, instead of how the counselor wishes to proceed in the session.
- Pick up on what the client is saying, rather than being distracted by personal thoughts.
- Make a request: "I was thinking about something else while you were talking. Do you mind telling me that again?"
- Observe: "I see your tears."
- Show interest in what the client is saying.
- Say, "I can be just like that at times."
- Self-disclose when appropriate.
- Comment: "That's painful. That really hurts."

- Ask questions to understand more clearly what the client is saying.

- Show interest in the internal workings of the client: "What are you feeling right now? Do you feel that in your body?"

THREE WAYS TO INTEGRATE CONTEMPLATION INTO COUNSELING

So far, we have focused on one manner in which contemplative prayer can be integrated in counseling: by the counselor's presence. There are two other main methods by which we can bring contemplation into our work with clients: using insights derived from contemplative prayer to inform our work and explicitly teaching our clients how to practice contemplative prayer.

Contemplative prayer contains certain practices, attitudes, and truths. For example, the emphasis in contemplative prayer is the present moment. It entails learning to be open, instead of blocking out or reacting to the unfolding experience. It is about discovering how to pay attention. Yes, there will be distracting thoughts, but we get better at letting them go and returning our focus to the present moment. Contemplative prayer is training in compassion and acceptance. At its core, contemplative prayer is the belief that we are all vulnerable and weak, but our practice of sitting with God in silence teaches us to meet our shortcomings with gentle acceptance. The emphasis in contemplative prayer is on the power of connections, the strength that comes from being in relationships.

How do we communicate these truths to our clients? Do we impart them in some sort of intellectual or classroom manner? No, instead we share them through our way of being. Our clients experience how we move, how we speak and behave, how we ask questions and respond. Out of their personal encounters with us, they begin to absorb and possess these same truths. Can we embody this way of being if we are not active participants in contemplative prayer? Of course not.

The third way that contemplation is integrated into our counseling work is by explicitly teaching our clients how to practice contemplative prayer. As we discussed in the preceding paragraph, if we hope to impart some truth to our clients, we must demonstrate that truth in how we live, move, and talk. How much more important is it for us to have our own regular routine of contemplative prayer if we are teaching our clients how to practice contemplative prayer?

To illustrate this point, the developers of MBCT (mindfulness-based cognitive therapy; Segal, Williams, & Teasdale, 2013) make an analogy with swimming instruction: "A swimming instructor is not someone who knows the physics of how solids behave in liquids, but he or she knows how to swim. It is not just an issue of credibility and competence, but of teachers' ability to embody from the inside the attitudes they invite participants to cultivate and adopt" (p. 79). Since we expect our swimming instructors to know how to swim, it is reasonable, if we are teaching contemplative concepts, for our clients to expect us to have our own practice of contemplative prayer.

Is it unreasonable to expect counselors who are adopting a contemplative-oriented approach to counseling to practice contemplative prayer themselves? Can't counselors instruct their clients about the value of presence, openness, attentiveness, acceptance, compassion, and resonance? Can't counselors simply teach interested clients about centering prayer? I have concluded that it is essential for counselors to have their own discipline of contemplative prayer.

Secular counselors who practice mindfulness-based forms of counseling have arrived at this same conclusion. Thomas Pedulla (2013) writes,

> In order to bring mindfulness effectively into the therapeutic relationship, the therapist must have his or her own mindfulness meditation practice. . . . Unless one is personally willing to engage in the practice over time, one probably shouldn't attempt to teach mindfulness skills or conduct mindfulness-based psychotherapy. (p. 157)

Although contemplative prayer may seem simple to learn and put into use, integrating it into one's way of being and one's way of conducting counseling requires practice. It is not a way of being and interacting with clients that comes overnight. Instead, it requires a commitment on the part of the contemplative counselor to regularly undertake the discipline of contemplative prayer. Having a practice of one's own is a prerequisite for engaging in this contemplative approach to counseling.

THE COUNSELOR'S PRACTICE

The world's most famous hiking trail, the Appalachian Trail, runs near my home in western North Carolina. Before one sets out on the AT, it only makes sense to learn about the trail by reading educational literature. But eventually, if hikers want to *know* the AT, if they want to experience it for themselves, they have to get out on the trail. It is the same with contemplative prayer. In order to truly know contemplative prayer, you must get out on the trail. You must practice.

So, how do we go about establishing our own practice? Before examining this issue, let's address a more basic question: Do I have the right attitude for beginning my journey into contemplative prayer? Why begin the trip if we don't even have an attitude that will sustain us throughout our travels?

We now know that several attributes are needed to ensure that, once begun, we will continue on the contemplative path. They are patience, discipline, and a willingness to slow down. First, we recognize that patience is required to engage successfully in contemplative prayer. We know that we will get discouraged with contemplative prayer if we expect quick results. Instead, the transformative process that comes about by spending time alone with God in silence is typically subtle and gradual. We must be patient because changes are generally noticed over time, in retrospect.

Next, we must approach contemplative prayer with a disciplined attitude. Waiting and resting in God's presence requires a regular practice. It isn't a day hike or something we do intermittently. Instead, it is an exercise we do almost every day, week after week, at the same time. Practicing on a regular basis for a set amount of time will require discipline. Thomas Keating (1999) says that the only no-no in contemplative prayer is to skip your daily time alone with God in silence.

Finally, maintaining a commitment to the contemplative path requires a certain mentality. We must embrace the value of slowing down. Our culture tells us to go fast and to always be doing something. The discipline of solitude and silence invites another approach. We must be willing to slow down and do nothing. This is a countercultural attitude.

Do you have or want to have the preceding attitudes? If so, you are a good candidate for the contemplative journey. Here are a few practical suggestions for beginning your practice:

1. Set aside a space. Find a place that you will go to on a regular basis. My place is the sofa in my den. Make sure this place is quiet, comfortable, and free from distractions. Make sure you will not be disturbed (Moon, 2004).

2. Set aside a time of day to practice. In my case, I have attached contemplative prayer to a daily, routine activity. I spend my time alone with God right after breakfast because eating breakfast is something I do seven days a week. For you, it could be after taking a shower, right after getting home from work, or just before you go to bed. The key is to pick a routine activity that you do virtually every day. It is a mistake to think that you can "squeeze it in" sometime during your day. Instead, it needs to be done on a regular basis, five to seven days per week (Gehart, 2012).

3. Set a realistic length of time to practice. There is disagreement among teachers on this point. Thomas Keating (1999) suggests starting out at twenty minutes, two times per day. Other teachers recommend starting out with a short amount of time and gradually building up (Gehart, 2012). According to this approach, you might start off with two minutes. Once you feel that the time is too short and that you want to do more, increase your time to five minutes. Continue with this approach, incrementally increasing your time until you get to twenty minutes. As a practical suggestion, use some type of timer that does not tick. Using a timer will keep you from checking your clock and wondering how much time has passed.

4. Follow a clear set of guidelines. Throughout this book, we have studied the four guidelines set forth by Keating (1999) for centering prayer. Keep these instructions in the forefront of your thinking:

   - Choose a sacred word as the symbol of your intention to consent to God's presence and action within.

   - Sit comfortably and with your eyes closed, settle briefly, and silently introduce the sacred word as the symbol of your consent to God's presence and action within.

   - When you become aware of thoughts, return ever so gently to the sacred word.

- At the end of the prayer period, remain in silence with eyes closed for a couple of minutes (p. 139).

5. Commit to practicing for eight weeks. Your practice may be easy or difficult. As you spend time alone with God in silence, your mind may be calm or restless. Just keep going and try not to evaluate your practice too soon. For eight weeks, just keep sitting with God, following the guidelines for centering prayer. Then, after eight weeks, you can look back on your journey. Has anything changed? Do you want to continue your practice?

It is important to stay on the trail and not get lost. There are clear indicators that you are on the Appalachian Trail. The same is true of the contemplative journey. Here are clear landmarks that you can look for (Pollack, Pedulla, & Siegel, 2014). The first sign that you are on the contemplative trail is that you are developing an orientation to the present moment. The second marker is an increased ability to refocus your mind when you become aware that your attention has wandered. The third signal that you are on the right path is greater skill in letting go of troubling thoughts (e.g., judgment, worries, obsessive ideas, etc.). The final sign that you are on track is a realization that you are becoming kinder to yourself.

The contemplative trail has a starting point and a destination. The point of origination is where we are right now. God takes us just as we are, with all of our shortcomings and weaknesses, with simple trust in Jesus. Accepting us as traveling companions, he empowers us by the Spirit. The goal is transformation. The destination is to become like Jesus, to take on his character. As we travel alongside the Spirit, the Spirit shapes us more and more into the image of God.

Reaching the destination requires a departure. We must leave the territory with which we are familiar and head out into an unfamiliar landscape. The key question is: Are you ready to start the journey? You are prepared. You have a divine traveling companion. The destination is a good one. Now, it is up to you. There is no better time than today to begin your practice.

CONCLUSION

In this chapter, we have observed that contemplative prayer fills a substantial gap within the discipline of counseling. Contemplative thought reveals the qualities needed by counselors, and mounting scientific evidence suggests that contemplative prayer may help us develop such traits. The attitude that we have focused on the most is the counselor's presence.

Our loving presence radically alters the way we show up for and engage in counseling sessions. Instead of simply playing a professional role—saying and doing all the expected things—we appear genuinely. The choice offered in this chapter is clear. We can focus on counseling techniques, or we can concentrate on a whole new way of being.

Presence encompasses a comprehensive way of being. As a result of our presence, our clients observe that we are with them in the present moment. We are open to where they are at that moment in time. Our clients feel our compassion for and acceptance of them. They sense that we are attuned to both the verbal and nonverbal messages that they are sending. We are not just talking on a conscious level but also communicating at a level beneath words. They experience our curiosity as we ask evocative questions, digging ever deeper to understand them. Somehow they feel connected to us. They leave our office with the sense that they have experienced a "professional form of love" (Siegel, 2010, p. 245).

The relationship we establish with our clients—one characterized by presence—can set in motion the process of change. In our presence, their threat response system begins to settle down, and they start to feel safe. Exposed to our love, their fear slowly dissipates. Imitating our openness, they examine old, stubborn narratives about their identities and consider new ways of viewing themselves. Experiencing compassion, they face their shame, come out of hiding, and are willing to be seen. Feeling a sense of companionship, they no longer feel alone. With a sense of connection, they bravely examine emotions and sensations that were previously hidden. And finally, because of our acceptance, they approach and consider thoughts and reactions that they had previously avoided. Presence is at the heart of healing.

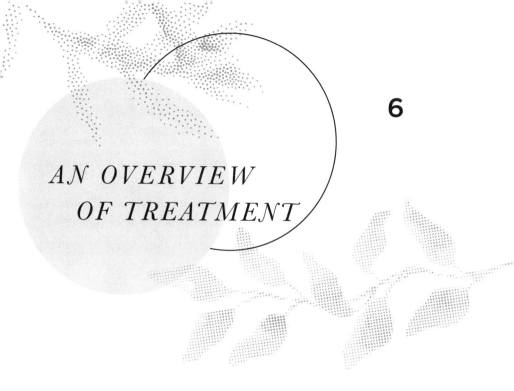

6

AN OVERVIEW
OF TREATMENT

EQUIPPED WITH EXPERIENCE in and a proper understanding of contemplative prayer, we are better prepared to assist clients in the process of change. The methods we use in counseling are called interventions. I am careful to say that we assist because a Christian contemplative attitude recognizes that the Spirit is the primary agent of change.

There are two leading beliefs when it comes to selecting interventions (Corey, 2013). The first approach to interventions is called an integrative approach. This path uses techniques drawn from many approaches and uses strategies from different models of counseling. Multimodal therapy, rational emotive behavior therapy (REBT), and reality therapy are examples of the integrative approach. These models draw upon techniques that address various dimensions of the person: physical, emotional, intellectual, and behavioral.

The second approach emphasizes one dimension of the person. For example, a cognitive therapist assumes that the best way to facilitate change is by focusing on a person's thinking process. On the other hand, a behavior therapist operates on the premise that alterations in behavior are a prerequisite for bringing about a difference. An emotion-focused therapist will argue that counseling is most effective when we target emotions. Finally, some therapists contend that the best way to nurture change is by focusing on physical sensations and movement.

Unlike models that target one aspect of the person, our Christian contemplative-oriented model is multidimensional and integrative. Built upon a Christian understanding of the human experience, this model focuses on four elements of the human person: body, emotions, intellect, and behavior. Theologian Dallas Willard (2012b) points out that a Christian view of the human person is essentially holistic and focuses on the integration of all of these dimensions.

THE BODY AND CONTEMPLATIVE PRAYER

Therefore, I urge you, brothers and sisters, in view of God's mercy, to offer your bodies as a living sacrifice, holy and pleasing to God— this is your true and proper worship.

ROMANS 12:1

Why have I picked the body as the first dimension to study? First, because contemplative prayer is a bodily behavior (Willard, 2006). Also, all the capacities of emotions, cognitions, and behavior are grounded in the human body (Mann, 2006). The body is an untapped resource in addressing the issues that bring clients to counseling.

Willard (2006) suggests that the role of the body is probably the least understood aspect of our spiritual formation. Therefore, we have our work cut out for us as we attempt to understand the role of our bodies in contemplative prayer and counseling.

The following questions will introduce our contemplative study of the body:

1. What is the role of the body in contemplative prayer?

2. What should our attitude be toward the body?

3. What is the language of the body?

4. What is its role in our relationship with God?

5. What is its connection to emotions, thoughts, and behavior?

We must first accept that resting in God's presence is something that we do with our bodies. Prayer is not something we do just with our minds or spirits.

No, contemplative prayer is a physical act. Have you noticed that your body doesn't just drift into God's presence (Willard, 2012b)? We don't just accidentally find ourselves sitting with God. No, we consciously, intentionally place our bodies before God in prayer. In wordless, trusting openness to Jesus, we arrange to sit with God on a daily basis.

What an amazing privilege it is that we—ordinary people—can walk into God's presence. Prior to the death of Jesus, if Jews wanted to come close to God, they would go to the temple. However, they could only enter the courtyard, where they would offer animal sacrifices. They could not go into the temple—a place that represented the presence of God. Only the priests could enter the temple itself. And only one person—the high priest—could enter the most sacred part of the temple, called the holy of holies.

This Old Testament sacrificial system radically changed with the death of Jesus. Unlike the Jews, who had to remain in the courtyard offering animal sacrifices, we can come directly into the presence of God. We can approach God in prayer and place our bodies before God as a "living sacrifice" (Rom 12:1).

What attitude should we have toward this body that we bring to God in prayer? First, we must learn to see it as a good thing. It is "holy and pleasing to God" (Rom 12:1). The body is such a marvelous thing that, in Scripture, it is compared to a temple: "Do you not know that your bodies are temples of the Holy Spirit, who is in you?" (1 Cor 6:19). In his letter to the Christians in Corinth, Paul was making reference to the most beautiful, important structure in the city: the temple of Aphrodite. As temples of the real God—not a Greek god—our bodies are to be valued and cherished.

One indicator that God values bodies is that God, in the form of Jesus, inhabited one. What an amazing concept—that God revealed himself in a body. Jesus came in the flesh, taking a human body: "The Word became flesh and made his dwelling among us" (Jn 1:14). I like how William Meninger (1996), one of the cocreators of centering prayer, puts it: "God turned the tables and took on *our* image and likeness so that we might be restored to *God's* image and likeness" (p. 90). This act of coming in the flesh—incarnation—supports the centrality of the body in the life of Jesus. If it was central to him, it must also be primary to us. We must cherish it and take care of it. Our body is inhabited by the Holy Spirit.

But to care for our bodies, we must first learn to feel at home in them. Many of our clients (and perhaps we as counselors) are not well connected to their bodies (Ogden & Fisher, 2015). They may view their bodies as a problem, being hypercritical of them and even disliking them. They may see their bodies as something to be fixed or repaired. They may even ignore them. Our clients may even be like a character that James Joyce (1990) described in *The Dubliners*: "Mr. Duffy lived a little distant from his body" (p. 84). They may be so detached from their bodies that they don't attend to the messages their bodies send.

Scripture teaches us to cherish and protect our bodies. In his letter to the Christians in Ephesus, Paul wrote, "No one ever hated their own body, but they feed and care for their body" (Eph 5:29). His assumption is that we will love our bodies and look after them. To accomplish this, it is essential for us to feel connected to our bodies.

Once we get in touch with our bodies, we begin to listen to them. Our bodies are always communicating. As John O'Donohue (1999) observes, "The human body is a language that cannot be silent" (p. 59). What is the language of the body? The body is clearly not speaking in words. Instead, the body is "speaking" through habits of posture, movement, vocal cues, and facial expressions.

Contemplative prayer is embodied. Once we accept this reality, we will become more attentive to what our bodies are "saying" to God during our times of silent prayer. Being more attuned to our bodies while sitting with God in silence will cause us to consider important questions: What am I doing with my hands? Is my body comfortable? How is my breathing? What is my posture? What I do with my body reveals a lot about my attitude as I approach God in prayer. The language of my body affects the quality of my prayer and impacts my time spent with God.

Once we accept the power of the body, it can become a powerful agent of transformation. Scripture teaches us that the body has great potential for influencing our thinking: "Offer your bodies as a living sacrifice. . . . Be transformed by the renewing of your mind" (Rom 12:1-2). Notice that the work we do with our bodies precedes a change in our mental processes. In addition to our thinking, the body has the capacity to alter two other important dimensions of self: emotions and behavior.

In order for our bodies to be agents of change, we must pay attention to our bodies' nonverbal messages (Ogden & Fisher, 2015). These body-based processes include our facial expressions, breathing, posture, and movement. Our feelings, thoughts, and behavior are altered as we "work with" these habits of the body. To "work with" our bodies means to experiment with different facial expressions, new ways of breathing, and altered posture. As we modify our habits of movement, we discover that our mood has shifted, our thoughts are different, and our behavior has improved.

This emphasis on body-based processes is important within the context of contemplative prayer. For example, we "work with" our eyes. Does it help you pray if you close your eyes or keep them open? We work also with posture. Are you sitting in a way that is comfortable and that fosters alertness? (Remember, you want to sit without pain, if that is possible, and stay awake for twenty minutes.) Perhaps you are too slouched or too rigid in your posture. We work with breathing. If thoughts distract you, does focusing on your breathing help you let go of your thinking and help you return your attention to God? We work with movement. Does sitting still for a few minutes help calm your body, mind, and emotions so that you can settle into your time of prayer?

THE BODY AND COUNSELING

A Christian contemplative view of the body sheds tremendous light on the counseling process. Several principles set forth in the preceding section inform how we work with the body in counseling:

1. Valuing the body.

2. Listening to the body.

3. Bringing awareness to the body.

4. Facilitating congruence between nonverbal and verbal messages.

In counseling, we are not only working with clients' behaviors, emotions, and thoughts. We are also welcoming their bodies into the counseling process. This means that we must nurture our clients' connection with their bodies. We do this primarily by including their bodies in the conversation. We ask the following kinds of questions: "What is happening in your body as you talk about that?" "Where do you feel the stress in your body?" Or we make the following types of observations: "I noticed that your voice got quieter as you remembered that." "You sat upright as you were telling that story." "I see the pain in your face."

Our clients are communicating with us even when they aren't using words. Most of the messages they send us are being transported via body language. And these signals are being transmitted in milliseconds. Long before they formulate and speak words, their bodies have communicated many things. Therefore, we must become adept at reading their body language.

Our clients' bodies speak an entirely different language, one in which we must become fluent. This language relies upon such things as tone of voice, gazes, movements, facial expressions, breathing patterns, and skin color (Solomon & Tatkin, 2011). Their bodies are telling us if they are getting agitated or withdrawing. If our clients are getting worked up, the following changes happen: vocal pitch goes up, volume increases, tone becomes sharper, skin color changes, movements happen faster, and bodies become more rigid. For clients who are shutting down, their body language is different. Their pitch goes down, their volume decreases, their tone sounds dead, they move more slowly, and their bodies begin to crumple.

One of our biggest goals is to help our clients become aware of their bodies. In the beginning of our work together, they will probably not know the messages that their bodies are transmitting. Unbeknownst to them, their bodies are sending messages via habits of posture, gesture, and movement. We must learn to work with their bodies and bring attention to what their bodies are communicating. Our job is to help them develop a vocabulary that describes their physical sensations. Our task is to explore with them the movement, posture, and physiology of their bodies. As we help them describe their physical sensations, they achieve greater wholeness and health.

One of our primary goals in counseling is to help our clients communicate more effectively. This requires a congruence between the messages they send with their words and the signals they transmit with their bodies. What a challenging undertaking! To accomplish this task, we must help them pay greater attention to both their nonverbal and verbal messages. Does the information being transmitted in the form of words match the message being sent through their bodies? Assisting clients as they develop congruence in this area will help bring about greater stability and calmness as they attempt to address the problems that bring them to counseling.

EMOTIONS AND CONTEMPLATIVE PRAYER

He answered, "I heard you in the garden,
and I was afraid because I was naked; so I hid."
GENESIS 3:10

Emotions are an unavoidable part of contemplative prayer. They cannot be bypassed. How do clients experience them as they engage in the discipline of solitude and silence? How do clients respond to emotions while they are opening themselves to the presence of the Spirit of Christ? Ultimately, the manner in which our clients deal with and express their emotions—and much of this learning occurs in the context of contemplative prayer—will influence the outcome of our work together.

We are missing a thorough Christian understanding of emotions. Yes, we have a superficial knowledge of them, but we lack a deep comprehension of our emotional landscape, an apprehension that is shaped by Christian concepts. For example, how well do we discern the role of emotions in the story of Adam and Eve? Yes, we know that Adam was afraid and that he hid (see Gen 3:10), but we need to dig deeper into Adam's story—and our clients' stories. A sound Christian psychology of emotions will ask Adam—and our clients—tough questions. Do you know what you are feeling? Can you name it? (We take for granted that Adam knew what he was feeling, but did he?) Do you understand the cause of your emotion? Have you made sense of it? Are you thinking and acting in a clear way? (Had Adam even thought through his plan? I doubt it.) Why are you blaming your wife (see Gen 3:12)?

Take another familiar passage that deals with emotion: "'In your anger do not sin': Do not let the sun go down while you are still angry" (Eph 4:26). Superficially, we recognize that anger can get us into trouble. We acknowledge the necessity of dealing with it quickly. However, at a deeper level, how do we regulate it so that it doesn't cause problems? And what is the Christian way for moving past it sooner rather than later?

Christian contemplative prayer shines a light of understanding on this series of questions. As we sit gazing at God, we can sharpen our awareness of emotions, develop a healthy attitude toward them, and learn to deal with them effectively. As we set out to develop a deeper Christian understanding of emotions, we will use three questions to guide us into the emotional side of contemplative prayer:

1. What causes emotions to arise while we sit silently with God?

2. How can we respond to the emotions that spring up?

3. What should our attitude be toward emotions?

Emotions are primarily concerned with safety. In other words, emotions serve an appraisal or judging function: Is the situation good or bad? We tend to think of spending time with God alone in silence as a pleasant and safe experience. However, it is not quite that simple because we really aren't alone. We are also with our minds, which are happy to wreak havoc during our quiet time. Our minds are prone to leave the present, peaceful moment in search of more troubling times, that is, our past and future.

Let's examine the process of how our minds wander off to the past and future in order to see how this is connected to painful emotions. I will use Bob as an example. In silent prayer, his intention is to give God his attention. However, his mind drifts off to an upcoming event. His mind begins to think about a meeting with his boss that is scheduled for later in the day. Bob wants to be well prepared to ensure that the meeting goes well. But then his mind begins to remember a previous appointment he had with his supervisor. Attached to this memory are painful emotions because at that earlier meeting Bob's supervisor hinted that she was thinking about getting rid of his position. The feelings associated with that encounter—fear and anger—then appear as he sits in prayer.

Let's examine in further detail how the process of visiting the future during contemplative prayer may be attached to painful emotions. Often as we think about upcoming events, we automatically begin to anticipate and plan for potential problems. Let's check in on Bob's time of contemplative prayer again. Bob is sitting quietly with God when his mind drifts off to the appointment with his supervisor later in the day. He imagines problems that might emerge and thinks about how he might successfully handle them. At one level, this seems like simple problem solving, but on another plane Bob's mind is preparing for a threatening situation. Any real or perceived sign of danger that registers on our mind during contemplative prayer will arouse painful emotions.

Once an emotion arises during contemplative prayer, will I respond to it in a Christian way? What is my attitude toward the feeling? How will I relate to it? How will I regulate my emotion? Will I manage it in a way that helps me maintain emotional balance? Or will I respond to it in a way that puts me out of balance? Our response to these questions—over time—will determine if we grow and heal.

Describing two unproductive approaches to emotions may illuminate a more appropriate response. The first ineffective method is *restraint*. This may take the appearance of shutting off the feeling because it is too intense, unfamiliar, or confusing. As I run away from the sensations, it may not even register with me that I am having a feeling. In short, I am avoiding and being inattentive to the emotion. It seems as if my thinking brain has turned off my emotional response to the situation. I may find myself getting caught up in thinking about the emotion during my time of contemplative prayer.

The second ineffectual way of regulating emotions shows up as *surrender*. I know that I am feeling something, but it feels so strong that I just give in to it. I don't do enough to regulate the sensations as they wash over me, flooding me. It seems as if the emotion is drowning out my thoughts as I experience a sense of being cut off from logical thinking. I may find myself being consumed or distracted by the emotion during my time of solitude and silent prayer.

While I am quietly praying, what is a more balanced or effective approach to regulating emotions? The first step is to notice the internal emotional response. Instead of avoiding it, I actually take time to pay attention to it and know what I am feeling. Perhaps I am feeling some type of emotional discomfort. It may be registering as some type of sensation in my body: tension in my neck, discomfort in my stomach, a tight sensation in my chest. The next step is to welcome it. Instead of trying to get rid of the emotion, I listen to the information that it wants to share. I pause to accept the emotion, as opposed to rejecting it. The final step is to name it. This means that I put a label on the emotion. Is it anxiety, sadness, fear, or anger? Instead of turning off my thought processes, I use my thinking mind to attach words to the feeling. Once I have labeled it, I turn my attention back to God. I don't want to get too far off my original intention, but I do want to deal effectively with the emotion that arises.

Emotions, once triggered, organize how we think and act. They even activate various physical responses. We must deal with feelings in a Christian way in order to develop the character of Jesus. We need to catch early signs that emotions are stimulating certain systems within our body. We don't want emotions to gain control of our thinking minds. It is important to channel our emotions into constructive behaviors.

Isn't this what Jesus did? Let's look at one example. In a story told by Mark (Mk 10:13-16), people were bringing children to Jesus, but his disciples were attempting to stop them. The passage tells us that Jesus was "indignant" (Mk 10:14) with his disciples. Did he recognize how the emotion was stirring in his body? I believe so. Did he let the feeling interfere with accomplishing his goal? It is obvious that this didn't occur. Just the opposite happened. Motivated by indignation, Jesus overcame barriers (Mk 10:15) so that he could take "the children in his arms" (Mk 10:16). The strong feeling—akin to anger—moved Jesus toward loving behavior.

We need a deep understanding of emotions for two reasons. First, they emerge within the context of contemplative prayer—and life—so we need effective strategies for relating to them. Second, our client's ability to recognize and regulate them is central to a productive counseling experience.

EMOTIONS AND COUNSELING

Many of our clients, when they come to counseling, are overwhelmed with emotions. They don't understand where their painful feelings originate, and they lack control over where their emotions take them. Most of the time their emotions are moving them to fight, flee, or freeze. They are often caught in a vicious cycle: painful emotions → reactive thoughts and behavior → painful emotions.

We can help them regulate their painful emotions as we promote the following attitudes: awareness, acceptance, and reflecting. With *awareness*, we help our clients learn how to pay attention to their internal emotional experiences (Harris, 2009). We facilitate the process of awareness by helping them consider the physical sensations that accompany their emotions: "Perhaps that feeling in my chest is one of sadness." Awareness is about helping our clients observe their feelings.

With *acceptance*, we are teaching our clients to welcome their emotions. I use this analogy with my clients: "Can you treat your emotion like a guest in your house?" We help our clients learn to attend to each emotion and to listen to the information that it wants to share. Instead of trying to control their emotions or make them go away, we want them to understand their emotions. Clients discover that they can only let go of an emotion when they welcome it and attend to it. I say to my clients, "The next time you experience an emotion, notice how you relate to it. Do you want to reject it or accept it?"

Reflecting refers to the process of focusing on and slowly examining the emotional situation (Johnson, 2004). As we teach our clients to reflect on an emotion, they learn to step back and make sense of it. As they make meaning of it, they verbalize the feeling, putting a label on it. By putting the emotion into words, they alert themselves to the action tendency embedded in the emotion. For example, if I say, "I am angry," then that alerts me to the tendency to attack or to inflict pain. By verbalizing the feeling, my client becomes less apt to act upon it.

As our clients engage in a regular practice of contemplative prayer, they acquire knowledge of how to manage their feelings. They discover that effective methods of regulating emotions—if practiced regularly, over time—can turn into character traits. And, finally, they learn how to convert their strategies for balancing emotions into essential personal and relationship skills.

THE MIND AND CONTEMPLATIVE PRAYER

> *For God hath not given us the spirit of fear;*
> *but of power, and of love, and of a sound mind.*
> **2 TIMOTHY 1:7 (KJV)**

Is contemplative prayer simply another self-improvement project? Absolutely not. Our purpose is simply to present ourselves to God, as Paul instructs us in Romans 12:1, so that we are open to his power and presence. As we orient ourselves toward God, the Spirit is transforming us into the image of God. We are beginning to take on the character of Jesus—which is love.

In this section, we are focusing upon our innate faculties for thinking and knowing. You may be wondering, "Why didn't we begin our examination of human dimensions at this location? Isn't thinking the place to start?" Our study didn't originate with thinking because I didn't want you to think of contemplative prayer as simply a way of the mind. It is a major mistake to accept the idea that people are primarily thinking beings (Strobel, 2013).

Instead, people are fundamentally loving beings (Strobel, 2013). God first loved us; then he called us to love him in return with all our heart, soul, strength, and mind (Lk 10:27). This is a holistic kind of love. It involves loving God with our whole beings, not simply our minds. As theologian Kyle Strobel (2013) contends, "Thinking is not the bedrock of the human person. We are most fundamentally lovers" (p. 59). Because we are not primarily thinking beings, I postponed this topic until now. I wanted us to explore the physical and emotional dimensions before taking on the intellectual arena.

It is now time for this topic because contemplative prayer is dependent upon how we use our minds. Does your mind work correctly? Is it aimed in the right direction? What are the traits of a good thinker? Is your thinking connected to love? Does your mind keep you on track? Do you exercise good thinking habits? Have you established patterns of good thinking? Our clients' answers to these questions will determine whether they reap the potential benefits of counseling.

The questions that I have just raised are aimed at the intellectual dimension. We function intellectually because we possess innate thinking abilities: memory, language, the desire for understanding, the disposition to seek God, and so on. But the real question is, Do we use our mental faculties well? Intellectual capacities by themselves do not allow us to function at a high thinking level. These abilities must be developed, and one way our minds are trained is through contemplative prayer. Recognizing the relationship between contemplative prayer and development of the mind, Strobel (2013) quotes Jonathan Edwards (1703–1758) as saying, "The business of the Christian ought to be very much [in] contemplation and the improvement of the faculties of his mind in divine things" (p. 129).

As clients improve the faculties of their minds in the context of contemplative prayer, they change the way they think. They begin to develop the character traits of a good thinker. One of the traits we want to nurture in our clients is wisdom. Wisdom was evident in the life of Jesus at an early age. Luke tells a story of Jesus at the age of twelve (Lk 2:41-52). Jesus was "in the temple courts, sitting among the teachers, listening to them and asking them questions. Everyone who heard him was amazed at his understanding and his answers" (Lk 2:46-47). See his mind at work—listening, asking, understanding, answering. Luke writes, "Jesus grew in wisdom" (Lk 2:52).

As we engage in contemplative prayer, the Spirit of God wants to produce within us the physical and emotional character traits of Jesus. But how about the intellectual character traits of Jesus? Does the Spirit desire to produce within us the mind of Christ? I believe so. Paul writes to the Christians in Corinth, "We have the mind of Christ" (1 Cor 2:16). He provides Christians in Philippi with similar encouragement: "In your relationships with one another, have the same mindset as Christ Jesus" (Phil 2:5). Scripture is telling us that our minds can operate according to the same intellectual virtues that Jesus' mind possesses.

As we consider the role of the mind in contemplative prayer, it behooves us to ask a fundamental question: What is the purpose of the mind? What am I trying to accomplish with my mind as I engage in contemplative prayer? Our goal is knowledge. Unfortunately, far too often we have confused knowledge with the contents of the mind, with believing the right things. But knowledge is far more than information. Knowledge has more to do with *how* we think, as opposed to *what* we think. According to Christian philosophers Roberts and Wood (2009), knowledge is about understanding and seeing for yourself.

As we spend time alone with God in silence, the mind has an aim and direction. Paul captures this idea when he writes, "Set your minds on things above" (Col 3:2). He is not instructing us to focus on a place. Instead, he is telling us to direct our attention to God. The thing the mind most wants to know is God. Strobel (2013) writes, "Contemplation, therefore, is setting your mind on God" (p. 129). At the heart of contemplation is the assumption that the mind needs something upon which to focus. Strobel (2013) adds, "In contemplation your mind is captivated by the object of beauty—God in Christ" (p. 131).

As we focus our attention on God in contemplative prayer, our minds grow in both knowledge and love. Love and knowledge go together. When Jesus said, "Love the Lord your God with all your heart and with all your soul and with all your mind" (Mt 22:37), he made it clear that the mind is intended to be used in the service of love. We must combine our love of God with our knowledge of God. We don't seek knowledge of God for purely intellectual reasons. Instead, we want to know him in love. This is "knowing God affectionately" (Strobel, 2013, p. 97).

In contemplative prayer, we come face-to-face with the nature of the mind. It has a tendency to take its focus off of God. Why is that? First, the mind would rather center on itself. It likes to concentrate on its own workings: remembering, problem solving, creating stories, and feeling. When we try to target our attention on God, focusing away from the mind, the mind rebels. In its rebellion, it wanders from one thought to another. Our first challenge is a wandering mind.

The second challenge is that my mind wants me to focus on myself. When I try to center on God during contemplative prayer, my mind rebels by concentrating on me. What are my plans? How am I feeling? What problems am I facing? How are my relationships working out? Is my work fulfilling? Am I happy in my marriage? Even though the mind was designed to focus on God, it has become disoriented. As a result, it prefers to concentrate on me.

We must admit the truth about our minds. They are disorderly, rebellious, and stubborn. We soon discover as we try to center our attention on God that we have little control over our minds. Unwanted, intrusive thoughts show up to occupy our attention. What are we to do? How do we react to them? We have two common responses. The first is to give in to these thoughts, allowing them to occupy our minds. The second response is to fight them. We try to stop them and push them out of our minds. This is ineffective and requires too much effort.

What are we to do? It is clear that the mind needs discipline. Training occurs within the context of contemplative prayer. When we notice that a thought has captured our attention and turned our focus away from God, we simply turn our concentration to a word that reminds us of our intention to center on God. We don't fight the thought. Instead, we turn our attention to something else. In doing so, we simply let go of the intrusive thought.

Contemplative prayer takes on a predictable pattern. First, we focus on God. Then we lose focus. And then we return our focus to God. The cycle happens over and over. But, as we continue in this process, an amazing change occurs. Our minds are being trained. Over time, the mind of Christ is being cultivated within us.

In the discipline of solitude and silence, we make ourselves available to the transforming power of the Spirit. This transformation happens at various dimensions of our being: physical, emotional, and behavioral. But this change also occurs in our thinking processes and habits. Scripture encourages us to "be transformed by the renewing of your mind" (Rom 12:2). As our mind is renewed, we become better thinkers. But we also become better lovers—better lovers of God, others, and ourselves.

THE MIND AND COUNSELING

In contemplative prayer, our clients directly encounter and learn about the nature of their minds. Our objective is for them to learn how to handle their minds effectively. We can better assist them in this regard as we stay focused on two goals:

1. Helping clients develop an awareness of how their minds work.

2. Supporting clients as they learn how to respond effectively to their thought processes.

Modern psychological research has uncovered five faulty mechanisms of the mind (Harris, 2009). First, the mind traps us in negative stories. Second, our minds carry us out of the present into the past and future. Third, false ideas show up under the guise of "truth." Next, the workings of the mind distort our perceptions. Finally, the thoughts of the mind are intrusive. Let's examine each of these mental processes in turn.

The mind likes to tell stories. A story is the mind's way of making sense out of an event, interaction, or emotion. A narrative has a plot: who, what, where, when, and why? Within a flash, our minds have created a story that explains the cause of the situation or our experience. And oftentimes the story is a very negative account of others and ourselves.

As our minds are writing this fiction, they engage in time travel. That is, they carry us into both the past and the future. First, the present interaction triggers memories of similar incidents in the past. The mind replays an old fight, disappointment, or grievance. As we relive a time when someone hurt us or let us down, a present interaction can become even more painful. Or our minds take us into the future, showing us a scary picture of what our lives will be like in the future. Memories of the past and speculations about the future become intermingled with the original plot line of our distressing story.

The next step in the thinking process is predictable. We begin to believe the stories, or thoughts, created by our minds. Because the mind is so convincing, we accept these negative thoughts as the "truth." More likely than not we won't even ask ourselves, "Is my mind telling me the truth?" The painful story seems so obviously true that we just take it for granted. The thoughts created by our minds are extremely hard to give up.

The workings of the mind make it difficult for us to see clearly. As a result, our minds distort our perception of two people (Harris, 2009). First, we lose sight of ourselves. We are so lost in thought that we forfeit the values—to be kind, loving, considerate—that typically guide our actions. Second, we lose touch with others. We can no longer see the other person clearly because all we can see are our negative thoughts about that individual. The other gets lost in our negative story about what is wrong with her or him. All we can see is the cloud of dust and dirt stirred up by our thinking processes.

Finally, thoughts are intrusive. It seems as if they have a life of their own. We didn't intend to think all these bad things about ourselves or others, but for some reason, as soon as our mood takes a turn for the worse, our thinking follows right along. If we are angry, our minds churn out thoughts to justify our anger. If we are hurt, our minds create a story about how mean and selfish the other person is. We may not want to have these thoughts, but they show up anyway.

When our minds speak to us this way, we have three options (McKay, Lev, & Skeen, 2012). We suppress them, hold on to the thoughts tightly, or let them go. The irony with the first choice is that trying to suppress thoughts actually makes them stronger. Our second option is to get caught up in our thoughts. We give them our attention and treat them as if they are true. We dwell on them, replay them, and immerse ourselves in them.

The third option—letting thoughts go—is what we learn to do in contemplative prayer. This last option can be broken down into three steps (D. Siegel, 2010b). The first step is watching. This is the brief moment when you notice that a thought has captured your attention.

Step two is to earmark the thought as simply a thought. Let me use Melinda, who was bothered by depression, to illustrate the process of labeling. In our first session, she declared, "No one can be trusted." At this point, she equated her ideas with the truth. However, with time, her practice of contemplative prayer helped her learn how to identify the thought as a thought. As she reached step two, her original statement was replaced with this one: "There is that story again, the story about not being able to trust anyone." Notice that labeling removes the sentiment that the belief is true. Instead, the thought is now classified as simply a thought.

The next step—letting go—comes fairly easily once we have completed the first two steps. With the third step, we make the choice to turn our attention to some other thought. We have decided that the negative thought no longer deserves our attention.

Learning to let go of thoughts can be liberating for our clients. Instead of being lost in negative thinking, they can choose to focus on ideas that promote personal happiness. Instead of being bound by painful beliefs ("I am incompetent"; "I can never measure up") that are false, they are free to concentrate on ideas that promote their well-being. Our goal is to help clients develop an awareness of what their minds are doing. With this knowledge, they can then cultivate a mind that works well.

BEHAVIOR AND CONTEMPLATIVE PRAYER

Dear children, let us not love with words or speech but with actions.
1 JOHN 3:18

Now, we turn our attention to action. Contemplative prayer clearly relies upon certain behaviors. But, as we begin to examine the behavioral dimension, we must be clear about the answers to certain questions:

1. What are the antecedents to action?

2. What is the role of behavior in contemplative prayer?

3. What is the process by which we integrate action into counseling?

It would be a mistake to start contemplative prayer—or counseling for that matter—with an emphasis on action. To do so would get us focused on the wrong thing. Jesus made it clear that the inside, what we can't see, is more important than the outside, actions that we can observe. He illustrated his point by referring to common kitchen dishes. Speaking to the Pharisees, Jesus said, "You clean the outside of the cup and dish, but inside they are full of greed and self-indulgence" (Mt 23:25). He told them, "First clean the inside of the cup and dish, and then the outside also will be clean" (Mt 23:26). Instead of starting with actions, we must begin with the inside.

The inside refers to the heart. Dallas Willard (2012b) teaches us that the heart is synonymous with our spirit. It is the core of our being. The heart is the source of our actions. As Jesus said, behavior comes "from within, out of a person's heart" (Mk 7:21). This is where we must start—on the inside. Before focusing on behavior, we must focus on the heart. This is how the process goes: start with the inside (the heart); the outside (actions) naturally changes.

So how do we alter our hearts? Obviously, on our own, we can't change our hearts. Only God can initiate and carry out this interior transformation process. We can embark upon a self-improvement project—reading our Bibles more, attending church more frequently, volunteering to help out at church—but these things won't alter our hearts. Only God can reach us at the center of our being and bring about the transformation of our hearts.

So we discover an important truth as we engage in contemplative prayer. We discover that action is taking place, but most of that action comes from God. As we sit alone with God in silence, God's grace—"the action of God in our lives" (Foster, 2008, p. 184)—is at work. Our job is to simply surrender to the love of God. Our role in the change process is to remain connected to the vine (see Jn 15:1-8). As we open up to the Father, by the power of the Spirit, we are being conformed into the image of the Son.

Even though the discipline of solitude and silence is effortless, it is not about doing nothing. It does require our cooperation—our action—in small ways. For example, we *move* ourselves to a place of prayer. We *sit* (hopefully with a posture that fosters comfort and alertness) for twenty minutes. We *close* our eyes. These are observable actions. But then there are interior actions as well. For example, we *notice* when our mind has wandered. We *return* our attention to God. We *give* God our loving attention. We *consent* to the action of God.

Contemplative prayer opens us to the transforming work of the Spirit. We are developing the character traits of Jesus. We are cultivating important physical, emotional, and intellectual virtues. These virtues are on the inside. It is out of these interior traits that we want our actions to emerge.

All these virtues are rooted in love. Contemplative prayer begins in love and culminates in love. God invites us into his loving presence, by which we are transformed. Then sitting with God in silence leads to our actions, which are loving. Our actions grow out of God's love, which is in us. Loving action does not come from biting our tongues and willpower. Instead, it emerges naturally from the new people that we are becoming. Actions grow out of character. It goes like this: God's love leads us to contemplative prayer → contemplative prayer leads us to love → love shapes our character → character directs our actions.

This progression ends with character directing our actions. What does this mean? It means that our behavior is always guided by a question: Is this action consistent with love? So often, our behavior is guided by other motivators. We do things to look good. We hope that our actions will lead to some kind of personal reward or benefit. Our behavior often grows out of fear or guilt, but ultimately we want our actions to be consistent with virtuous character traits. The goal of our actions is to reveal the love of Jesus that is within us.

BEHAVIOR AND COUNSELING

In the last section, we explored a contemplative view of action. We unearthed some important principles that can guide us as we work with our clients' behavior:

1. Sitting precedes action.

2. Action grows out of good character.

3. Love is the basis of action.

In this section, we will explore the relationship between these ideas and good counseling.

In contemplative prayer, we learn that sitting precedes action. How do we relate this principle to counseling? We want our clients to learn to pause before they act. During this time, they reflect upon their thoughts and feelings. We ask, "What is happening in you? Has something been triggered for you?" We help them consider the interior experiences—physical sensations, thoughts, and feelings—that precede the impulse to do something.

Ultimately, good actions are the outgrowth of good character. We can help our clients identify and name their behaviors, but it serves no use to judge their actions. Our focus needs to be on interior matters of the heart. Once that changes, the behaviors will surely fall in line.

As counseling progresses, we want to encourage our clients to engage in behavioral experiments. In other words, we support them as they try out proactive loving (Fishbane, 2013). What is proactive loving? First, it is expressed when our clients take responsibility for their own behavior: "I am accountable for how I acted. I cannot blame another person for my actions." Second, proactive loving occurs when they begin to see that they have a profound impact upon others.

Counseling is about our client's behavior. Our goal is to help them make thoughtful choices to engage in behaviors that are guided by and inspired by interior processes—the character of Jesus. Ultimately, we want them to slow down and choose behaviors that reflect a loving character.

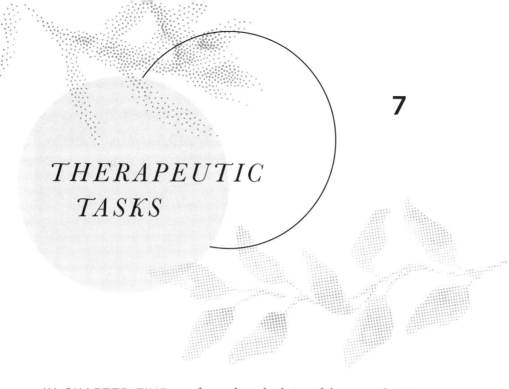

THERAPEUTIC
TASKS

IN CHAPTER FIVE, we focused on the *being* of the counselor. Now we are turning to the *doing* of the counselor, another essential element in our contemplative-oriented approach to counseling. In our new paradigm, we are interested in the art and science of both—being and doing. As counselors, our aim is to combine and balance these two basic sides of counseling. Our objective is to be a loving presence while employing productive interventions.

In our contemplative model of counseling, we acknowledge the tension that comes from trying to balance these two facets of counseling. We don't want to convey the idea that only techniques matter. Neither do we believe that a counselor must embody all the qualities of a loving presence before he or she sets out to practice a contemplative-oriented way of counseling. It is my experience that we must engage in both sides of counseling at the same time. In other words, we are learning the skills of this approach while we are developing the qualities needed of an effective counselor.

The evolution of motivational interviewing (MI) is a good example of this principle. William Miller and Stephen Rollnick, the developers of MI, acknowledge that their initial emphasis was simply upon techniques. Over time, though, they realized that something important was missing. What was it? Miller and Rollnick (2013) determined that they had failed to convey the "underlying spirit of MI, its mind-set and heart-set" (p. 124). As a result, they began to highlight the four elements of the spirit of MI: partnership, acceptance, compassion, and evocation. They began to emphasize both being and doing.

Eleven fundamental interventions are employed within our contemplative-oriented approach to counseling:

- teaching contemplative prayer

- engagement

- exchanging information

- reflection

- tracking

- hold and wait

- silence

- empathy

- validation

- evocative responding

- proactive loving

In the following section, I will spotlight the hallmark intervention of this model: teaching clients how to practice contemplative prayer. I point out that there are two methods for implementing contemplative prayer: formal and informal. In the formal procedure, the emphasis is on sitting in silent prayer for a specified period of time. The formal approach that I use in my model is centering prayer. In contrast, an informal program emphasizes the application of contemplative prayer in everyday life. In my contemplative-oriented method of counseling, I highlight the formal scheme so that is where I will begin our discussion. However, since an informal approach may be useful for some clients, I will also introduce this plan.

TEACHING CONTEMPLATIVE PRAYER

In the first part of this section, we will explore how to introduce and teach centering prayer in the context of counseling. For many clinicians, the idea of bringing contemplative prayer into counseling can feel overwhelming and frightening. Where do we start? Is there a process to follow? How do I know if this is an appropriate intervention with a client? I will address these questions in this section.

How we introduce centering prayer to clients makes a significant difference in whether they actually adopt a practice of their own. There are three steps that I follow: (1) determining if a client is a good candidate, (2) teaching centering prayer, and (3) follow-up.

Step one: Determining readiness. As a counselor, since you are practicing and experiencing the benefits of contemplative prayer, you may be tempted to recommend it to every person who enters the door. This should be avoided. Contemplative prayer is not for everyone or for every issue. Initially, we must determine the client's potential for actually practicing contemplative prayer. We must first ask ourselves: "Does contemplative prayer fit their need? Will they benefit from the practice?"

There are several clear indicators that it is not the right time for introducing a client to contemplative prayer (Gehart, 2012). We should not advance centering prayer to clients if they are (1) in a current crisis or chaotic situation, (2) lacking a sense of ownership about the problem, (3) feeling overwhelmed or exhausted by life circumstances, or (4) actively experiencing psychotic, manic, or trauma symptoms. With these clients, we can delay introducing them to contemplative prayer until their situation has changed or improved.

On the other hand, there are indicators that clients may be good candidates for contemplative prayer. First, clients' goals for counseling are a good match for contemplative prayer. For example, their aim is the reduction of fear and anxiety. Or they are motivated to let go of troubling thoughts. Maybe they tell you they want to face a situation that they have previously avoided. The clients' objective may to be build self-esteem. All these goals fit well with the principles and practice of contemplative prayer.

A second common indicator is that the clients are currently—or previously— engaged in spiritual practices. Clients tell you that they are looking for ways to form a better connection or relationship with God. They have tried reading Scripture and prayer, but they are searching for something else. They report benefitting from spiritual disciplines but wonder if something else might help. Knowing that you are a Christian counselor, they have expressed an interest in knowing about other Christian practices.

The clearest indicator that a client is a good candidate is that the client is directly asking for your help. For example, the client may say, "I have heard a lot about mindfulness, but is there a Christian form of contemplation?" Another example is: "My relationship with God is really important. Do you know of practices that might help me grow closer to God?" Clients have told me: "I don't want to use medication if I don't have to. Are there natural resources within my faith that might help?"

We may be tempted at this point to charge in with information about contemplative prayer, but it still isn't the right time. There are three suggestions offered by motivational interviewing (MI) that I find useful at this point: (1) ask permission, (2) explore prior knowledge, and (3) query interest (Miller & Rollnick, 2013).

Let's explore how these suggestions might show up in the context of a counseling session. Asking permission may sound like this:

- Would it be all right if I tell you something about contemplative prayer?

- Would you like to know about a type of prayer called contemplative prayer?

We might use the following types of questions to explore the client's prior knowledge:

- What do you know about prayer?

- Have you heard about contemplative prayer? What do you know?

- How do you think you might benefit from a Christian practice such as contemplative prayer?

Querying interest might appear in this way:

- What would you be most interested in knowing about contemplative prayer?

- Do you have any specific questions about contemplative prayer?

I find these suggestions useful for several reasons. First, they enhance clients' willingness to hear what you have to say. Next, they prevent you from telling the clients what they already know. Finally, they let you know what a client is most interested in learning. Approaching clients in this way is likely to increase their receptivity to what you are going to teach them (Miller & Rollnick, 2013).

Now that we know a client has a sincere interest in and desire to learn about contemplative prayer, what do we do? We pause long enough to consider the primary impediment to practicing contemplative prayer—irregular practice. By highlighting this challenge, we hope to generate commitment by the client to engage in the practice regularly for a period of time (Gehart, 2012).

When we invite clients to practice centering prayer regularly, we are asking them to make a significant change in their lifestyle. We are requesting a lot of our clients when we ask them to take twenty minutes out of their day to stop and do nothing, just sit in silence. This is so at odds with the values of our American culture. The emphasis in our society is on pleasure—eating cupcakes, drinking delicious drinks, watching television, playing video games, and so on. We live in a system that encourages people to get quick fixes in illegal drugs and legally prescribed medications. By highlighting the challenge of taking time out of their busy days for contemplative prayer, we are shifting the clients' attention away from "Will I be good at this?" to "Will I do this at all?"

When asking clients to consider contemplative prayer, adopting a collaborative stance is useful (Gehart, 2012). Our clients should know that we are extending them a genuine invitation. Consequently, they are free to decline our invitation of including contemplative prayer in treatment. We express our belief that contemplative prayer is not for everyone. We are not putting pressure on our clients because we know this will not help them begin a meaningful journey into contemplative prayer.

Step two: Teaching centering prayer. We have taken our time at step one. We have cautiously and carefully approached step two. Now we are ready to begin. My method is to teach centering prayer during the session, making the following moves: (1) summarizing the key elements of centering prayer, (2) practicing together in session, and (3) leaving time for follow-up.

The key elements of centering prayer are captured in the four guidelines set forth by Keating (1999):

- Choose a sacred word as the symbol of your intention to consent to God's presence and action within.

- Sit comfortably and with your eyes closed, settle briefly, and silently introduce the sacred word as the symbol of your consent to God's presence and action within.

- When you become aware of thoughts, return ever so gently to the sacred word.

- At the end of the prayer period, remain in silence with eyes closed for a couple of minutes (p. 139).

I convey these guidelines to my clients in the following way:

1. Choose a sacred word to use throughout our exercise. This word ought to be short: *Jesus, Abba, love, peace,* or something similar. Stick to this one word throughout our exercise.

2. Remember the intention or purpose of our time of prayer. Our goal is to be open to God's presence. We are turning our minds and hearts toward God and away from distracting thoughts.

3. What to do about posture, eyes, and hands? It is best to sit with a relaxed, yet erect posture with both feet on the floor. I tell clients: "If you feel uncomfortable with your eyes closed, you can keep them partially open with a soft gaze a few feet in front of you. Rest your hands comfortably on your knees or in your lap."

4. How to deal with distracting thoughts? I say, "If you notice that you are in thought—the word *thought* also refers to emotions or physical sensations—gently bring to mind your sacred word as a way of turning your attention away from the distracting thought."

5. What is the process? For the time you spend in centering prayer, the process looks like this: freedom from thought → distracted by thought → use sacred word to let go of thought → enter quiet → distracted by thought → repeat.

Miller and Rollnick (2013) provide guidance that can be useful as we offer our clients instructions in centering prayer. First, it is important to avoid long monologues. Instead, we need to provide information in small doses, making sure that the client is staying with us. When we divide the recommendations into bits and pieces, we can check in with our clients, making sure that they understand and soliciting their questions. The following dialogue illustrates how this conversation might begin:

COUNSELOR: The first step is to pick a short word, like *Jesus, Abba, love,* or *peace,* that you will use during our exercise. Have you picked a word?

CLIENT: Yes, I have a word.

COUNSELOR: Our only purpose during this exercise is to be open to God's presence. We are going to turn our attention away from normal things you might think about. Does this make sense?

CLIENT: Am I trying not to think about anything?

COUNSELOR: Well, it is likely that thoughts will enter your head during our exercise. That is okay. But when they arrive, just focus on your word long enough to let go of the thought.

CLIENT: Is it like a mantra? Do I keep saying the word over and over?

COUNSELOR: No, it's not quite like that. You only use it until the thought glides away. Then you stop using the sacred word until you notice another thought. Are you getting it?

After offering the client some information about centering prayer, it is time to practice together. As Basil Pennington (1999), one of the co-developers of centering prayer says, "We should never share Centering Prayer with anyone without leading them into their first experience of it. It is an experiential prayer. The teaching will mean nothing until the experience is had" (p. 176). I generally set a timer for three to five minutes, assuring my client that I will keep my eyes closed and that I will be in prayer until the timer makes a noise.

After we have engaged in centering prayer for a few minutes together, I ask my client questions such as:

- How did that go?
- Do you have any questions?
- How did you go about refocusing?
- Can you tell me about your experience?
- Did any unpleasant feelings come up for you?

Part of the follow-up entails developing a plan for clients to use at home. I ask the following series of questions in order to help them develop a realistic and doable plan: (1) "Do you have a daily routine activity to which you can attach your time of centering prayer?" (2) "Are you able to have two sessions of twenty minutes each? If not, how many minutes is doable for you?" (3) "What will you use as a timing device?"

I often disclose my own answers to these questions with my clients. I tell them that I attach my time of centering prayer to breakfast. After breakfast, which I have every day at home, I move into the den and sit on my sofa for centering prayer. After setting the timer on my smart phone for twenty minutes, I sit silently until my phone begins to chirp.

Step three: Follow-up. When clients return to sessions after a time of practice, we need to take time to follow up with them about their experience, finding out what worked and what didn't. There are several common issues that emerge (Gehart, 2012). For example, clients often have questions about how to stay focused. They may need to explore barriers that are interfering with their practice. Perhaps they desire help coming up with a more realistic practice schedule. In addition, they may want to discuss thoughts and emotions that came up for them during their times of centering prayer.

When I work with couples, they often wonder if practicing together is a good idea. Research indicates that engaging in centering prayer with another person can be beneficial, but practicing together can also trigger relationship dynamics. For example, what if one spouse is more disciplined and can stick to a regular plan better than the other spouse? This can soon become a source of struggle. The more organized spouse can become critical. The other spouse can feel pressured into practicing. Our goal is to avoid these types of problems.

I offer these suggestions to couples (Gehart, 2012). First, only practice together if you have positive feelings for each other. Next, experiment with different meanings of the phrase "practicing together." This usually means practicing at the same time, but it can also mean practicing in separate spaces at the same time. Finally, develop a plan that both of you think is doable. Can you come up with a time of day and length of time that is mutually agreed upon? Commit to practicing together for three weeks. At the end of that period, have a discussion in which you decide if a joint practice is working for you.

For several weeks after beginning their practice, clients continue to have questions about the principles of centering prayer. These are some common questions that come up:

- How do I focus on God? That seems so vague to me.

- So many thoughts come up for me during centering prayer? What am I supposed to do about that?

- I get so restless when I'm sitting. How do I handle that?

- I'm not very good at this. How can I get better?

- What's the purpose of this anyway? What is supposed to happen?

I use the scheme suggested by Miller and Rollnick (2013) for exchanging information: elicit-provide-elicit (EPE). The first step is to elicit questions from your client. During follow-up sessions, you may ask your client:

- What kind of questions have come up for you about your centering prayer practice?

- Is there anything you are wondering about in regard to your practice?

- Is there any information that I can help you with?

The second step is to provide information. Remember to focus on what your clients want to know. Make sure that you address their questions. Try to use simple, everyday language. Give small amounts of information and then give your clients time to reflect. By asking your clients what they already know about the topic, you can avoid giving them unnecessary recommendations. Assure them that it is okay for them to disagree with you.

The final step is to elicit once again. Now you are checking back to inquire about your client's understanding, interpretation, or response to what you have just said. Using this approach, you investigate at regular intervals after sharing a small piece of information. There are many different ways to elicit at this point in the process. It may sound like this:

- Centering prayer is a prayer of intention. Does that make sense to you?

- Centering prayer is more about what God does and less about what you do. What do you make of that?

- Centering prayer is about opening up to God's presence. What words would you use to describe how this is for you?

- Centering prayer is a way of saying, "Here I am." The next step is up to God. I wonder what this means to you?

Some clients continue their routine while others ultimately discontinue their practice. For this second group, it is vital to honor what they have settled on. It may not be the right time for these clients. Your ability to accept their decisions will be important in maintaining a safe relationship with them. It is critical that they not feel judged or as if something is wrong with them if they don't practice. As always, we maintain the position that centering prayer is not for everyone.

Throughout the process of teaching centering prayer, we must maintain an attitude of love and humility. As Pennington (1999) says, "We know we cannot actually teach prayer. We can only show others how to open the space so the Holy Spirit can teach them" (p. 152). We always want to "teach" our clients in a spirit of love. This love allows clients the freedom to find an approach that is meaningful and doable for them. Pennington (1999) adds that we should always maintain "a radical freedom in regard to method" (p. 43).

INFORMAL CONTEMPLATIVE PRAYER

Is there another contemplative option for clients who choose not to practice formal contemplative prayer? Yes, and that choice is informal contemplation. *Informal* refers to the application of contemplative skills in everyday life. In mindfulness-informed models of counseling such as acceptance and commitment therapy (ACT) and dialectical behavior therapy (DBT), informal contemplative practices are a significant part of the treatment programs. So, in our Christian contemplative-oriented approach to counseling, we ought to consider this—that is, informal contemplative prayer—as an alternative for our clients.

Several examples of informal contemplative prayer are available for us. Undoubtedly, the best-known proponent of informal contemplative prayer is Brother Lawrence, a plain, humble Carmelite friar of the seventeenth century. Working as a lay brother at a monastery in Paris, France, he was assigned menial tasks, such as working in the kitchen and shoe-repair shop. In his little classic *The Practice of the Presence of God*, Brother Lawrence taught us how to remember God's presence in the midst of our daily activities. Formal times of prayer did not appeal to Brother Lawrence, but he found great joy in being aware of God's presence while engaged in his work. Brother Lawrence (1977) writes, "Even in the busiest times of my work, I banished and put away from my mind everything capable of diverting me from the thought of God" (p. 74).

Frank Laubach (1884–1970), a missionary in the Philippines, serves as another wonderful example of how to engage in informal contemplative prayer. Unlike Brother Lawrence, who practiced God's presence while cooking in the kitchen, Laubach used his interactions with others as a reminder to turn his attention to God. Laubach (2007) writes, "I must learn a continuous silent conversation heart to heart with God while looking into other eyes and listening to other voices" (p. 72). One of his "experiments" in informal contemplative prayer was to use the event of making eye contact with others as a reminder to be aware of God's presence. As he became more regular in bringing God back to his mind, Laubach (2007) noticed, "I feel like one who has had his violin out of tune with the orchestra and at last is in harmony with the music of the universe" (p. 10). (This quote reminds me of the quality of resonance that we discussed in chapter five.)

More currently, Christian psychologist Gary Moon teaches us that we can be aware of God's presence in the midst of daily tasks. Moon (2004) offers us several examples of events from the day that can be used as cues to direct our minds toward God. Every time we approach a red light or stop sign, we can remember that we are in God's presence. Taking a drink can prompt us to turn our inner gaze toward God. Getting out of bed every morning can be a reminder to shift our loving attention to God. As we develop these habits of returning to an awareness of God's presence, we are engaging in informal contemplative prayer.

CONTEMPLATIVE-INFORMED INTERVENTIONS

Engagement. Speaking of centering prayer, Pennington (1999) writes, "Christian prayer is love; it is a communication in love. It is the encounter between two free persons" (p. 43). Likewise, counseling is a relationship between two individuals. Every relationship begins with a period of engagement. Miller and Rollnick (2013) write, "Engaging is the process by which both parties establish a helpful connection" (p. 26). Without engagement, our clients are unlikely to fully enter into the counseling experience. Therefore, the skill of engagement is essential and becomes the foundation for everything that follows.

There are four common behaviors—or traps—that interfere with engaging (Miller & Rollnick, 2013). First, counselors can fall into the assessment trap. When this happens, the counselor and client take on certain roles. The counselor asks lots of questions while the client responds with short answers. The first pitfall has a direct link to the second one: the expert trap. Asking lots of questions sets up an expectation—that the counselor will provide the fix or answer after he or she has collected enough information. The third snare is the premature focus trap. The problem here is that we start trying to solve the presenting problem prior to actually forming a trusting, helping relationship with our client. The last behavior that can interfere with engaging is called the blaming trap. Looking for someone to blame for the problem can undermine our efforts to form a helpful connection.

By keeping three issues in mind, we have a better chance of engaging with our clients. First, we must keep our clients' goals in mind. Why are they coming to see us? What is it that they want out of counseling? Second, we must tune in to their expectations. In other words, how do they think we might be able to help? Finally, we must attempt to inspire a sense of hope. The client wants to know what you do and how it helps. By presenting a positive and honest picture of your ability to assist them, clients become encouraged about a brighter future. All these factors help form the connection we need to move forward with our clients.

Reflection. Engaging is a process, and a fundamental skill we rely upon during this phase is reflection. At the heart of reflection is the client's experience. What is the client encountering? What is the client's stance toward his or her circumstance? How does the client talk about what he or she is going through? How does the counselor reflect the client's experience? What are the different elements of the counselor's reflections? These are the questions that will guide our discussion in this section.

What are the different elements that make up what we call *experience*? An experience has physical, mental, emotional, and behavioral components. In my practice, my reflections focus on five specific areas: (1) the initial trigger, (2) the body sensation, (3) the emotion, (4) meaning making, and (5) action tendency (Johnson, 2004). The trigger refers to the event that sets all the other processes in motion. What was the threat? The body sensation refers to the physiological arousal that occurs once the client's threat response system is activated. What physical sensations did the client meet with? The threat response is accompanied by some emotion: anger, fear, surprise, shame, or another. What was the client feeling? The client is always trying to make sense out of the situation that triggered the threat response system. What did it mean to the client? And finally, the sense of danger sets off some automatic behavior in the client. We usually refer to this as fight-flight-freeze. What did the client do? Notice that the client's experience affects every dimension of human nature.

It is important to observe a client's stance toward an experience. There are two postures that clients take (Wallin, 2007). They can be *embedded* in their circumstances, or they can take a *reflective* stance toward them. An embedded frame of mind takes the elements of experience (e.g., cue, bodily sensations, emotion, and meaning making) and interprets them to be reality. There is only one view of the event, that is, our own. When a wife, from an embedded stance, says, "My husband doesn't like me," she is expressing this as a fact versus her interpretation of the facts, which might be wrong. When our clients are caught in this posture, they are on automatic and are constrained to habitual patterns of thinking, feeling, and doing.

There is another posture toward experience that we want to promote within the context of our contemplative approach to counseling, a reflective stance. In this frame of mind, we invite our clients to distance themselves from the incident so they can bring it into focus, see it clearly, and put it into words. From a reflective stance, our client might say, "I tell myself that my husband doesn't like me, but that might not be the case. At that moment, though, when he is raising his voice, it really feels that way." Once clients move from embeddedness to reflectiveness, there is the possibility that they can alter their thoughts and feelings about the situation and, then, their responses to the event.

We must be aware of how words are being employed in counseling because, with reflection, we are using language in a very specific way. Cozolino (2016) informs us that clients use three levels of language to talk about their experiences: reflexive, internal dialogue, and self-reflection. *Reflexive* language is as automatic as walking or breathing. We can employ this type of language without even thinking. The following interaction between two people illustrates reflexive language. The first person asks, "How are you?" The other person responds, "Fine. How are you?" The person who started the conversation then replies, "Fine. See you later." The interaction is so automatic that they both say "fine," even though something may be bothering one or both of them. At this level of language, the response is more like a motor reflex than a true expression of how the person feels.

The second level of language is called *internal dialogue*. This position refers to the conversations that go on in our heads. This private talk differs in content and tone from reflexive language. Unlike reflexive language, which can be kind, pleasant, and positive with others, internal dialogue can be harsh, critical, and negative toward self. Internal dialogue, which allows for private thoughts, is often driven by fear and shame.

There are other unique differences between reflexive language and internal dialogue. Reflexive language reveals how we have been taught to converse with others while internal dialogue reflects how we feel about ourselves. Reflexive language keeps us in line with the group while internal dialogue keeps us in line with the guidance that our parents instilled in us as children.

Without our help, our clients are prone to bounce back and forth between the first two dimensions of language, but we want to guide them to the third level: *reflective*. Reflection is a language of thoughtful consideration. Our clients move to this position when they can step back from their experiences and look at the flow of feelings, sensations, reactions, thoughts, and actions. At this level, our clients are able to think about their bodily, mental, emotional, and behavioral reactions. They slow down long enough to become consciously aware of their reactions and to put them into words.

Our goal with reflection is to guide our clients to the self-reflective level of language. At this plane, change begins to take shape. Reflexive language and internal dialogue are both habitual, and they simply maintain existing ways of feeling, thinking, and acting. On the other hand, reflective language creates an opportunity for flexibility—the ability to engage in new emotional, cognitive, and behavioral responses.

Tracking. A skill that goes hand in hand with reflection is tracking. Tracking could even be considered a component of reflection. Tracking is how we "stay with" what a client is experiencing, moment by moment (D. Siegel, 2010a).

Tracking has several important elements: (1) staying in the present, (2) assisting with awareness and expression, (3) noticing shifts, and (4) slowing down.

First, tracking involves communicating with clients about their experience in the here and now. Instead of capturing what a client experienced in the past, tracking is about this point in time. We are reflecting on our clients' emotions, narratives, and behavior in real time: "What are you sensing, feeling, thinking, and doing right now?" Tracking directs the client's attention to the experience that is happening at this moment: "Your facial expression just changed. What is happening?"

An amazing thing happens as clients become more aware of and able to express their experience: the incident unfolds or shifts in the moment. As we hold the event up to the light, as we slowly turn it around and examine it, a new experience emerges. For example, one of my clients was examining his fear that his wife might forget about him in the midst of a social situation. As we slowly examined and put his fear into words, something new came into his awareness: "I see that I get angry with her when I experience this fear. It is like I blame her when I become afraid." The experience was unfolding right in front of us in real time.

Hold and wait. Tracking has one more key characteristic. It is so important that we classify this element as a separate intervention. It is called "hold and wait" (Solomon & Tatkin, 2011). Tracking requires us to slow down the pace of counseling. Moving at a steady and deliberate tempo, we are able to observe subtle signals. Then we can reduce our speed even more to actually hold and examine our client's experience.

In order to track the client's experience, we must go slowly. Like animal trackers of old, we must proceed at an unhurried pace, attentive to the faint signs of footprints. It is as if the slow pace allows us to "hold" the client's experience long enough for it to be truly seen. We say to our client, "Let's pause here and notice what you are feeling. What is it like for you? Do you feel it in your body?"

If we don't move at a slow pace, we are sure to miss important signs. We want to assist our clients in noticing their own experiences. It is almost as if we invite them to be co-trackers: "Can you see that? Do you notice that sensation? Do you feel that? What are you noticing right now?" Tracking is about helping clients pay close attention to the details of their physical, mental, and behavioral tendencies. Then we invite them to put their experiences into words. Tracking allows a client to feel the experience, check it out, and explore it.

Silence. Silence is an important tool in counseling. Sometimes we guide the session to a resting place by inserting a pause in the session. Miller and Rollick (2013) call it a "pregnant pause" (p. 265). Perhaps the client has stopped talking, and we join them in their silence. At other times, we request silence by saying, "Can we just pause here for a second? This seems so important that I just want it to sink in." Silence gives us time to think about the client's experience.

Silence is a wonderful space between words. There are moments when we just need to take a break from talking. This pause gives us time to let the immediate experience sink in. Perhaps the client has just recognized a hidden emotion or memory from the past. There may be no reason to speak at this time. Maybe the client just needs to be seen.

As we pause in silence, the experience of counseling has time to sink in. There is no need to talk. There is no need to rush on. We are simply giving the client—and ourselves—time to reflect. Some counselors complain, "I don't have time for this." I agree with Miller and Rollnick (2013), who say, "If you don't have a lot of time, you can't afford not to do this" (p. 266). In other words, sometimes the fastest way to change is by taking pauses, by embracing silence.

Empathy. Another skill that supplements reflection is empathy. Accurate empathy requires the skill of reflection. And reflection without empathy is ineffective. Empathy is often viewed on a cognitive level, as a mental recognition of our client's situation or condition. However, when we move to the somato-affective level, empathy becomes an expression of sharing our clients' experiences. In real time, in addition to examining our clients' thoughts, we are also sharing in their sensory and emotional experiences (Solomon & Tatkin, 2011).

The word *empathy* comes from the German word *einfühlung*, which means "to feel into" (Johnson, 2004). When we are empathic at a somato-affective level, we are actually feeling in our bodies what our client is experiencing at an unconscious level (Fishbane, 2013). In this way, we can sense emotions that are just coming into a client's awareness. But as we track and reflect a client's experience, it comes into fuller awareness and expression.

As we move into this dimension of empathy, Mona Fishbane (2013) offers a couple of precautions. First, empathy involves self-regulation. We don't want to become so upset in the face of our client's pain that we fall into distress. Just imagine, what if your client is sharing a sad story, and you start sobbing? You have lost perspective and are caught up in your own reactions. This is not empathy, and it is not helping your client. We must be able to regulate our own emotions. Tearing up a bit in response to your client's story can be deeply meaningful for your client, but your empathy is being regulated.

Empathy also requires a healthy boundary between you and your client. This boundary between self and other is crucial to the process of empathy. We cannot open ourselves to the pain of others if we are going to get lost in the experience. We want to engage with our clients and share in their experience, but we must maintain healthy boundaries. These boundaries provide the safety that both we and our clients need in the context of counseling.

Several key ideas are being expressed by counselors as they employ the skill of empathy (Johnson, 2004). First, we are sending the message that we are open to their experience: "I want to slowly and carefully observe your experience." Second, accurate empathy communicates to clients that their experience makes sense: "It makes sense that you are feeling angry about that." (Now, of course it won't make sense to you if you have not clearly reflected the meaning-making part of the experience.) Next, we let clients know that we are willing to linger at, feel, and explore their experience until it makes sense. Finally, empathy sends the message that we are ready to help hold, support, and contain the sensations, emotions, and thoughts that come up for them during the conversation.

Empathy has a powerful effect on clients (Johnson, 2004). As the counselor accepts the client's experience—that is, doesn't judge it—the client tends to feel safe. In this environment, the client's fears begin to lessen. The client feels accepted, understood, and comforted. The client feels safe, seen, and acknowledged. With this assurance, clients can open up more to their own experiences. They can let down their defenses and explore what they are going through in greater detail. In this context, clients can begin to revise and reshape their experiences: "This sensation in my stomach is a sign of fear. Underneath my anger is a fear of not being good enough. Maybe the way I see my spouse is faulty. Perhaps I don't have to walk away when I feel that impulse."

Validation. Reflecting on what it is like to be this client, tracking his or her experience, and communicating empathy leads us to the next skill: *validation.* Through validation, we communicate to our clients that they are entitled to their experience: "No wonder your body is keyed up. This situation feels threatening to you. It makes sense that you get angry because this looks dangerous to you. Of course, you have an urge to go on the attack." Notice that validation is explicitly stated. Your statements reveal that you are deeply engaged with what your client is living through. Your clients cannot doubt that you are offering them acceptance.

Acceptance, in which validation is embedded, has a powerful impact on clients. Your acceptance assures them that they are in a safe place and that you are their ally. As a result, they can become more engaged in their own experience—noticing it, holding it in awareness for a while, and expressing it. Finally, they can move to a place of revision, expanding upon what they are encountering. In other words, maybe something else or something more is going on than meets the eye.

Evocative responding. It is clear by now that a client's experience is tentative, unclear, and emerging. As we reflect, track, empathize, and validate, new sensations, thoughts, and feelings begin to appear in real time. We witness experiences moving from *out of* clients' awareness *into* their awareness. We are working between the unconscious and consciousness as experiences move from one level to the next.

The skill we use for working with emerging aspects of our clients' experience is called *evocative responding* (Johnson, 2004). With evocative responding, we capture elements of the clients' experience that are just outside of their awareness. We do this by guiding them to the leading edge of what they are going through, to that experience that is just barely inside their awareness. We are not discussing old, habitual ways of responding to and making sense of a situation. Instead, we are at the edge of a new experience. And then we take our clients one step further. We immerse them a little more in the leading edge of what they are encountering. Through the use of several means—slowing down, using imagery, using their words, repeating their words—we make the experience a little more intense. As the sensation or emotion becomes a little more profound, new elements of the circumstance begin to arise. Clients becomes even more engaged in the present moment.

And, as they do so, their experience is expanded. That which was once unknown can now be connected to conscious awareness. Happenings that were once in the dark can now be included in their narratives.

Reflection, combined with tracking, empathy, validation, and evocative responding, becomes a powerful force for a client. Over time, clients feel safe. They think that you can be trusted. Their anxiety diminishes. They become more open to their own experiences, and their self-awareness is expanded. As Miller and Rollnick (2013) observe, "Healing is not primarily a process of dispensing expertise. The opportunity to follow and reflect on one's experience is valuable" (p. 49). As we employ the skills of reflection, our clients feel secure enough to keep going. They move from a habitual set of experiences to an expanded set of experiences.

Proactive loving. By employing the skills that we have been identifying in this section, we further our objective to increase our clients' awareness of their habitual patterns of responses. Coming to our last intervention, it is now time to focus upon one particular aspect of our clients' experience—action. With empathy and validation, we help them see and acknowledge their automatic behavioral reactions. Then we assist them in building the skills of *proactive loving* (Fishbane, 2013)

What is proactive loving? It is about taking responsibility for one's interactional patterns. Proactive loving requires a willingness to make thoughtful choices and a commitment to change. Clients get to this place first by becoming aware of their reactions and then by taking responsibility for the way they treat themselves, others, and God.

Once clients are more aware of their habitual behaviors, what will they do? Our job is to help them step back and think through their options and to finally promote choices that will help them create the kind of loving relationships—with self, others, and God—that they really want. Love is an active, not a passive, verb. Instead of being reactive, we want our clients to be proactive in their loving.

The skill of proactive loving puts the focus on our clients: "What are *you* doing? How do *you* want to change your behavior?" With the awareness they have gained of their automatic responses, we help our clients map out a different set of actions. And then we support them as they risk taking desired steps. Of course there will be setbacks, but they will continue to refine the ways they interact with themselves, others, and God.

As we promote proactive loving by our clients, we continue to employ the other core skills. We continue to reflect with them upon the sensations, thoughts, and emotions they experience as they attempt to reach out in love. We track, hold, pause, empathize, and validate. All our interventions— and our way of being—help them feel protected. In a context of acceptance and safety, we continue to assist our clients as they build more loving ways of behaving.

THE RELATIONSHIP BETWEEN CENTERING PRAYER AND CORE SKILLS

It is no accident that these eleven techniques show up within our contemplative-oriented approach to counseling. Rather, these core skills are embedded in the principles and practices of centering prayer. Engaging in the practice of centering prayer leads us and our clients directly to the basic interventions of this model. In this section, we will briefly show the connection between the practice of centering prayer and our key skills.

Engagement. At the heart of contemplative prayer is the conviction that we are in a relationship with God. And in this relationship, we are sharing our experience with God while God is sharing his experience with us. These encounters may not be expressed with words, but they are nevertheless communicated. Contemplative prayer is about forming a connection with God. Everything else is built upon this foundational assumption.

Exchanging information. In contemplative prayer, God is teaching us something. He is teaching us about transformation. Instead of it being something that we work at, it is something that we receive. As Foster (1992) says, "The primary purpose of prayer is to bring us into such a life of communion with the Father that, by the power of the Spirit, we are increasingly conformed to the image of the Son. The process is transformation" (p. 57). The end result of contemplative prayer is transformation of character.

Reflection. Centering prayer is an experience—our own. I remember the day I had a difficult discussion with my doctor about my eyes. She informed me that I was probably going to lose vision in my right eye. (Future tests disproved this initial prognosis.) The next day, as I sat down to pray, I was overwhelmed with fear. It was terrifying to think that I might become blind in my right eye! That morning, I could feel the heaviness in my chest. I could feel that sick feeling in the pit of my stomach. I tried to imagine what it would mean to live with vision in only one eye.

All these experiences accompanied me into my prayer room. The trigger was the danger of losing my eyesight. The emotion was one of fear. The physical sensations were heaviness of heart and an ache in my stomach. My mental efforts to make sense out of how this would alter my life were meaning making. My time of centering prayer was not devoid of these experiences. Instead, these experiences were right at the core of my prayer.

What was I to do with these experiences? I didn't want to push them away and repress them. Neither did I want them to be the center of my attention because this was my twenty minutes to focus on God. Therefore, I set about letting go of these experiences each time one would arise. The fear emerged, and I turned to my sacred word in order to affirm my intention to be open to God. When I became aware of uncomfortable sensations in my body, I shifted my attention to God. As thoughts captured my attention, I used my word again to gently turn my attention back to God.

Centering prayer is a time of dealing with the five elements of experience. This morning, as I sat with God for twenty minutes, I heard the screeching of hawks in the trees behind my house. (These hawks, as they perch in the trees in my backyard, are a beautiful sight.) In reaction to their sound, I automatically started to get off the sofa in order to view these magnificent creatures. Then I caught the urge, the action tendency. I remembered: *No, I'm here to be with God for these twenty minutes.* Using my sacred word, I sank back into the sofa, turning my attention away from the experience that had momentarily captured my interest.

Tracking. In centering prayer, we pay attention to the experience—a sensation, an urge, an emotion, a narrative—that appears at that moment. We notice it, and we might even label it: "This is an urge to scratch my nose." "This is a worry." "This is planning." But, using our sacred word, we let go of the experience as we return our attention to God.

Hold and wait. Centering prayer requires a willingness to take a break from the normal activities of the day. In this practice, we determine that it is a good thing to push the pause button. Peter Kreeft (2000) observes, "Prayer is like a railroad crossing" (p. 31). We need to stop, look, and listen. Centering prayer begins by stopping. We must stop everything else we are doing.

Silence. Richard Foster (1992) says that contemplative prayer is "progress toward silence" (p. 155). In centering prayer, we enter into a wonderful form of communication that takes place beneath words. We discover the beauty of taking a break from talking. We find that there is a wonderful place between words called silence.

Empathy. When we enroll in the school of contemplative prayer, we learn about empathy. During our twenty minutes of centering prayer, we attend to our feelings. We not only recognize them on a cognitive level—"this is anxiety"—but we are also aware of them on a somato-affective level. In centering prayer, we learn to welcome our emotions. We don't judge them, resist them, or react to them. Instead, we gently return to our sacred word, letting our emotions go.

Validation. In contemplative prayer, we learn not only to empathize with our own experience but to validate it: "Of course you are having physical sensations, feelings, and thoughts. That only makes sense. You have slowed down enough for these experiences to rush in. You are not distracting yourself so of course they are going to come to the forefront of your mind." So, within validation, there is no judgment of the experiences that emerge during our times of silent prayer. There is only a gentle acceptance.

Evocative responding. During centering prayer our experiences are oftentimes heightened. Contemplative prayer has been described as effortless—God's Spirit is doing the real work—but it is not about doing nothing. Instead of being passive, we are actually doing some things: sitting erect, noticing the emergence of thoughts, returning to the sacred word, consenting to the action of God, and so on. And all these actions can sometimes have the effect of bringing new experiences to conscious awareness. Is this a bad thing? No, this is simply an unloading of our unconscious.

Proactive loving. In contemplative prayer, we settle into the fundamental character of the relationship between self and God: love. Love is at the center of centering prayer, and love is not passive. We discover that love is active. Centering prayer is about opening up to both the presence and the action of God. As we sit in silence, God's love is activated in our lives. We may not feel it at the moment, but we receive the gift of God's love by faith.

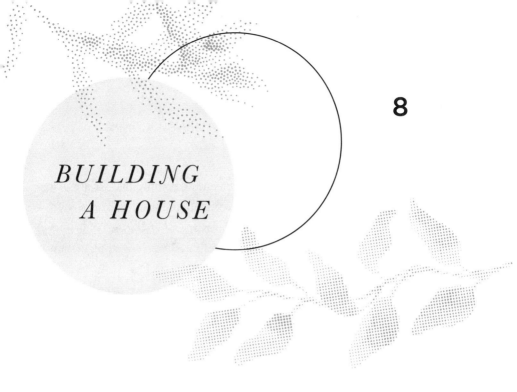

BUILDING
A HOUSE

WE HAVE BEEN describing an approach to counseling that is rooted and grounded in Christian contemplation. Combining the insights of three domains—science, theology, and Christian contemplation—we have explored the three building blocks of theory building: (1) understanding the client's situation—that is, case conceptualization; (2) establishing a helping relationship; and (3) utilizing effective interventions for accomplishing the goals of treatment. After probing these components of counseling theory, we are still left with an important question: What is the treatment process? This topic gets at the steps that can be used for promoting the change we desire. The purpose of this chapter is to address this question.

Adopting a metaphor used by John Gottman (2011), our approach to treatment can be compared to building a house. Our dwelling place has four levels: (1) making a connection, (2) reaching inward, (3) moving out, and (4) integration. When looking at an edifice, we may find it easy to overlook an important part of the building—the substructure. Therefore, we will begin our description of the change process by identifying the nine principles of which our foundation is composed.

FOUNDATIONAL PRINCIPLES

To be a sound structure, a house must have strong base. The foundation of our new paradigm is composed of the following nine elements, all of which are rooted in Christian contemplation.

Relationship. Contemplative prayer rests on the premise that we are in a relationship with God. Contemplative prayer is about forming a connection with God. Likewise, counseling is about another kind of engagement—one between counselor and client. This relationship is characterized by certain essential qualities.

Presence. God's presence is the bedrock of contemplative practice. Contemplative prayer is about consenting or opening up to "God's presence and action within" (Keating, 1999, p. 139). "In contemplation, we just sit. God's Spirit is present. We are present" (Wilhoit & Howard, 2012, p. 124). And, what do we do in God's presence? Tom Schwanda (2014) answers by telling us that contemplation is a "willingness to wait and rest in God's presence" (p. 68). We are simply resting in God's embrace. In the context of counseling, the client is supported by the counselor's presence. Daniel Siegel (2010a) argues that the counselor's presence is "the most important element of helping others heal" (p. 1).

Present moment. When we come into God's presence, we do so in the here and now. As Christian philosopher Peter Kreeft (1989) reminds us, "God lives in the present and enters the present only" (p. 135). In counseling, we prioritize the present moment. What is happening in the room right now? That is the time in which we reside.

Attentiveness. "Christian contemplative prayer is attending to the presence of the Spirit of Christ" (Coe, 2014, p. 151). Evan Howard (2008) adds, "Without attention there is no prayer" (p. 311). With attentiveness, we focus our minds and hearts on God. It is a loving kind of consideration. And when our concentration wanders, we learn to catch it and lead it back again to its target: God. It is the same in counseling. We learn to be attentive and attuned to the present moment that we are sharing with our clients.

Experience. Basil Pennington (1999) teaches us that centering prayer is "an experiential prayer. The teaching will mean nothing until the experience is had" (p. 176). Contemplation is "something we experience" (Wilhoit &

Howard, 2012, p. 112). In the same manner, a key to this model is the counselor's emphasis on the client's experience.

Silence. For Richard Foster (1992), contemplative prayer is "progress toward silence" (p. 155). Peter Kreeft (2000) adds that contemplative prayer is the "practice of God's presence without words" (p. 28). Silence is about the scarcity of words. It is about opening up to other levels of communication. In our model of counseling, we assist clients in finding language for expressing what they are going through. However, we also invite them into areas of their experience that are beyond words. We introduce them to stillness and silence so they can notice the nonverbal messages of their bodies.

Openness. In contemplative prayer, we open ourselves to God's presence. Contemplative prayer is about unlocking the door of our life, inviting God in (see Rev 3:20). Openness is about being receptive, that is, receiving the present experience of contemplative prayer. The event may not be what we anticipated or even desired, but we trust that God is at work at some unseen level. In this model of counseling, we emphasize the counselor's willingness to accept the present-moment experience: What am I experiencing now? What is my client experiencing now? We open the door to receiving what the clients are going through while at the same time maintaining a healthy boundary. We don't want to get lost in their process. In a spirit of openness, we fluctuate between words and silence. Daniel Siegel (2010a) reminds us, "Being open may require we let go of the tendency of words to dominate our present awareness" (p. 106).

Acceptance. Contemplative prayer is training in acceptance. It is humbling in contemplative prayer to discover how quickly and often the attention of our minds and hearts wanders away from God. But an important element of concentration is learning how to bring it back to its target: God. And, as we relocate our attention, we learn to do so with gentle acceptance. As Thomas Keating (1999) instructs us, "When you become aware of thoughts, return ever-so-gently to the sacred word" (p. 139). From a counseling perspective, acceptance concerns itself with receiving things as they are right now. Acceptance is about not having to change, remove, or judge the here-and-now experience of the client. It is about welcoming the client's sensations, thoughts, and emotions at this present moment.

Integration. The famous Puritan, Richard Baxter (1615–1691), is quoted as saying that contemplation "opens the door between the head and the heart"

(Beck & Demarest, 2005, p. 250). In contemplative prayer, the different dimensions—head, heart, body, and soul—are integrated with one another. Contemplative prayer unites the various components of the human person. Likewise, integration is a key objective of our approach to counseling. As Goldstein and Siegel (2017) point out, "Integration is the basis of health" (p. 280). With integration, we bring together elements that are often disconnected or omitted from counseling. We connect words and silence. We integrate the body, mind, and heart. We coordinate conscious and unconscious processes.

Upon a firm foundation composed of these solid principles, we begin building the four levels of our house.

STAGE ONE: MAKING A CONNECTION

Client's process. Regardless of the problem with which our clients present, our way of working equips us with the knowledge that there are primary concerns just below the surface. The two issues that we want to address at stage one are (1) an activated threat response system and (2) fear. We assume that our clients' threat response system is on high alert because of fear. They are detecting real or perceived threats to their well-being. As a result, we assume that the clients' bodies, minds, emotions, and behavior have been hijacked by this threat-generated fear. If a client's autonomic system is activated, he or she may appear anxious and overly talkative. On the other hand, if the threat response system has deactivated the autonomic system, the client will appear lethargic, quiet, and reserved.

We assume that our clients are on high alert because they do not feel safe within the framework of their primary relationships. Perhaps they are feeling misunderstood, unwanted, and in danger within the context of their relationship with others. They may be feeling very alone. Not only do they feel that others have an adverse view of them, but they may be experiencing a negative perspective of themselves. They may be feeling that they are not good enough, that they are deeply flawed.

The counselor's objectives. During stage one, the counselor has three main goals:

- To generate a connection with the client.
- To create an environment of safety for the client.

- To help regulate the client's affect.

Therapeutic relationship. In our approach—and in stage one—we emphasize seven qualities of the counselor. These traits are (1) presence, (2) openness, (3) attention, (4) acceptance, (5) compassion, (6) resonance, and (7) love. These attributes are not so much about what the counselor does as they are about the counselor's way of being. Cozolino and Davis (2017) remind us, "Sometimes the best thing to do, especially at first, is to do nothing" (p. 61). Our way of being with the client is key to accomplishing the goals of stage one. As we demonstrate these qualities through our actions, clients begin to calm down, experience safety, and feel a connection with us.

Therapeutic interventions. The primary interventions used in stage one are as follows: (1) engagement, (2) reflection, (3) validation, (4) hold and wait, (5) silence, and (6) teaching contemplative prayer.

1. Engagement. As Miller and Rollnick (2013) write, "Engaging is the process by which two parties establish a helpful connection" (p. 26). Without engagement, the client will not fully enter into the counseling experience. Everything else builds upon this intervention. To engage effectively with our clients, Miller and Rollnick (2013) suggest that we explore the following questions: Why is the client coming to see you? What does the client want out of counseling? How does the client think you might be able to help? What is the client hoping that you will be able to help him or her accomplish?

In the process of engaging with our clients, we must avoid certain pitfalls. First, we must abstain from an assessment that takes the form of questions by the counselor and answers by the client. In my practice, I make use of an intake form in order to gather this type of information, but the client fills out this form before the initial session. Second, we must avoid sending our clients the message that we are trying to fix them or solve their presenting problem in the first session. This is premature. Establishing a connection is our first order of business.

2. Reflection. With this skill, we communicate that we are following and understanding what they are going through—their thoughts, feelings, and behavior. In stage one, clients are typically embedded in their experience. This means that they have only one view of what is happening—their own. They even suppose that they have an accurate view of their situation. They have not yet learned the difference between reality and perceptions. Typically, clients are also focused on events and behaviors. With the skill of reflection, we communicate that we are following their view of the situation and interactions. Our reflections are often about surface behaviors because this may be all that a client can focus on at this stage of therapy. However, we want to avoid the trap of trying to change or alter a client's behavior at this point in therapy because this would be premature.

3. *Validation.* A key intervention in stage one is validation. Through validation, we communicate to our clients that they are entitled to their experience. Validation is embedded in acceptance, which is the opposite of judgment and blame. We send the message that their behavior makes sense in light of how they are feeling about the event and making sense of the situation. We assume that they are doing the best they can at this moment in time.

4. *Hold and wait.* We teach our clients that counseling is most effective when we proceed at a slow pace. Too often we move at a speed that is too fast for our minds to process—for both counselor and client. Therefore, we must "hold" the conversation long enough for its contents to be held to the light and seen.

5. *Silence.* There are times when we insert pauses into the session. This space between words is called silence. In silence, we take breaks from talking. Silence allows time for the experience of counseling to sink in. Taking a recess from words is helpful when our clients are experiencing either high or low autonomic arousal. Pat Ogden and Janina Fisher (2015) recommend grounding as a valuable tool when clients are struggling with either hyper- or hypo-arousal. Grounding is the physical process of being aware of our legs and feet and their connection to the ground or floor. We might say to clients, "Can you press your feet against the floor? Can you stomp your feet on the floor to sense your legs?" For clients who are feeling overwhelmed, off balance, or "knocked off their feet," this silent physical experience can settle their nerves and help restore a degree of calmness.

6. *Teaching contemplative prayer.* In chapter seven, we spelled out the steps for teaching contemplative prayer: (1) determining readiness, (2) teaching centering prayer, and (3) follow-up. After determining that a client is a good candidate for contemplative prayer, I summarize the key elements of centering prayer, providing the information in small doses. Dividing the knowledge into

bits and pieces, I check in with clients, seeing if they understand and responding to any questions they might have.

After offering the client some information, I take time to practice centering prayer together with my client for three to five minutes. Remember, this is an experiential prayer. Teaching is useless if the client doesn't have the experience. After having the brief experience, I take time to debrief with my client: "How did that go? Do you have any questions?" We then take time to develop a plan for the client to follow at home.

The clients' own practice of contemplative prayer is important to the treatment process for several reasons. Through their own experience, they learn about (1) the importance of body posture; (2) how the mind is distracted by physical sensations; (3) the internal workings of the mind—that is, thoughts and emotions; (4) how to return attention to God with acceptance; (5) how to be at home in the body; (6) staying in the present moment; and (7) being open to and resting in God's presence. All these lessons become valuable tools for the work that lies ahead.

Transition. There are important signs that indicate it is time to transition into stage two. First, we notice that clients are putting their trust in us. They are becoming more engaged in the treatment process. Next, as a result of their sense of safety, they are beginning to open up about more issues. Third, we can tell that they are becoming more regulated in their affect. The client who was initially deactivated is becoming more talkative and displaying more energy. On the other hand, the activated client is beginning to relax and is less talkative. Finally, the client is becoming interested in mental experiences that are beneath the surface behaviors. We are now determining that it is time to move on to stage two. As we do so, we don't dismiss the strategies and goals of stage one. Instead, we are simply adding another level or floor to our house.

CASE ILLUSTRATION: ALLEN, PART ONE

Before proceeding to the next stage, I will begin sharing the true story of my work with Allen, with his permission. I hope that his case and excerpts from our sessions will open a window for you to view into our contemplative-oriented model of counseling.

Allen came to see me at the age of thirty-eight. He was married with two children, an older adolescent daughter and an eleven-year-old son. At the age of twenty, after completing two years of college, Allen had discontinued his education in order to become a firefighter. He married at the age of twenty-seven. After getting married, Allen became active in his church, serving as the youth and young adult pastor.

Referred to me by his family doctor, Allen was suffering from chronic anxiety and uncontrollable high blood pressure. His symptoms first appeared after the death of his paternal grandfather and Allen's own gallbladder surgery. These two significant events occurred in the same month, three years before Allen made his first appointment to see me. During these three years, his symptoms had gotten progressively worse. By the time Allen came in, he was taking four blood pressure medications, but his blood pressure was still not under control.

The loss of his grandfather and Allen's own health problems destabilized Allen's life. His grandfather was the one person that Allen confided in and from whom he sought counsel. Without him, Allen had no one to turn to for advice. Allen was reluctant to confide in his wife, telling me, "I don't want to stress her out." It took the doctors three months to correctly diagnose Allen's gallbladder problem. During that time, he became extremely ill, almost dying.

After his grandfather's death and his own close encounter with death, Allen became preoccupied with and spent more and more time ruminating about his own death. In his profession as a firefighter, Allen had witnessed many deaths, some the result of heart attacks and strokes caused by high blood pressure. "If they died from high blood pressure, then so could I," Allen lamented in one of our early sessions.

I worked with Allen over a period of fourteen months. For the first ten months of counseling, we met an average of two times per month. For the last four months of treatment, our sessions were at one-month intervals. Even though I had twenty-four sessions with Allen, I have included excerpts from only sixteen sessions. Instead of providing all these selections at one time, I have divided them into four sections. The first set of excerpts will be offered first to illustrate the issues, tasks, and interventions of stage one. After our discussion of stage two, I will offer another set of excerpts to illustrate stage two. I will follow the same approach for stages three and four.

EXCERPTS FROM STAGE ONE WITH ALLEN.
SESSION ONE

Gregg: What brings you in to see me?

Allen: I am having health problems due to anxiety and stress in my life. My biggest health issue is high blood pressure.

Gregg: It makes sense that you are concerned about your health. I understand your desire to get your blood pressure under control.

(This response illustrates both reflection and validation.)

Gregg: How do you think I might be able to help, and what do you hope that we can accomplish together?

(This is an example of engagement.)

Allen: The main reason I came to see you was because my doctor told me that you are a Christian. I'm a Christian, and I was selective in who I was willing to see. I am hoping that the Lord might be able to do something through you that might help me handle my stress and anxiety.

Gregg: I can tell that your relationship with the Lord is important. With the Lord's help, I hope that some wonderful changes can happen with your health and in your life.

Gregg: Do you have other concerns?

(More of engagement.)

Allen: I'm worried about how I'm becoming an angry person. I've noticed in the past two months that I'm getting snappy, harsh, and even mean with my wife, son, and daughter. I'm afraid of crossing that line and hurting someone.

Gregg: I can tell that worries you. It makes sense that anxiety can lead to anger, but you don't want to do something that you would later regret.

(Again, this illustrates a combination of reflection and validation.)

SESSION TWO

Allen: It seems like anxiety is in control of my life. I find myself sitting for hours on end, just worrying about problems. The biggest thing I worry about is dying. I'm really afraid of dying.

Gregg: I really appreciate your willingness to talk about your fears. It makes sense that you don't like how anxiety is bothering you.

(An example of both reflection and validation.)

Gregg: Do you feel the anxiety or stress right now in your body?

(This illustrates my attempt to bring the session into the present moment and to explore nonverbal messages.)

Allen: Yeah, I can really feel it in my shoulders.

Gregg: Can you do something for me? Can you try to make your shoulders even tighter? And then release the tension. Do it again. Do you feel that?

(While I wait for Allen to increase and reduce muscular tension, I am employing the use of silence.)

Allen: Yeah, I can tell the difference.

Gregg: Can you do something else? Can you just feel your body sitting on the sofa? Notice the pressure points where your arms touch the sofa, where your back rests against the sofa, and where your legs hit the sofa. Can you notice that?

(This illustrates the use of hold and wait.)

Allen: Yes.

SESSION THREE

Gregg: I remember you telling me in our first session that you are a Christian. Can you tell me about your relationship with God?

(This is my first attempt to explore Allen's relationship with God.)

Allen: My relationship with God is extremely important. However, I haven't felt as close to him lately. I would really like to feel closer to him.

Gregg: Would you mind telling me about your religious practices?

Allen: Well, going to church is important. Also, praying is very important.

Gregg: Have you ever heard of a type of prayer called contemplative prayer?

(An example of determining his readiness for contemplative prayer.)

Allen: No, can't say that I have.

Gregg: Would you mind if I told you a little about it?

Allen: No, not at all.

Gregg: Well, contemplative prayer is praying without words. We just sit in God's presence, glad to be hanging out with him. We aren't looking for anything other than to be with God. Even though relaxation is not the purpose, many people find that it is a wonderful byproduct of contemplative prayer.

Allen: Sounds interesting.

Gregg: Would you be interested in practicing for a few minutes right now? I will practice along with you.

Allen: Okay.

Gregg: (I hand Allen the four guidelines for centering prayer and then take a few moments to explain the procedure. After asking him if he has any questions, we sit together for five minutes.) How did that go?

(Example of teaching centering prayer.)

Allen: Good. My mind was wandering for most of the time though.

Gregg: That's okay. Were you able to use your sacred word to let go of thoughts?

Allen: I think so.

Gregg: Would you be interested in practicing some at home?

Allen: Yes. I think the morning would be the best time for me to try it.

Gregg: The biggest problem is finding time. What is your typical morning like?

Allen: My mornings are hectic. I get up like a ball shot out of a cannon. I am up and out of the house in fifteen minutes. I think the way I start out the day is part of my problem. Maybe I could get up an hour before leaving and do this prayer for ten to twenty minutes.

Gregg: Sounds good. Give it a try.

SESSION FOUR

Gregg: How did your prayer time go?

(This illustrates follow-up.)

Allen: I did it five mornings this week. I call it God-and-me-time. My biggest problem, though, was that my mind kept drifting away. Is that normal?

Gregg: I like that name: God-and-me-time. Yes, everyone's mind wanders when they practice contemplative prayer. The key is to just keep letting go of thoughts, remembering that you are just spending time with God.

Gregg: Did you notice anything else this week?

Allen: Yeah, it felt comforting to think about God being with me. When I was praying, it was like I wasn't alone with my worries. I told myself that it wasn't the time or the place to worry. I thought that it was just time to be with God, so I was able to let go of my worries for a little while.

SESSION FIVE

Gregg: Are you aware that you are talking faster today than normal? What's happening inside?

(This illustrates hold and wait.)

Allen: The best way to put it is that my mind and body are having a cramp.

Gregg: That's a great image you just gave me. Can we slow down and look at that some? A cramp. Can you help me understand what you mean by that?

(More of hold and wait.)

Allen: Yeah, it's like I feel so tight inside. I feel like I have a lot of pent-up energy. It feels out of control, like I can't control it.

Gregg: It's like all this energy wants to come out, but you don't know what to do with it. Is that right?

(Example of reflection.)

Allen: Yep.

Gregg: What's been going on today?

Allen: I got into another argument with my daughter today. I confronted her with a bad decision she had made, but she didn't want to listen. She got so angry. It went badly, like I thought it would.

Gregg: You want the best for your daughter, but you are afraid that talking to her isn't helping. And when it doesn't go well, you get real upset. Is that right?

(This is reflection.)

Allen: Yeah.

Gregg: Will you do something for me? Put both of your feet on the floor. Can you notice how it feels for your feet to rest on the floor? Can you feel the pressure points? Wiggle your toes a little inside your shoes. Just take a few moments to really pay attention to your feet.

(This illustrates a combination of silence and wait & hold.)

Gregg: I think it was great that we talked about how arguments with your daughter set off a lot of anxiety. I wonder if you could be curious about and look for other things that set off or trigger anxiety?

Allen: I'll do that.

STAGE TWO: REACHING INWARD

Client's process. The primary issues we want to address in stage two are avoidance, shame, and hidden functions. (These underlying issues were discussed in depth in chapter four.) Since most clients are dealing with feelings of shame, they are worried about what the counselor thinks about them. Due to their fear that the counselor will discover the things that clients believe about themselves ("I am dumb, bad, not good enough," etc.), clients are hesitant to share their inner processes with the counselor.

Clients coming for counseling often have had few, if any, opportunities to engage in self-reflective conversations. They have had little experience with noticing their thoughts, emotions, and physical sensations. Dan Hughes (2017) observes, "They are reluctant to turn their gaze toward qualities that they assume are inadequate, bad, or unlovable" (p. 170). Perhaps they have never been in a situation where a significant person shows interest in their thoughts, feelings, and wishes. Whether it is from lack of opportunities or deep feelings of shame, clients may have lost curiosity about their internal experiences.

Clients who come for treatment have often developed a pattern of avoidance. They have learned to steer clear of conversations about their inner lives. Talking about their feelings of loneliness, inadequacy, fear, and anger may not feel safe to explore. They evade by getting distracted, asking an endless series of questions, remaining quiet, disagreeing, or simply not listening. They come to counseling with the belief that they must hide their experiences.

Finally, clients are typically unaware of the unconscious processes that are behind most of their physical, cognitive, emotional, and behavioral functions. They assume that they can accurately capture their thoughts, emotions, and behaviors in words. Unbeknownst to them, there is a world of visceral reactions, emotions, memories, and intuitions going on outside of their awareness. Many of these hidden functions express themselves in quick, automatic reactions—bodily sensations, strong emotions, and impulses to act—that show up during the session but are unseen by the client.

The counselor's objectives. During stage two, the counselor adds four new goals. The counselor wants to help the client become:

- Curious about and able to talk about their internal world.

- Aware of messages being expressed by their body.

- Vulnerable and willing to talk about their perceived failings and shortcomings.

- Willing to work at the edges of their conscious experiences.

Therapeutic relationship. In stage two, we remind ourselves that it isn't so much what we do, but who we are, that brings healing to our clients. Goldstein and Siegel (2017) use a catchy acronym PART—presence, attunement, resonance, trust—to remind us of the fundamental stance that we take in counseling. Presence is about an openness that we have to our client's experiences, a receptivity that filters out our expectations and judgments. Attunement refers to our attention to the client's internal world, the thoughts, feelings, and sensations that drive their external visible actions. Resonance is about allowing ourselves to enter into the experiences of our clients without losing our own sense of self. Trust is what the client feels as a result of our qualities of presence, attunement, and resonance. (These qualities are discussed in great detail in chapter five.)

Daniel Siegel (2010a) uses another acronym, COAL—curiosity, openness, acceptance, love—to capture the manner in which we approach our clients' experiences. We are familiar with the elements of openness and acceptance, but what about curiosity? Hughes (2017) offers a useful description of curiosity. It is about the release of assumptions, evaluations, and shaming. Every experience by the client is met with acceptance. Thoughts and feelings are not judged as right or wrong. Hughes (2007) also states that certain behaviors may not be welcomed—especially the ones that threaten the safety of the client and others—but the thoughts and feelings that led to these behaviors are always admitted. Finally, curiosity conveys our deep fascination with our client's internal world. It conveys a wide-eyed desire to know the client. When the counselor demonstrates curiosity, along with openness and acceptance, the client experiences love.

Therapeutic interventions. The primary interventions used in stage two are as follows: (1) reflections, (2) tracking, (3) empathy, and (4) evocative responding.

Reflections. At the heart of reflection is the client's experience. Reflections focus on five areas of the client's experience: (1) the initial trigger, (2) the body sensation, (3) the emotion, (4) meaning making, and (5) action tendency. Our aim with this intervention is to teach the client a new language, one that is called reflective. At this level, our clients are slowing down enough to direct their attention to their bodily sensations, thoughts, and feelings. They are now exploring their own nonverbal messages and minds in ways that were previously unavailable to them. We offer reflections to help clients recognize and gain awareness of processes that were previously avoided.

Tracking. Tracking is a component of reflection. Tracking is how we "stay with" our client's experience. Tracking focuses on the present moment. When we reflect what the client is sensing, feeling, thinking, and doing right now, we are tracking. We say things like, "What is happening now? I see the expression on your face changing. Can you help me understand what is happening? How does that feel in your body right now? When you say that, does a new thought or feeling show up?" Slowing down and staying with what the client is going through allows the experience to evolve into something new, which emerges right in front of us.

Empathy. Empathy occurs on two planes. The first is cognitive: intellectually understanding what the clients are expressing with words. However, we believe that the somato-affective level of empathy is necessary. At this dimension of empathy, we are sharing in our clients' sensory and emotional experience. We are fully open to our clients and experiencing their worlds along with them. Hughes (2017) describes empathy as our ability to be touched by the client and his or her world. Rather than being a detached observer of our clients, we allow ourselves to enter into what the clients are experiencing. Fishbane (2013) reminds us to remain emotionally regulated and to maintain healthy boundaries even as we enter into this somato-affective level of empathy.

Evocative responding. As we hold our client's present circumstance up to the light, it turns into something else. The technique we use for working with the emerging aspects of a client's experience is called evocative responding. With this skill, we lead our clients to the edge of their awareness, to something that is just barely inside their awareness. Our responses might be: "Did you notice your voice get shaky as you were just saying that? What do you think that means? When your voice gets shaky, what emotion are you feeling? As you talk about being angry, what physical sensations are you aware of?" As we immerse them a little more in the happenings of the present moment, what they are going through becomes a little more intense, and, as this happens, new elements of the experience begin to appear. It is as if the experience is moving from the darkness into the light.

This transition from darkness to light is another way of saying that that which was unconscious—or hidden—is becoming conscious. Using a captivating metaphor, Peter Levine (2017) describes less conscious states as "glowing embers" (p. 134). Having a wood stove, I am familiar with this image. Sometimes when my fire is on the verge of extinction, I puff vigorously on the remaining red cinders. Exposed to increased air, the burning coals begin to pulsate; then they quickly catch fire. Evocative responding is like blowing on the glowing embers of the unconscious until it bursts into flame—or into full view.

Transition. How do we know when it is time to go to the next floor of our treatment process? We are looking for certain signs. At the beginning of stage two, our clients were guarded in the way in which they discussed their experiences. They seemed to lack curiosity in, and even avoided, talking about their internal world. They seemed embedded in their circumstances and lacked the ability to explore present-moment experiences.

By the end of stage two, we notice that a shift has occurred. They are now curious and interested in exploring their inner world. Having developed the ability to reflect on what they are going through as it is happening, they are now more willing to work at the edges of their conscious experiences. They are able to express thoughts and feelings that they were once too afraid to verbalize. They have discovered that important messages are being spoken beneath the words, through their bodies. They are now willing to be seen and known by us. We are now prepared to move on to stage three. We don't forget about the methods and practices that we employed at stages one and two. No, we are simply enlarging our approach.

CASE ILLUSTRATION: ALLEN, PART TWO

Before moving on to stage three, let's check in with Allen's progress in stage two.

EXCERPTS FROM STAGE TWO WITH ALLEN.
SESSION EIGHT

Gregg: Since our last session, have you noticed anything that triggers the anxiety?

Allen: Yes, getting a call at work sets if off almost every time.

Gregg: What's a call?

Allen: A call is when we get called out to a location because of a problem like a fire or injury.

Gregg: So the thing that sets off the anxiety is getting the call. Right?

(This is a reflection of the trigger.)

Allen: That's right.

Gregg: Are you aware of the thoughts that get activated when you receive the call?

Allen: Yeah, the thought is, *This is going to be bad! Someone is going to die or be hurt. It won't turn out good.*

Gregg: I can sense how you kick into high gear so quickly. Your mind is telling you that there's only one possible outcome, a bad one. And your body also gets revved up. Do you feel the tension right now?

(This illustrates a combination of reflection, tracking, empathy, and evocative responding.)

Allen: A little. I can feel my shoulders tensing up.

Gregg: Okay. Can you take a moment to tighten your shoulders just a little bit more and then release the tension?

(This is an example of evocative responding.)

SESSION TEN

Allen: The way I manage anxiety is by sticking to a routine. I do the same thing every day. I go to the same places, the same restaurants, the same stores.

Gregg: You tell yourself that doing the same thing will reduce the anxiety. Can you tell me how that works for you?

(This illustrates reflection of his action tendency.)

Allen: I think so. By going to the same places, I feel like I have some control. Nothing is going to catch me by surprise. If I go to an unfamiliar place, I feel out of control.

Gregg: I think I see. Let's go slowly here. A routine gives you a sense of control. Is that right?

(This is reflection, tracking, and evocative responding.)

Allen: Yeah, one way to control anxiety is to control everything.

Gregg: Do you mind saying that again? That seems real important.

(More evocative responding.)

Allen: Okay, one way to control anxiety is to control everything.

Gregg: The expression on your face changed right then. What is happening?

(More tracking, empathy, and evocative responding.)

Allen: I am seeing how I try to control everything. I'm afraid to put myself in new situations. I feel kind of embarrassed to admit that.

Gregg: It makes sense that you would try to control everything given how your mind tells you that that is the only way to control the anxiety. Of course you would stick to routines. It would be scary to do something spontaneous, wouldn't it?

(This illustrates validation and evocative responding.)

Allen: Probably, but maybe I should try it—I mean, do something spontaneous.

Gregg: If you want to, try that this week.

SESSION TWELVE

Allen: You won't believe this. I was out with my wife and did something totally spontaneous. I pulled into a bakery that we had never been in before and told my wife, "Let's try this place out." She looked at me like I had lost my mind. She said, "You don't do stuff like this. What has gotten into you?"

Gregg: You sound pretty happy with yourself. Wow, you broke out of your routine. How did you do that?

(This illustrates a combination of reflection of emotion and empathy.)

Allen: I just told myself, "Try something out of the ordinary. Maybe it won't be that bad."

Gregg: Was it bad?

Allen: No, not at all.

STAGE THREE: MOVING OUT

Review. At the first and second floors of our house, we have been working with our clients' threat response system. At stage one, our primary objective was to calm our clients' nervous systems, along with their fears. In stage two, our aim was to move our clients from a posture of avoidance to one of approach. For too long, our clients steered clear of their inner world of thoughts and feelings and were cut off from the wisdom of their bodies. At the second level of our building, we were attempting to increase their awareness of these three dimensions: cognitions, emotions, and physical sensations. At stage three, we continue working with the clients' threat response system, but our focus has become enlarged so that we include the clients' behavior.

Client's process. Behavior is embedded in the clients' threat response system. We call it the fight-flight-freeze response. When the clients' alarm bells goes off, they automatically engage in one or more of these behaviors. In stage one, they may have identified some type of undesirable behavior: "I have a short fuse." "I drink too much." "I've been having an affair." "My wife caught me using pornography." "I avoid conflicts." "I have trouble saying no." "I keep putting things off." Hopefully, they noticed that we reflected their behavior back to them in an accepting manner. But, in addition, they may have observed that we didn't make their behavior the target of treatment.

Moving into stage two, they observed that we were still not focused on their behavior. If they talked about their troubling actions, we listened and reflected, but we paid more attention to the inner world beneath the surface actions. To them, it seemed as if we wanted to expand the discussion—to explore thoughts, feelings, and sensations that they had previously ignored. Now, in stage three, they observe that the focal point has finally turned to their problematic behavior.

The counselor's objectives. In this model, we postpone our efforts to change the clients' behavior until stage three. Our assumption is that our clients will have a difficult time changing their automatic behaviors if they have not calmed their threat response system, becoming more aware of it and its hidden functions. Now, at stage three, we believe that clients are more prepared and equipped to change their undesired actions. At stage three, the counselor wants to help clients:

- Gain greater awareness of how they relate with themselves, others, and God.

- Develop more loving behaviors toward self, others, and God.

Therapeutic relationship. We bring the same way of being to the third floor that we demonstrated at the first and second levels. From a contemplative perspective, the qualities that are necessary are (1) presence, (2) openness, (3) attention, (4) acceptance, (5) compassion, (6) resonance, and (7) love. From an interpersonal neurobiology (IPNB) perspective, we approach our clients with COAL—curiosity, openness, acceptance, love. In addition, from an IPNB viewpoint, the fundamental stance of the counselor is one of PART—presence, attunement, resonance, trust.

Hughes (2007) uses another acronym to capture the essential qualities needed by an effective counselor: PACE—playfulness, acceptance, curiosity, empathy. The last three traits have already been discussed in detail, but the property of playfulness is new to us. Since Hughes specializes in working with children, it is not surprising that he introduces this important attribute. The dimensions of playfulness are (1) an openness to all the client's experiences, not just the ones that seem difficult, (2) bringing a lightness to the conversation, (3) conveying an attitude of confidence in one's ability to manage the situation, and (4) focusing more on the client's experience of the event as opposed to the event itself.

Therapeutic interventions. The primary interventions used in stage three are (1) reflections and (2) proactive loving.

Reflections. At stage three, we are primarily reflecting upon the clients' relationship with themselves, others, and God. As we reflect with our clients concerning their relationship with themselves, we are examining four main areas: (1) experience of body, (2) encounter with mind, (3) self-acceptance, and (4) construction of self. (These areas are discussed in great detail in chapter three.)

We engage in reflective conversations with our clients concerning how they relate to others. Again, we focus on certain areas: (1) taking responsibility, (2) practicing presence, (3) remembering intentions, and (4) demonstrating acceptance. In addition, we are careful in stage three to reflect upon our clients' relationship with God, if they are open to this dimension of their lives. (Again, these topics are explored in chapter three.)

Proactive loving. With this skill, we are attempting not only to increase our clients' awareness of their behavior but also to alter their actions. The steps we take to bring about change are (1) taking responsibility, (2) setting intentions, (3) developing a plan, (4) initiating action, and (5) follow-up.

The first step is to address the clients' level of responsibility (Fishbane, 2013). At stage one, they were focused on blaming someone else, but now it is time for our clients to accept responsibility for their own actions. Isn't this the lesson Jesus was teaching when he said, "Why do you look at the speck of sawdust in your brother's eye and pay no attention to the plank in your own eye? . . . First take the plank out of your eye" (Lk 6:41-42)? Of course, our clients' natural tendency is to see the faults and shortcomings of others, but now it is time for them to assume responsibility for their own actions.

Many times, our clients do not have clear intentions or they have forgotten them. An intention is the direction in which one wants to go. Before our clients can act in proactive loving ways with themselves, others, and God, they must first establish a desirable endpoint. How do they want to treat themselves, others, and God? In what ways do they want to be more loving? Of course they will lose track of their direction, but with practice they can return again and again to their new intentions.

We must help our clients develop a plan for being more loving. A plan refers to actions that our clients are able to put into writing. The client answers these questions: "How do I want to treat myself better?" "In what specific ways do I want to act differently with my family, my neighbors, my co-workers?" "What would I be doing differently if I were responding in love toward God?"

Now it is time for our clients to put their plans into action. This takes great courage because the clients are attempting to move from being reactionary to responding. Now, they are attempting to focus on their own behaviors versus those of others. With greater self-awareness of their own bodies and minds, they are better equipped to notice when their threat response system is being activated. This new consciousness will hopefully deter them from reactionary behaviors and into ones that are more loving.

Of course, change is a process. Clients will attempt repeatedly to employ these proactive forms of behavior, not always succeeding. They will need our acceptance, empathy, and validation. In stage three, we will reflect with them upon their attempts at proactive loving: (1) "What were you sensing?" (2) "What were you feeling?" (3) "How did you make sense out of it?" (4) "How did you behave?" As they follow up with us about their intentions and plans to engage in proactive loving behaviors, we communicate that we are amazed by their efforts, understanding of their setbacks, and inspired by their successes. We let them know that they are not alone.

Transition. There are signs that we are approaching the last floor of our house. First, we notice that our clients are experiencing success in relating with themselves, others, and God with new patterns of behavior. Second, we are aware that our clients are beginning to coordinate many of the lessons they have been learning throughout the treatment process. It now looks as if our clients are ready to move to stage four.

CASE ILLUSTRATION: ALLEN, PART THREE

Before moving to a discussion of stage, let's witness Allen's progress in stage three.

EXCERPTS FROM STAGE THREE WITH ALLEN.
SESSION FIFTEEN

Allen: Because of our work together, I have become more aware of how I just sit around stewing over my problems.

Gregg: You see that that isn't helping you.

(This illustrates reflection, that is, taking responsibility.)

Allen: Yeah, I have become isolated from my family. In addition, I have put on almost twenty-five pounds.

Gregg: You want to treat your family and yourself better.

(This is an example of the intention part of proactive loving.)

Allen: Right.

Gregg: Let's think of what you want to do differently. How do you wish you were acting?

(This is more about proactive loving, that is, remembering intentions.)

Allen: Maybe I could get up and take a walk every time I catch myself worrying. That way I'm not just sitting there stewing, and I'm also burning some calories. Maybe I could start playing basketball with my son in the driveway. That way we're doing something together, and I'm getting some exercise.

Gregg: Those sound like great ideas. How many times a week do you want to get outside with your son and play ball?

(Here we are developing a plan for proactive loving.)

Allen: How about I set a goal of two to three times.

Gregg: Great!

SESSION SEVENTEEN

Gregg: You were telling me that you have one idea stuck in your head when you go out on a call. The thought is, *This is going to be bad.* Did I get that right?

(This illustrates reflection of mind.)

Allen: Right. From the time we get the call to the time we arrive, that's what I'm thinking.

Gregg: You know how you've learned during your God-and-me-time to let go of distracting thoughts? Do you think we could apply that lesson to this situation?

Allen: I'm open. What do you have in mind?

Gregg: Well, when you get the call, what if you let go of the old thought, *This is going to turn out badly*, and give yourself another option? For example, you could say to yourself, *I have a chance to help someone. They will be better off because of me. Even if something bad happens, my being there will keep it from being worse.*

(Here we are setting intentions and developing a plan.)

Allen: That sounds worthwhile to think about.

SESSION NINETEEN

Allen: Last night, I got real angry with my daughter. I caught her in the hallway and was real snappy and harsh with her. I said some mean things to her.

Gregg: You sound like you regret how you acted. Is that so?

(In this reflection, I am helping Allen take responsibility.)

Allen: Yeah, that's not like me. This is not who I am. I was raised to act better than that.

Gregg: You seem sad about how you acted.

(Another reflection.)

Allen: Yes, but mostly I'm just mad at myself. I ask myself, *Why are you acting like this? What is your problem? Can't you get a grip on yourself?*

Gregg: You're really feeling down on yourself. I wonder what it would sound like if you were being kind to yourself right now?

(This reflection focuses on self-acceptance.)

Allen: I'm not sure what you mean.

Gregg: You know how you can get distracted during your God-and-me-time? Remember how you come back to God's presence without being mean to yourself. You are gentle with yourself.

Allen: Okay.

Gregg: I mean that you could talk to yourself like you talk to a good friend. It might sound like this, *You're under a lot of pressure, so of course you will blow it at times. The good thing is that you are working on your issues. God is helping you. You and Gregg are working together on this. You are not alone. It will get better.* How does that sound?

(This reflection continues to target Allen's self-acceptance.)

Allen: Good!

SESSION TWENTY

Allen: You won't believe this. The other day, I felt the impulse to light into my daughter, but I caught myself and said to her, "I have something I would like to discuss with you. Let me know when you have time to talk." She looked at me like I had lost my mind. Then I just smiled and walked off. I would have never done that in the past.

Gregg: You sound really happy about this. Change is nice. What does your story illustrate?

Allen: It shows that I'm trying to be less controlling of my daughter. I'm willing to accept her more. I need to give her a choice about if and when she wants to talk.

Gregg: You're becoming less controlling. You realize that you can't control everything and that's okay. You're becoming more accepting of your daughter. Way to go.

(This illustrates both a reflection—construction of self—and the follow-up part of proactive loving.)

STAGE FOUR: INTEGRATION

Client's process. From the first session until now, our clients have been grappling with an important question: Who am I? Their sense of identity has been embedded in their threat response system. Not only have their bodies been energized, their emotions aroused, and their actions self-protective, but their sense of self has been limited. Many clients enter and continue in the treatment process with a dark and negative view of self.

The counselor's objectives. During stage four, the counselor has two major goals:

- To assist clients in developing a new definition of self.

- To help clients develop a new story of their changes.

The counselor's process. Typical clients enter counseling with a narrative about self that is decidedly negative. There is a dark shadow that hangs over their view of self. Our goal is to help them rediscover their true identity. This process comes about as we help them identify and let go of old narratives that they hold on to about who they are. This change doesn't come about by directly confronting their old stories. Instead, a new sense of self appears as we reflect with them on present-moment experiences, allowing new experiences to surface in real time during our sessions. An enlarged view of self emerges as we reflect with clients on their efforts and successes at implementing new patterns of behavior.

Finally, a new narrative emerges as we review with them the changes they have made in the following areas: (1) emotional, (2) physical, (3) cognitive, and (4) relational.

1. *Emotional.* We review with clients how they are processing and regulating their emotions differently. They are more aware of their emotions, more accepting of their emotions, and better equipped to express their emotions.

2. *Physical.* We reconsider with clients their increased awareness of their bodies. They are now more attuned to signs that their threat response system has been activated. Along with greater self-awareness, they have words to describe the sensations that they feel in their bodies.

3. *Cognitive.* We have helped clients discover the difference between reality and perspective. Our clients now have the ability to identify how they make meaning out of an experience. They see how their minds can get oriented in a negative direction, and they have the ability to redirect their thinking.

4. *Relational.* Clients are now able to describe changes in their behavior toward self, others, and God. They see how they have become loving in their behavior. These modifications show up specifically in how they are more present, responsible, intentional, and accepting in their behavior.

CASE ILLUSTRATION: ALLEN, PART FOUR

We can now see how Allen has resolved his concerns with the help of contemplative prayer.

EXCERPTS FROM STAGE FOUR WITH ALLEN.
SESSION TWENTY-ONE

Allen: I have some good news. I had an appointment with my doctor yesterday. My blood pressure has gone down thirty points since I started seeing you. You remember how I was on four blood pressure medications. Now he is cutting me back to two.

Gregg: That's great news. I know you were very concerned about your health when we started. I can feel the relief you have.

Gregg: Do you remember how you were so afraid that you were going to drop dead of a heart attack or stroke? What has happened to that fear?

Allen: I still think about dying from time to time, but it isn't on my mind very often. I don't dwell on it anymore.

Gregg: It's nice to be free of that worry.

(I am helping Allen form a new definition of self. We are talking about how he is developing a new story about the physical and emotional areas of his life.)

SESSION TWENTY-TWO

Gregg: How have your relationships with your family members changed since we first started?

Allen: When I first started, I had isolated myself from my family. I just sat around stewing. Now I feel so much love for my family. I've become much more involved with them. For example, my son and I are playing basketball together two or three times a week. I can play so much more now than when we first started playing.

Gregg: I can tell that you're pleased with being more engaged with your son and more active.

(This is a new story of the relational and physical dimensions of his life.)

Gregg: How are things now with your daughter?

Allen: When anxiety was in control, I was very controlling. That only made her mad. She still gets mad at me, like the other day. When she stopped talking, I said, "Well, I guess we aren't going to get this figured out right this second." She was waiting for me to get angry, but when I didn't, she looked at me like I was crazy.

Gregg: You realize you don't have to control every situation. That's nice.

(We continue to develop a new definition of self.)

SESSION TWENTY-THREE

Allen: I have God-and-me-time every morning. I feel so much closer to God now than when I started. This is the greatest tool you've given me.

Gregg: Out of all the strategies we've tried, it's amazing to hear you say that sitting quietly with God is the most valuable thing that you will take away from counseling.

(This is a new story of Allen's relationship with God.)

SESSION TWENTY-FOUR

Allen: When I first started counseling, I felt out of control. Anxiety controlled my life. But now I see anxiety when it starts creeping up on me. And when I see it, I know that I have some strategies that work.

Gregg: At first, anxiety managed you, but now you manage it. Is that right?

(We are developing a new definition of self.)

Allen: Yes, I feel so good that anxiety is not in control of me. I had become someone I didn't know.

Gregg: Now you see a new Allen. You don't feel helpless in the face of anxiety. You feel capable of handling it.

(We continue working on a new definition of self. We are focused on the emotional side of Allen's life.)

Allen: Yeah, now I know how to deal with anxiety. I have some good tools.

Gregg: I'm so happy for you.

TRANSITION

It is now time to make the final transition of counseling: termination. Hopefully, this decision is made in a collaborative way as both you and the client acknowledge that it is the right time to end the treatment process.

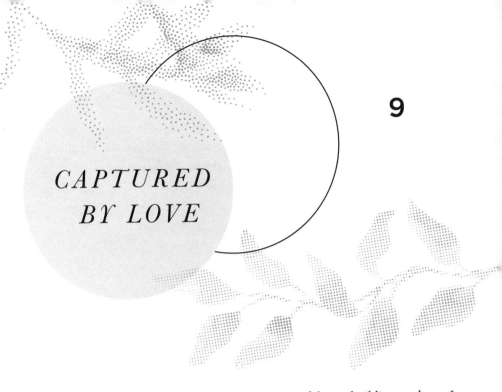

CAPTURED
BY LOVE

I HAVE PRESENTED the various elements of theory building, and now I am ready to add our last fundamental ingredient: the goal of counseling. As Corey (2013) observes, at the core of all theoretical orientations are goals that are essential to the success of counseling. Without a clear purpose, it is unlikely that treatment will be productive.

All too often we are tempted to focus treatment on our clients' presenting complaints. If our clients believe that their problem is emotional in nature—depression, anxiety, or some other—we establish goals that concentrate on their emotions. On the other hand, if our clients suggest that the essence of their concern is behavioral—drinking, people pleasing, or something else—then we set out to implement behavioral changes. Finally, if our clients complain that their problems are related to their thinking—low self-esteem, ruminations, or another—we target our goals at this level of their functioning.

The goals of counseling are diverse (Corey, 2013). The aim of one counselor may be to make the unconscious conscious, while another may focus on increasing a client's social interest. Some counselors will want to increase their clients' level of self-awareness in order to expand their choices. One counselor will attempt to eliminate maladaptive behaviors while the purpose of others is to alter the way the client thinks. Helping clients find better ways of meeting their needs or heightening their sense of self-agency may be the goal of other counselors.

In general, the main goal of most counselors is to assist the client in bringing about change in one of the following realms: thinking, feeling, or behavior (Corey, 2013). We perceive that the client is experiencing a symptom in one or more of these dimensions and then set out to remedy this particular problem. Our purpose is to eradicate or solve the problem as soon as possible.

Our contemplative-oriented approach to counseling radically alters the target of counseling. Even though we are interested in improving our client's functioning in the areas of emotions, cognitions, and actions, that is not the overall goal. We shift our purpose away from symptom reduction to something else more important. And this relocation of focus profoundly affects the guiding principles, tone, and approach of the way we work.

The target of our contemplative-oriented approach is love. We want to enhance our clients' ability to love and be loved. First, we want our clients to experience our love and God's love for them (Moon, 2012). Then, from this base, our ultimate goal is for clients "to be in love with God and others" (Moon, 2012, p. 145).

We must expand our understanding of how love pervades, illuminates, and determines the treatment process. Yes, love is the end—or goal—of counseling, but it is also the means. Not only do clients need love, but clinicians need it as well. As counselors, we first receive love from God. Then we serve as vessels of love to our client. And then, having received our love and God's love, our clients are able in turn to love God, others, and self. Christian psychiatrist Timothy Jennings (2013) writes, "It is love that heals and restores" (p. 58). He adds, "There is only one remedy, one cure, one solution for sin and the destruction it causes. It's love" (p. 208).

Secular mental health professionals have reached the same conclusion. Carl Rogers (1967), the most influential psychologist of the twentieth century, believed that counselors must provide "a kind of love for the client as he is, providing we understand the word love as equivalent to the theologian's term *agape*, and not in its usual romantic and possessive meanings" (p. 94). More recently, Daniel Siegel (2010a) has suggested that we must offer our clients a "professional form of love" (p. 245).

Throughout this project, we have attempted to maintain a respectful dialogue between theology, science, and Christian contemplative thought. We will continue to maintain this posture as we explore how the goal of love is supported by research in all three of these disciplines.

THEOLOGY OF LOVE

We turn to theology because it helps us understand the nature of God's love. Our basic theological belief is that God's chief attribute is love: "God is love" (1 Jn 4:8). From theology, we also learn that humans have the capacity to imitate God. In other words, since God loves, humans have the potential to love in similar ways. This idea is captured by the apostle John: "Since God so loved us, we also ought to love one another" (1 Jn 4:11).

In this section, we will explore theologian Thomas Oord's (2010) insights into the theology of love. Our discussion will contain ideas about (1) a definition of love, (2) three forms of love, and (3) the theological basis for self-love.

Definition of love. Oord (2010) defines love this way: "To love is to act intentionally, in sympathetic response to others (including God), to promote overall well-being" (p. 15). This definition contains four elements: (1) action, (2) intention, (3) sympathy, and (4) promotion of overall well-being.

First, love is action. Love is contained in the behavior itself. We often attribute love to an action if the consequences are good. But, according to this view of love, behavior can be loving even if it results in a disastrous outcome. The assumption is that those who love do not entirely control the consequences of their actions.

Second, were my intentions in the right place? The answer to this question determines if an action is loving or not. This question gets at the second component of love—that love is intentional. Love is not determined by the outcome of one's conduct. Love does not look behind, at what happened as a result of my behavior. Instead, love is prospective, looking at what I am hoping will happen. What is my aim? What is my purpose? What do I desire to happen? These are questions about the intention of love.

The third element of love is sympathy. In choosing this term, Oord realizes that it can be confusing and controversial. However, he selects it for its technical and philosophical purposes. In these respects, the word *sympathy*—derived from the Greek word *sympatheō*—highlights how humans are mutually influencing. In other words, the one who loves is deeply affected by the other person. The lover is influenced at a deeply internal level. To sympathize is to "feel with" (Oord, 2010, p. 19). This description of sympathy is reminiscent of Daniel Siegel's (2010a) concept of "feeling felt," which he says is the simplest way of describing love.

Why does Oord choose the word *sympathy* instead of *empathy*? The term *sympathy* is disliked by the discipline of psychology because it carries overtones of pity, condescension, or distance. However, the philosophical term *sympathy* could not be further from these descriptions. For Oord, *sympathy* means that we are feeling the feelings of others. Our own experience, at a deep internal place, is being profoundly affected by the other person. Having chosen the term *sympathy*, Oord graciously admits that the terms *sympathy* and *empathy* can be interchanged.

Another component is needed in order to label an action as loving. This final element of love gets at the aim of love. We know that love is intentional, but what is its target or purpose? The aim of love is to promote the overall well-being of the other. What does this term *well-being*—derived from the Greek word *eudaimonia*—mean? It is a good life, one in which we develop our strengths, realize our potential, and become what it is in our nature to become (Haidt, 2006). Oord agrees that well-being pertains to one's quality of life. Looking to the life of Jesus for insight into the meaning of *well-being*, Oord selects the following quote: "I have come that they may have life, and have it to the full" (Jn 10:10).

When the goal of counseling is love, we naturally promote our clients' well-being by enhancing the cognitive, physical, emotional, and relational areas of their lives. But our target is beyond or greater than one or more of these dimensions. Improvement in these areas may naturally occur, but this improvement is the byproduct of love rather than the aim of counseling.

This understanding of love applies to the love that both God and humans express. Just as God promotes our overall well-being, God calls us to advance the overall well-being of others. This makes sense because we are made in God's image, *imago Dei*. In light of this truth, it is reasonable to assume that we can be imitators of God. It makes sense that we have the potential to love as God loves. As Stephen Post (2003) puts it, "To be created in God's image means that we are created *for* love *by* love" (p. 20).

Of course, an accurate theology of love highlights the source of all love— God. All love originates and springs from God. Without God, love is impossible. Our love for God, others, and even self is empowered and inspired by God. We have the choice of responding appropriately or inappropriately to God's love. However, when we do respond appropriately, we are inspired by God to promote the well-being of others.

Perhaps an illustration may help. Let's imagine living in ancient times in a small village, and in the center of that community is a well. Water is directly available to us if we go to that fountainhead. We can even put fresh water from that wellspring into a container and deliver it to others. If we so choose, we can deprive ourselves of water and fail to distribute it to others. However, if we do provide others with fresh water, it is obvious that we are not the source of that water. It comes from something bigger than ourselves. We are simply carriers of the gift of water. We have it because we have drawn from its source.

Three forms of love. Theologians agree that there are three forms of love, associated with the following Greek words: *agape, eros,* and *philia.* Each type of love fits with our basic description of love, but each goes beyond and adds something distinct to our original definition of love. What do these terms mean? How does each form of love differ from the other varieties of love? How does each kind adhere to our fundamental definition of love? These are the questions that we will address in this section.

Agape love refers to the context in which a lover promotes the overall well-being of the other person. The situation is one in which the person being loved intends ill will or harm for the one who loves. When confronted by this malevolent intent, the lover continues to advance that which is best for the other person. In other words, *agape* repays evil with good. In this regard, *agape* is dissimilar to the other two forms of love.

Unlike *agape,* which is a response to ill will, *eros* is a reply to something else. It grows out of the lover's assessment that the other person is of great worth. *Eros* is an affirmation of the loved person's perceived importance. *Eros* reaches out toward that person who is valued and works to that person's advantage. When *eros* is expressed, it tends to carry emotional content. It is emotional in nature.

Because of its emotional component, *eros* has sometimes been equated with sex and romance. However, it is a mistake to identify *eros* with these behaviors. Of course, sexual behavior and romance can be an expression of *eros* love when it seeks to advance that which is best for the loved one. However, it is obvious that not everyone who engages in sex or romantic behavior is seeking to promote the overall well-being of the other person.

Finally, *philia* is identified with terms like *mutuality* and *reciprocity*. *Philia* love captures how—or the manner in which—the lover attempts to promote the overall well-being of the loved one. It is done in a spirit of teamwork. What distinguishes it from the other forms of love is its cooperative nature.

In review, the three forms of love are similar, yet distinct. They are alike in that they all attempt to promote the overall well-being of the other. However, *agape* is different in that it continues to advance the good of the other even when confronted with evil. *Eros* is unique in that it sees value in the other and then promotes the well-being of that person in response. *Philia* is unlike the other types because it seeks to contribute to the quality of the loved one's life by working in a cooperative manner.

These three forms of love can be expressed by both God and God's creatures. These types of love are sometimes mixed. And, even though multiple kinds of love are present, it may be that one form predominates. While promoting the overall well-being of the other, *eros* and *philia* may be present, but *agape* may be holding the most power in response to the other person's intent to do harm at that particular moment.

In the context of this discussion, let's return to our earlier quote by Carl Rogers. Rogers (1967) instructed counselors to provide "a kind of love for the client as he is, providing we understand the word love as equivalent to the theologian's term *agape*, and not in its usual romantic and possessive meanings" (p. 94). In his admonition, he was steering counselors away from an inappropriate *eros* form of love and guiding them toward *agape* love. This is sound advice. I would add that engaging in a *philia* type of love is beneficial for the counseling relationship, as long as appropriate boundaries are maintained. Counseling is undoubtedly a collaborative venture.

In our discussion of love, we now turn to the issue of self-love. What does it mean? Is it appropriate? Based on our basic definition of love, self-love is operating when we promote our own overall well-being. We are attempting to strengthen our talents, advance our potential, and become the person who God has designed us to be.

Is engaging in this type of self-love the correct thing to do? According to Oord, self-love has a strong theological basis. He argues that God demonstrates self-love. God the Father clearly loves Jesus because Jesus said, "As the Father has loved me . . ." (Jn 15:9). And Jesus ardently proclaims his love for the Father: "I love the Father and do exactly what my Father has commanded me" (Jn 14:31). The Trinity is a community of love, each one loving the other members of the Godhead. As imitators of God, we must engage in self-love as does the Trinity.

Our ideas about love are grounded in theology, but what is science saying about love? We turn to this subject next.

THE SCIENCE OF LOVE

Science has a lot to teach us about love. Two scientific disciplines in particular—psychology and neuroscience—have presented us with research that sheds light on our understanding of this important topic. Each field provides its own distinctive evidence about love. However, their research often intertwines, providing us with corroborating data on the subject of love

The psychology of love. Within the field of psychology, attachment theory provides a firm foundation for building a solid science of love. The father of attachment theory, John Bowlby, was convinced that the mother-child bond was essential for healthy human development. In other words, for children to thrive and flourish, they must be loved. *Love* was simply defined by Bowlby as an attachment between two people.

Theoretical orientations that adopt attachment-based ideas (e.g., IPNB, EFT) espouse the view that love is the goal—and means—of counseling. Sue Johnson (2004), the originator of emotionally focused therapy (EFT) for couples, argues that attachment theory offers counselors a useful theory of love. Attachment theory provides counselors not only a way to understand clients' problems but also treatment goals and techniques for achieving them.

Psychology is keenly interested in the dynamics and mechanisms of love. These processes include how we interact with others, empathy, sensitivity to the suffering of others, compassion, and the ability to cross relational space. But what is it that interferes with the experience and expression of love? Here, psychology's study of love leads to the study of its antagonist, stress.

Stress has been a primary area of study for the field of psychology. We know that stress affects our bodies, thinking, emotions, and behavior. Once a threat is detected, the endocrine system releases adrenaline and cortisol, setting our bodies in motion. Stress mobilizes us for action—fight, flight, or freeze. As our body is being triggered, so too are our emotions. The emotions of anger and fear emerge as protective responses that move us toward, against, or away from the stressful situation. And, finally, stress affects our cognitions, generating negative thoughts about ourselves, others, and the situation.

But what does this have to do with love? Psychological research indicates that stress reduces our ability to love (Cousineau, 2018). Important behaviors associated with love—empathy, compassion, and closeness—are diminished by stress. As a result of stress, we are less empathic, less compassionate, and more prone to distance ourselves from others.

Psychological findings provide evidence that stress turns off love. Without love, people withdraw, become hostile, engage in negative thinking about others, become poor listeners, and are easily irritated (Gottman, 2011). Simply put, under stress, people become nasty and mean. Overwhelmed with stress, people lose the resources to feel or be kind (Cousineau, 2018).

Psychologist Louis Cozolino (2006) offers us great insight into the battle between love and stress. When love is silenced by stress, a predictable set of mechanisms is set in operation: our bodies are activated, we become avoidant, we experience a limited view of self, we feel shame, and various unconscious systems are turned on. However, when love is turned on, we are freed from fear and from the stress response system.

For the field of psychology, the main question is, How do we turn on the mechanism of love? To answer this query, psychology has turned primarily to neuroscience for answers. This is where the two disciplines overlap.

The neuroscience of love. In recent years, attention to love has been on the rise among neuroscientists. As advances in technology have occurred, especially with the advent of functional magnetic resonance imaging (fMRI), neuroscience has devised experiments that allow us to see how the brain lights up when we love (Johnson, 2013).

Turning first to the neurobiology of stress, neurobiologists tell us that the limbic system of the brain is always on. Scanning the environment, it is constantly alert to anything that feels threatening. Assessing that a situation is unsafe, the limbic system sounds an alarm called stress.

When stress and the accompanying emotion of fear are switched on, dramatic shifts occur in how the brain operates. Several key neurological changes have been identified. First, a scared amygdala shuts off activity in the left prefrontal cortex. Second, as activity in the left prefrontal cortex subsides, energy in the right prefrontal cortex increases. Finally, the functioning of the anterior cingulate cortex (ACC) is reduced.

The role of the ACC—which is situated between the frontal lobe and the limbic system—in love cannot be overestimated. Neuroscientist Andrew Newberg (2009) teaches us that the ACC bridges the gap between our limbic system and our prefrontal cortex. It connects our emotions with our cognitive skills, playing a crucial role in emotional self-control and problem solving. When the activity of the ACC subsides, the prefrontal cortex's ability to mitigate negative emotions emerging from the amygdala is hampered. Jennings (2013) adds that the ACC is the brain region where we experience love.

The greatest impediment to love that occurs in the face of stress is a surge in fear. According to neuroscience, brain structures operate in a seesaw fashion. In other words, as one brain activity goes up, another one goes down. When fear is switched on, love is turned off (Newberg & Waldman, 2009). The process of fear, which operates out of the limbic region, negates the power of love, which works from the middle prefrontal cortex and ACC (Cozolino, 2006).

According to psychologist Louis Cozolino (2006), fear actually outranks and outwits love in several ways. Operating from the right amygdala, fear is faster, automatic, and unconscious. Love, on the other hand, functioning out of the middle prefrontal cortex, is a slower and more conscious process. Newberg and Waldman (2009) agree that the functions of the prefrontal regions and the ACC—empathy and compassion—are slow when compared to the activity of fear.

We can conclude from neuroscience that a strategy is needed for quieting fear and turning on love. This leads us to our next section.

Neuroscience and contemplation. Recent findings in neuroscience indicate that contemplative practices can reverse the seesaw effect of stress. Within the context of training in contemplative practices, such as centering prayer and mindfulness, love goes up and fear goes down (Newberg & Waldman, 2009).

The neurological explanation for this phenomenon is fascinating. Certain brain functions change when a person consistently engages in contemplative practices over a period of time. First, activity in the brain shifts from the right prefrontal cortex to the left. This relocation of energy from the right to the left is associated with a desire to approach others instead of withdraw (Davidson & Begley, 2012). Second, when people engage in a regular practice of centering prayer, increased activation of the left prefrontal cortex inhibits or quiets the excited amygdala (Newberg & Waldman, 2009). As metabolism in the amygdala goes down, so does fear. Finally, contemplative practices stimulate the ACC (Newberg & Waldman, 2009). When the ACC—which controls empathy and compassion—is activated, our social awareness and concern for others increase.

According to neuroscience, contemplative practices alter the functioning of the brain, thus releasing the power of love. As Newberg and Waldman (2009) observe, people who contemplate become more sensitive to the suffering of others. When the ACC is stimulated, we resonate with the pain of others, allowing us to feel empathy. And, as neurobiologists Davidson and Begley (2012) observe, as contemplative practices relocate brain activity from right to left, practitioners are more willing to approach others. When contemplatives ask themselves, "Do I want to avoid or approach?" they are more likely to choose the latter and make a connection with others. As the amygdala becomes quiet, practitioners of contemplative practices experience fewer negative emotions, thus being less guided by them.

In recent years, as the psychology of love has met with the neuroscience of love, we have witnessed new research that demonstrates the interconnections between the two disciplines. Psychologist Marion Solomon (2017) speaks of "the brain in love" (p. 250). Psychologist Stan Tatkin (2011) claims, "We are wired for love" (p. 2). Finally, another psychologist, Mona Fishbane (2013), has authored a wonderful book titled *Loving with the Brain in Mind.*

Now that we have looked at scientific evidence about contemplation and love, let's view love from another angle, that of the Christian contemplative tradition.

CHRISTIAN CONTEMPLATION AND LOVE

We have discovered that love can be couched in both scientific and theological terms. But can love be expressed in the language of contemplative prayer? William Meninger (1996), one of the cocreators of centering prayer, answers with a resounding yes. Meninger describes contemplative prayer as a loving search for God.

Love is at the heart of contemplation. First, contemplative prayer begins with God's love for us. Prayer originates as God's movement in love toward us. Our loving search for God is, first of all, God's search for us. As John writes, "We love because he first loved us" (1 Jn 4:19). Our loving search for God is simply a response to his invitation to be in loving communion with him. This idea is captured in the Old Testament: "Before they call I [the LORD] will answer" (Is 65:24). And it is also expressed in the New Testament, "Your Father knows what you need before you ask him" (Mt 6:8).

How should we pray when we engage in contemplative prayer? Meninger's (1996) reply is, "Simply love God. Be in God's presence in that love" (p. 3). In contemplation, God loves us and we love God. It is that simple. To illustrate his point, Meninger (1996) tells the story of Saint John Vianney and the old man. Each afternoon, as Saint John entered the church that he pastored in France, he would see an elderly man sitting in a pew. When Saint John left the church later, the man would still be sitting in the pew. One day, Saint John went up to the elderly man and asked, "What do you do sitting here all afternoon, day after day?" "I don't do anything," he replied. "I just look at God and God looks at me" (p. 4). This story captures the essence of contemplative prayer. It is loving attentiveness. It is a loving gaze at God. No words are necessary.

And what happens as we sit in contemplative prayer? What transpires as we lovingly gaze at God looking at us in love? His love changes us. Meninger (1996) writes, "The love of God will do its work in transforming you" (p. 58). God's love restructures us at every level: physical, emotional, cognitive, behavioral, and relational. As we love God with our hearts, souls, minds, and strength (see Mk 12:30), each of these dimensions of the human person is transformed.

Contemplative prayer has a unique progression. First, we receive God's love. As Paul writes, "God's love has been poured out into our hearts through the Holy Spirit" (Rom 5:5). I like this image of the Holy Spirit emptying God's love into our lives. We are depicted as a vessel. We first receive love, it becomes ours, and then we pour it back out.

One clear outcome of contemplative prayer is love for others. We are first loved by God; then we love others. Jesus said, "As I have loved you, so you must love one another" (Jn 13:34). Later, it is recorded in the New Testament,

"Let us love one another, for love comes from God" (1 Jn 4:7). The motivation and means for loving others clearly comes from God. As Meninger (1996) observes, "We do not love with mere human love but with God's love" (p. 109). In loving others, we are being imitators of Jesus. As Paul writes, "Walk in the way of love, just as Christ loved us" (Eph 5:2).

In the school of contemplative prayer, we learn valuable lessons about love. Love begins with God. He searches for us and pours his love into our hearts. In response, every dimension of our being is transformed by love. Contemplation then turns to action as we are enabled to love God, self, and others. Love is poured into our lives; then we in turn pour it into the lives of others.

CONCLUSION

The method that we have championed in this book can be captured in one word: *love*. Love is at the center of our contemplative-oriented way of counseling. It is the goal of our approach, but it is also the means of accomplishing our aim. This program is *by* love *for* love. How does the dynamic of love pervade and inform every dimension of our new way of counseling?

1. *View of human nature.* Love informs the way we see our clients. Jesus' great commandment on love (Mk 12:30-31) reveals the various dimensions of the human person. As a result, we want to promote functioning in each of these vital areas: physical, emotional, cognitive, behavioral, and relational.

2. *Mechanisms of change.* Under stress, a predictable set of mechanisms is set in operation: our bodies are activated, we become avoidant, we feel afraid, and our cognitions turn negative. But when love is activated, we are freed from fear and the threat response system. This allows us to feel safe, switch to a posture of approach, discover our true selves, and express ourselves in a vulnerable manner.

3. *The role of the counselor.* Our lessons in love teach us that the most important element in counseling is our way of being. Our presence is so vital to the healing process. We present ourselves to our clients in ways that are loving and caring. As Siegel (2010a) writes, "The experience of caring for others with curiosity, openness, and acceptance can be seen as the core of what we experience as love" (p. 246).

4. *Contemplative prayer.* The distinctive feature of our contemplative-oriented model of counseling is contemplative prayer. The practice of contemplative prayer is a requirement for counselors who desire to implement this new paradigm. By sitting in God's loving presence, we can become a loving presence to our clients. Out of our own experience, we can then introduce contemplative prayer to clients when it is the appropriate intervention.

5. *Interventions.* Contemplative prayer, the hallmark intervention of this new model of counseling, is a loving search for God. The other key techniques of our approach are then grounded in and consistent with the law of love. We implement strategies from a posture of love: patiently, with kindness, in a humble fashion, with acceptance, always in a protective—or safe—manner, and with hope (see 1 Cor 13:4-7).

6. *Goal.* A distinctive feature of our contemplative model of counseling is its emphasis on love. We want our clients to directly experience God's love for them as they practice contemplative prayer. But we hope our clients will experience our love for them as well, love that we have learned in the school of contemplative prayer. It is through the experience of receiving love that our clients undergo change. And, as result of this transformation, we believe our clients will become more loving beings. Our desire is that they will love God, others, and self. All three sets of relationships are vital to their healing and growth.

The counseling process is a messy one. Sometimes we and our clients are moving forward in love. We see signs that they are feeling safe, facing the hard work of counseling, opening up, finding and strengthening new dimensions within themselves, and even resting in the love of God. But, at other times, we or our clients stumble. We or our clients feel threatened, try to hide, become overwhelmed with intense emotions and physical sensations, and act in confusing ways. When we stop to look at the terrain, we notice that we have been tripped up by fear. It is then that we need to pause, take a deep breath, and take hope in the following truth: "Perfect love drives out fear" (1 Jn 4:18).

REFERENCES

Anderson, C., & Granados, J. (2009). *Called to love: Approaching John Paul II's theology of the body.* New York, NY: Image Books.

Anderson, F. (2010). *Breaking the rules: Trading performance for intimacy with God.* Downers Grove, IL: InterVarsity Press.

Augustine, of Hippo, Saint. (1960/2014). *The Confessions of Saint Augustine* (J. K. Ryan, Trans.) (Reprint). New York, NY: Image Books.

Badenoch, B. (2008). *Being a brain-wise therapist: A practical guide to interpersonal neurobiology.* New York, NY: Norton.

Baer, J. (2015). *Cultivating good minds.* Retrieved from http://www.intellectual virtues.org

Baer, R. A. (Ed.). (2010). *Assessing mindfulness & acceptance processes in clients: Illuminating the theory & practice of change.* Oakland, CA: New Harbinger.

Beck, J. R., & Demarest, B. (2005). *The human person in theology and psychology: A biblical anthropology for the twenty-first century.* Grand Rapids, MI: Kregel.

Benner, D. G. (2003). *Surrender to love: Discovering the heart of Christian spirituality.* Downers Grove, IL: InterVarsity Press.

Benner, D. G. (2004). *The gift of being yourself: The sacred call to self-discovery.* Downers Grove, IL: InterVarsity Press.

Benner, D. G. (2010). *Opening to God: Lectio divina and life as prayer.* Downers Grove, IL: InterVarsity Press.

Benner, D. G. (2011). *Soulful spirituality: Becoming fully alive and deeply human.* Grand Rapids, MI: Brazos Press.

Bourgeault, C. (2016). *The heart of centering prayer: Nondual Christianity in theory and practice.* Boulder, CO: Shambhala.

Brown, B. (2012). *Daring greatly: How the courage to be vulnerable transforms the way we live, love, parent, and lead.* New York, NY: Penguin Random House.

Carey, B. (2008, May 27). Lotus therapy. *The New York Times*, p. F1.

Clinton, T., & Sibcy, G. (2012). Christian counseling, interpersonal neurobiology, and the future. *Journal of Psychology & Theology, 40*(2), 141-45.

Coe, J. (2014). The controversy over contemplation and contemplative prayer: A historical, theological, and biblical resolution. *Journal of Spiritual Formation & Soul Care, 7*(1), 140-53.

Coe, J., & Howard, E. B. (2014). The practice of contemplative prayer in an evangelical context. *Journal of Spiritual Formation & Soul Care, 7*(1), 60-61.

Corey, G. (2013). *The art of integrative counseling.* Belmont, CA: Brooks/Cole.

Cousineau, T. (2018). *The kindness cure: How the science of compassion can heal your heart and your world.* Oakland, CA: New Harbinger.

Cozolino, L. (2006). *The neuroscience of human relationships: Attachment and developing social brain.* New York, NY: Norton.

Cozolino, L. (2016). *Why therapy works: Using our minds to change our brains.* New York, NY: Norton.

Cozolino, L., & Davis, V. (2017). How people change. In M. Solomon & D. J. Siegel (Eds.), *How people change: Relationship and neuroplasticity in psychotherapy* (pp. 53-71). New York, NY: Norton.

Damásio, A. R. (1999). *The feeling of what happens: Body and emotion in the making of consciousness.* New York, NY: Harcourt Brace.

Davidson, R. J., & Begley, S. (2012). *The emotional life of your brain: How its unique patterns affect the way you think, feel, and live—and how you can change them.* New York, NY: Hudson Street Press.

Demarest, B. (1999). *Satisfy your soul: Restoring the heart of Christian spirituality.* Colorado Springs, CO: NavPress.

Edwards, K. J. (2015). When word meets flesh: A neuroscience perspective on embodied spiritual formation. *Journal of Psychology & Christianity, 34*(3), 228-39.

Ferguson, J. K., Willemsen, E. W., & Castañeto, M. V. (2010). Centering prayer as a healing response to everyday stress: A psychological and spiritual process. *Pastoral Psychology, 59*(3), 305-29.

Fishbane, M. D. (2013). *Loving with the brain in mind: Neurobiology and couple therapy.* New York, NY: Norton.

Foster, R. J. (1992). *Prayer: Finding the heart's true home.* New York, NY: HarperCollins.

Foster, R. J. (2008). *Life with God: Reading the Bible for spiritual transformation*. New York, NY: HarperCollins.

Fox, J., Gutierrez, D., Haas, J., Braganza, D. J., & Berger, C. (2015). A phenomenological investigation of centering prayer using conventional content analysis. *Pastoral Psychology, 64*(6), 803-25.

Frenette, D. (2012). *The path of centering prayer: Deepening your experience of God*. Boulder, CO: Sounds True.

Gehart, D. R. (2012). *Mindfulness and acceptance in couple and family therapy*. New York, NY: Springer.

Gehart, D. R. (2016). *Theory and treatment planning in counseling and psychotherapy* (2nd ed.). Boston, MA: Cengage Learning.

Germer, C. K. (2005). Teaching mindfulness in therapy. In C. K. Germer, R. D. Siegel, and P. R. Fulton (Eds.), *Mindfulness and psychotherapy* (pp. 113-29). New York, NY: Guilford Press.

Ginot, E. (2015). *The neuropsychology of the unconscious: Integrating brain and mind in psychotherapy*. New York, NY: Norton.

Goldstein, B., & Siegel, D. J. (2017). Feeling felt. In M. Solomon & D. J. Siegel (Eds.), *How people change: Relationships and neuroplasticity in psychotherapy* (pp. 275-90). New York, NY: Norton.

Gottman, J. M. (2011). *The science of trust: Emotional attunement for couples*. New York, NY: Norton.

Grenz, S. J. (2006). *Renewing the center: Evangelical theology in a post-theological era* (2nd ed.). Grand Rapids, MI: Baker Academic.

Gutierrez, D., Fox, J., & Wood, A. W. (2015). Center, light, and sound: The psychological benefits of three distinct meditative practices. *Counseling and Values, 60*, 234-47.

Haidt, J. (2006). *The happiness hypothesis: Finding modern truth in ancient wisdom*. New York, NY: Basic Books.

Harris, R. (2009). *ACT with love: Stop struggling, reconcile differences, and strengthen your relationship with acceptance and commitment therapy*. Oakland, CA: New Harbinger.

Hempton, G. (2009). *One square inch of silence: One man's quest to preserve quiet*. New York, NY: Free Press.

Hick, S. F., & Bien, T. (Eds.) (2008). *Mindfulness and the therapeutic relationship*. New York, NY: Guilford Press.

Howard, E. B. (2008). *The Brazos introduction to Christian spirituality*. Grand Rapids, MI: Brazos Press.

Howard, E. B. (2014). Is thoughtless prayer really Christian? A biblical/evangelical response to Evagrius of Pontus. *Journal of Spiritual Formation & Soul Care, 7*(1), 118-39.

Hughes, D. A. (2007). *Attachment-focused family therapy*. New York, NY: Norton.

Hughes, D. A. (2017). How children change within the therapeutic relationship: Interweaving communications of curiosity and empathy. In M. Solomon & D. J. Siegel (Eds.), *How people change: Relationships and neuroplasticity in psychotherapy* (pp. 167-83). New York, NY: Norton.

Jennings, T. R. (2013). *The God-shaped brain: How changing your view of God transforms your life*. Downers Grove, IL: InterVarsity Press.

John of the Cross, Saint. (1991). *The collected works of St. John of the Cross* (K. Kavanaugh and O. Rodriquez, Trans.) (Rev. ed.). Washington, DC: ICS Publications.

Johnson, M. E., Dose, A. M., Pipe, T. B., Petersen, W. O., Huschka, M., Gallenberg, M. M., . . . Frost, M. H. (2009). Centering prayer for women receiving chemotherapy for recurrent ovarian cancer: A pilot study. *Oncology Nursing Forum, 36*(4), 421-28.

Johnson, S. M. (2004). *The practice of emotionally focused couple therapy: Creating connection* (2nd ed.). New York, NY: Brunner-Routledge.

Johnson, S. M. (2013). *Love sense: The revolutionary new science of romantic relationships*. New York, NY: Little, Brown.

Joyce, J. (1990). *Dubliners*. New York, NY: Bantam Books.

Kabat-Zinn, J. (2003). Mindfulness-based interventions in context: Past, present, and future. *Clinical Psychology: Science and Practice, 10*(2), 144-56.

Keating, T. (1999). *Open mind, open heart: The contemplative dimension of the gospel*. New York, NY: Continuum.

Knabb, J. J., & Frederick, T. V. (2017). *Contemplative prayer for Christians with chronic worry: An eight-week program*. New York: Routledge.

Kreeft, P. (1989). *Three philosophies of life: Ecclesiastes: life as vanity; Job: life as suffering; Song of Songs: life as love*. San Francisco, CA : Ignatius Press.

Kreeft, P. (1992). *Back to virtue: Traditional moral wisdom for modern moral confusion*. San Francisco, CA: Ignatius Press.

Kreeft, P. (2000). *Prayer for beginners*. San Francisco, CA: Ignatius Press.

Kristeller, J. L. (2010). Spiritual engagement as a mechanism of change in mindfulness- and acceptance-based therapies. In R. A. Baer (Ed.), *Assessing mindfulness and acceptance processes in clients: Illuminating the theory and practice of change* (pp. 155-84). Oakland, CA: New Harbinger.

Laird, M. (2006). *Into the silent land: A guide to the Christian practice of contemplation.* New York, NY: Oxford University Press.

Laird, M. (2011). *A sunlit absence: Silence, awareness, and contemplation.* New York, NY: Oxford University Press.

Lambert, M. J. (1992). Psychotherapy outcome research: Implications for integrative and eclectic therapists. In J. C. Norcross & M. R. Goldfried (Eds.), *Handbook of psychotherapy integration* (pp. 94-129). New York, NY: Basic Books.

Lambert, M. J., & Simon, W. (2008). The therapeutic relationship: Central and essential in therapeutic outcome. In S. F. Hick & T. Bien (Eds.), *Mindfulness and the therapeutic relationship* (pp. 19-33). New York, NY: Guilford Press.

Langshur, E., & Klemp, N. (2016). *Start here: Master the lifelong habit of well-being.* New York, NY: North Star Way.

Laubach, F. C. (2007). *Letters by a modern mystic.* Colorado Springs, CO: Purposeful Design.

Lawrence, of the Resurrection, Brother. (1977). *The practice of the presence of God* (J. J. Delaney, Trans.). New York, NY: Doubleday.

Levine, P. A. (2017). Emotion, the body, and change. In M. Solomon & D. J. Siegel (Eds.), *How people change: Relationships and neuroplasticity in psychotherapy* (pp. 127-49). New York, NY: Norton.

Lewis, C. S. (1956a). *Mere Christianity.* New York, NY: Macmillan.

Lewis, C. S. (1956b). *Till we have faces: A myth retold.* New York, NY: Harcourt.

Madagáin, M. O. (2007). *Centering prayer and the healing of the unconscious.* New York, NY: Lantern Books.

Mann, M. H. (2006). *Perfecting grace: Holiness, human being, and the sciences.* New York, NY: T&T Clark.

Manning, B. (2000). *Ruthless trust: The ragamuffin's path to God.* New York, NY: HarperCollins.

May, G. G. (1991). *The awakened heart: Opening yourself to the love you need.* New York, NY: HarperCollins.

May, G. G. (2004). *The dark night of the soul: A psychiatrist explores the connection between darkness and spiritual growth.* New York, NY: HarperCollins.

McKay, M., Lev, A., & Skeen, M. (2012). *Acceptance and commitment therapy for interpersonal problems*. Oakland, CA: New Harbinger.

McMinn, M. R. (2012). An integration approach. In S. P. Greggo & T. A. Sisemore (Eds.), *Counseling and Christianity: Five approaches* (pp. 84-109). Downers Grove, IL: InterVarsity Press.

McMinn, M. R. (with Wilhoit, J. C.). (1996). Religion in the counseling office. In M. R. McMinn, *Psychology, theology, and spirituality in Christian counseling* (pp. 1-27). Wheaton, IL: Tyndale House.

Meninger, W. A. (1996). *The loving search for God: Contemplative prayer and the cloud of unknowing*. New York, NY: Continuum.

Merton, T. (1962). *New seeds of contemplation*. New York, NY: New Directions.

Merton, T. (1966). *Conjectures of a guilty bystander*. New York, NY: Doubleday.

Miller, S. D., Duncan, B. L., & Hubble, M. A. (1997). *Escape from Babel: Toward a unifying language for the psychotherapy practice*. New York, NY: Norton.

Miller, W. R., & Rollnick, S. (2013). *Motivational interviewing: Helping people change* (3rd ed.). New York, NY: Guilford Press.

Moon, G. W. (2004). *Falling for God: Saying yes to his extravagant proposal*. Colorado Springs, CO: WaterBrook Press.

Moon, G. W. (2012). A transformational approach. In S. P. Greggo & T. A. Sisemore (Eds.), *Counseling and Christianity: Five approaches* (pp. 132-56). Downers Grove, IL: InterVarsity Press.

Newberg, A., Pourdehnad, M., Alavi, A., & d'Aquili, E. G. (2003). Cerebral blood flow during meditative prayer: Preliminary findings and methodological issues. *Perceptual and Motor Skills, 97*(2), 625-30.

Newberg, A., & Waldman, M. R. (2009). *How God changes your brain: Breakthrough findings from a leading neuroscientist*. New York, NY: Random House.

O'Donohue, J. (1999). *Eternal echoes: Celtic reflections on our yearning to belong*. New York, NY: HarperCollins.

Ogden, P., & Fisher, J. (2015). *Sensorimotor psychotherapy: Interventions for trauma and attachment*. New York, NY: Norton.

Oord, T. J. (2010). *Defining love: A philosophical, scientific, and theological engagement*. Grand Rapids, MI: Brazos Press.

Pedulla, T. (2013). Depression: Finding a way in, finding a way out. In C. K. Germer, R. D. Siegel, & P. R. Fulton (Eds.), *Mindfulness and psychotherapy* (2nd ed.) (pp. 148-66). New York, NY: Guilford Press.

Pennington, M. B. (1999). *Centered living: The way of centering prayer.* Liguori, MO: Liguori/Triumph.

Pennington, M. B. (2001). *Centering prayer: Renewing an ancient Christian prayer form* (Reprint). New York, NY: Doubleday.

Pollack, S. M., Pedulla, T., & Siegel, R. D. (2014). *Sitting together: Essential skills for mindfulness-based psychotherapy.* New York, NY: Guilford Press.

Post, S. G. (2003). *Unlimited love: Altruism, compassion, and service.* Philadelphia, PA: Templeton Foundation Press.

Roberts, R. C. (2007). *Spiritual emotions: A psychology of Christian virtues.* Grand Rapids, MI: Eerdmans.

Roberts, R. C., & Wood, W. J. (2007). *Intellectual virtues: An essay in regulative epistemology.* New York, NY: Oxford University Press.

Rogers, C. R. (1961). *On becoming a person: A therapist's view of psychotherapy.* London, England: Constable.

Rogers, C. R. (1967). The interpersonal relationship: The core of guidance. In C. R. Rogers & B. Stevens (Eds.), *Person to person: The problem of being human* (pp. 89-103). Moab, UT: Real People Press.

Schore, A. N. (2012). *The science of the art of psychotherapy.* New York, NY: Norton.

Schwanda, T. (2014). To gaze on the beauty of the Lord: An evangelical resistance and retrieval of contemplation. *Journal of Spiritual Formation & Soul Care, 7*(1), 62-84.

Segal, Z. V., Williams, J. M. G., & Teasdale, J. D. (2013). *Mindfulness-based cognitive therapy for depression* (2nd ed.). New York, NY: Guilford Press.

Siegel, D. J. (2007). *The mindful brain: Reflection and attunement in the cultivation of well-being.* New York, NY: Norton.

Siegel, D. J. (2010a). *The mindful therapist: A clinician's guide to mindsight and neural integration.* New York, NY: Norton.

Siegel, D. J. (2010b). *Mindsight: The new science of personal transformation.* New York, NY: Bantam Books.

Siegel, D. J. (2017). *Mind: A journey to the heart of being human.* New York, NY: Norton.

Siegel, R. D. (2010). *The mindfulness solution: Everyday practices for everyday problems.* New York, NY: Guilford Press.

Simon, G. M. (2003). *Beyond technique in family therapy: Finding your therapeutic voice.* New York, NY: Allyn & Bacon.

Solomon, M. (2017). How couple therapy can affect long-term relationships and change each of the partners. In M. Solomon & D. J. Siegel (Eds.), *How people change: Relationships and neuroplasticity in psychotherapy* (pp. 247-74). New York, NY: Norton.

Solomon, M., & Tatkin, S. (2011). *Love and war in intimate relationships: Connection, disconnection, and mutual regulation in couple therapy.* New York, NY: Norton.

Sprenkle, D. H., Davis, S. D., & Lebow, J. L. (2009). *Common factors in couple and family therapy: The overlooked foundation for effective practice.* New York, NY: Guilford Press.

Stratton, S. P. (2015). Mindfulness and contemplation: Secular and religious traditions in Western context. *Counseling and Values, 60*(1), 100-118.

Strobel, K. (2013). *Formed for the glory of God: Learning from the spiritual practices of Jonathan Edwards.* Downers Grove, IL: InterVarsity Press.

Strobel, K. (2014). In your light they shall see light: A theological prolegomena for contemplation. *Journal of Spiritual Formation & Soul Care, 7*(1), 85-106.

Symington, S. H., & Symington, M. F. (2012). A Christian model of mindfulness: Using mindfulness principles to support psychological well-being, value-based behavior, and the Christian spiritual journey. *Journal of Psychology & Christianity, 31*(1), 71-77.

Tan, S.-Y. (2011). Mindfulness and acceptance-based cognitive behavioral therapies: Empirical evidence and clinical applications from a Christian perspective. *Journal of Psychology & Christianity, 30*(3), 243-49.

Tan, S.-Y., & Gregg, D. H. (1997). *Disciplines of the Holy Spirit: How to connect to the Spirit's power and presence.* Grand Rapids, MI: Zondervan.

Tatkin, S. (2011). *Wired for love: How understanding your partner's brain and attachment style can help you defuse conflict and build a secure relationship.* Oakland, CA: New Harbinger.

Thompson, C. (2010). *Anatomy of the soul: Surprising connections between neuroscience and spiritual practices that can transform your life and relationships.* Wheaton, IL: Tyndale House.

Thompson, C. (2015). *The soul of shame: Retelling the stories we believe about ourselves.* Downers Grove, IL: InterVarsity Press.

Tozer, A. W. (1948). *The pursuit of God.* Harrisburg, PA: Christian Publications.

Volf, M. (1996). *Exclusion & embrace: A theological exploration of identity, otherness, and reconciliation.* Nashville, TN: Abingdon Press.

Wachholtz, A. B., & Pargament, K. I. (2005). Is spirituality a critical ingredient of meditation? Comparing the effects of spiritual meditation, secular meditation, and relaxation on spiritual, psychological, cardiac, and pain outcomes. *Journal of Behavioral Medicine, 28*(4), 369-84.

Wachholtz, A. B., & Pargament, K. I. (2008). Migraines and meditation: Does spirituality matter? *Journal of Behavioral Medicine, 31*(4), 351-66.

Wallin, D. J. (2007). *Attachment in psychotherapy.* New York, NY: Guilford Press.

Wang, D. C., & Tan, S.-Y. (2016). Dialectical behavior therapy (DBT): Empirical evidence and clinical applications from a Christian perspective. *Journal of Psychology & Christianity, 35*(1), 68-76.

Weil, S. (2009). *Waiting for God* (E. Craufurd, Trans.) (Reprint). New York: Harper Perennial Modern Classics.

Wilhoit, J. C. (2010). Centering prayer. In J. Greenman & G. Kalantzis (Eds.), *Life in the Spirit: Spiritual formation in theological perspective* (pp. 180-97). Downers Grove, IL: InterVarsity Press.

Wilhoit, J. C. (2014). Contemplative and centering prayer. *Journal of Spiritual Formation & Soul Care, 7*(1), 107-17.

Wilhoit, J. C., & Howard, E. B. (2012). *Discovering lectio divina: Bringing Scripture into ordinary life.* Downers Grove, IL: InterVarsity Press.

Willard, D. (1988). *The Spirit of the disciplines: Understanding how God changes lives.* New York, NY: HarperCollins.

Willard, D. (1998). *The divine conspiracy: Rediscovering our hidden life in God.* New York, NY: HarperCollins.

Willard, D. (2006). *The great omission: Reclaiming Jesus's essential teachings on discipleship.* New York, NY: HarperCollins.

Willard, D. (2012a). *Hearing God: Developing a conversational relationship with God* (Updated and expanded). Downers Grove, IL: InterVarsity Press.

Willard, D. (2012b). *Renovation of the heart: Putting on the character of Christ.* Colorado Springs, CO: NavPress.

Young, M. E. (2005). *Learning the art of helping: Building blocks and techniques* (3rd ed.). Upper Saddle River, NJ: Pearson.

AUTHOR INDEX

SUBJECT INDEX

acceptance, 4-5, 9-10, 13, 15, 22, 46, 55, 57, 59-61, 63, 66-67, 96, 101-2, 106, 109-10, 114, 124-25, 144, 152, 154, 156, 159, 161-63, 170-71, 176-78, 180-81, 197-98

acceptance and commitment therapy (ACT), 4, 144

amygdala, 10, 69-70, 72, 80, 84, 194-95

apophatic, 25-26

approach, 1, 4, 6, 11-14, 16-18, 21-24, 37, 45, 47, 57-59, 61, 63, 69, 85-86, 92, 95, 98, 100, 104, 106, 110-12, 114-15, 117-18, 123, 135-36, 143-45, 147, 154, 157, 160-61, 164, 170, 173, 175-76, 187, 195, 197-98

attachment theory, 12, 192

attention, 2-3, 6-11, 14, 16, 22, 26-27, 29, 31, 33-34, 37, 39, 45, 51, 53, 55-57, 62, 72, 74, 82-83, 86-87, 91, 96-97, 99-104, 106, 108-9, 113, 119-20,

122-24, 127-28, 130-32, 139-41, 145, 149, 155, 158-59, 161, 164, 169-71, 176-77, 193

attunement, 7-8, 10, 22, 100-101, 170, 176

avoidance, 4, 69, 73-74, 83, 86, 92, 169, 175

awareness, 2-3, 5-9, 14, 54, 66, 73-74, 76, 80-82, 89, 91, 96, 99, 105, 119, 121, 124, 129, 131, 145, 149-50, 152-53, 156, 159, 170-72, 175-77, 182, 195

behavior,
  and contemplative prayer, 131
  and counseling, 133

body,
  and contemplative prayer, 116
  and counseling, 119

case conceptualization, 48, 59, 69, 157

centering prayer, 37-45, 50, 54, 83, 86-87, 89, 91-92, 96-97, 102, 110, 112-13, 117, 136-37, 139-45, 154-56, 158, 162 63, 167, 194-95

  and contemplative prayer, 38, 42
  and lectio divina, 38, 42
  scientific support of, 38, 43-45

Christian contemplative-oriented approach, 1, 12, 14, 16-17, 21, 37, 47, 57, 144

Cloud of Unknowing, The, 26, 41, 89

compassion, 4, 86, 96, 102-4, 109-10, 114, 136, 161, 176, 192-95

concentration, 12, 14, 16, 100, 102, 128, 158-59

consciousness, 80-82, 92, 152, 178

contemplative mindful practice, 11

contemplative prayer,
  and centering prayer, 38, 42
  compared with meditation, 24
  compared with mindfulness, 16
  counselor's practice of, 17, 47, 95, 198

ABOUT THE AUTHOR

 Gregg Blanton (EdD) is professor of psychology and human services at Montreat College. He is the founder of the Center for Contemplation and Marriage and is in private practice in Asheville, North Carolina, where he provides counseling and supervises counselors-in-training. A certified emotionally focused therapy (EFT) therapist, he has been motivated by his study of mindfulness to integrate contemplative practices—both mindfulness and centering prayer—into his practice of counseling.

Gregg is also the author of *Mind over Marriage: Transforming Your Relationship Using Centering Prayer and Neuroscience* and *The Three Minds of Marriage: How Psychotherapy, Neuroscience, and Contemplation Can Heal, Strengthen, and Transform Intimate Relationships*.

For more information, visit www.greggblanton.com.

CAPS

INTERNATIONAL

An Association for Christian Psychologists,
Therapists, Counselors and Academicians

CAPS is a vibrant Christian organization with a rich tradition. Founded in 1956 by a small group of Christian mental health professionals, chaplains and pastors, CAPS has grown to more than 2,100 members in the U.S., Canada and more than 25 other countries.

CAPS encourages in-depth consideration of therapeutic, research, theoretical and theological issues. The association is a forum for creative new ideas. In fact, their publications and conferences are the birthplace for many of the formative concepts in our field today.

CAPS members represent a variety of denominations, professional groups and theoretical orientations; yet all are united in their commitment to Christ and to professional excellence.

CAPS is a non-profit, member-supported organization. It is led by a fully functioning board of directors, and the membership has a voice in the direction of CAPS.

CAPS is more than a professional association. It is a fellowship, and in addition to national and international activities, the organization strongly encourages regional, local and area activities which provide networking and fellowship opportunities as well as professional enrichment.

To learn more about CAPS, visit www.caps.net.

The joint publishing venture between IVP Academic and CAPS aims to promote the understanding of the relationship between Christianity and the behavioral sciences at both the clinical/counseling and the theoretical/research levels. These books will be of particular value for students and practitioners, teachers and researchers.

For more information about CAPS Books, visit InterVarsity Press's website at www.ivpress.com/christian-association-for-psychological-studies-books-set.

Finding the Textbook You Need

The IVP Academic Textbook Selector
is an online tool for instantly finding the IVP books
suitable for over 250 courses across 24 disciplines.

---

ivpacademic.com
